CW01301919

BILLY CONN -
THE PITTSBURGH KID

Paul F. Kennedy

Bloomington, IN   Milton Keynes, UK
authorHOUSE

AuthorHouse™
1663 Liberty Drive, Suite 200
Bloomington, IN 47403
www.authorhouse.com
Phone: 1-800-839-8640

AuthorHouse™ UK Ltd.
500 Avebury Boulevard
Central Milton Keynes, MK9 2BE
www.authorhouse.co.uk
Phone: 08001974150

This book is a work of non-fiction. Unless otherwise noted, the author and the publisher make no explicit guarantees as to the accuracy of the information contained in this book and in some cases, names of people and places have been altered to protect their privacy.

© 2007 Paul F. Kennedy. All rights reserved.

No part of this book may be reproduced, stored in a retrieval system, or transmitted by any means without the written permission of the author.

First published by AuthorHouse 2/27/2007

ISBN: 978-1-4259-7344-5 (sc)
ISBN: 978-1-4259-7345-2 (hc)

Library of Congress Control Number: 2006910492

Printed in the United States of America
Bloomington, Indiana

This book is printed on acid-free paper.

ACKNOWLEDGEMENTS

This project began because I wanted to read a biography of a Pittsburgh sports hero, boxer Billy Conn. I discovered that none existed. Scores of far lesser boxers have had biographies written about them. Billy Conn's is long overdue.

The Conn family has been accessible and cooperative with their vast wealth of information, both written and oral. Mary Louise, Billy's widow, provided eyewitness accounts. The sons, Tim, Billy Junior, and Mike, knew their father into their adulthood and remember well the many stories he told them. Tim was especially helpful in doing the leg work of sifting through hundreds of newspaper and magazines articles in his father's memorabilia. My many long conversations with Tim over the past few years enhanced my understanding of the life and career of Billy Conn.

Other family members who provided information are Billy's brother Frank Conn and sister Mary Jane Cunningham Conn. Tim's son Ryan Conn maintains a wonderful web site, billyconn.net, of articles and photographs devoted to his grandfather.

I must also thank my wife Patty for her loving support and brutal critiques that made this a better book.

Many thanks to my sister and ace researcher, Marilyn Kennedy, who spent hours in the dusty microfilm of the Carnegie Library of Pittsburgh, and in the more pleasant aura of Mary Louise Conn.

Thanks also to Mike McGinley, Jack McGinley Sr., Nancy Kennedy, Mary Louise Kennedy, Carlos Ortiz, Gil Clancy, Kenneth Burke, Ronnie Conn, and the late Frank "Spacky" Delio.

Paul F. Kennedy

CONTENTS

Prologue		ix
Round One	Pittsburgh and "Sliberty"	1
Round Two	Moonie And Junior: "I Can Lick Any Kid In The Neighborhood"	16
Round Three	No Easy Road	24
Round Four	1935: Learning And Growing	27
Round Five	1936: Winning All The Way	36
Round Six	1937: Hitting The Big Time	56
Round Seven	1938: Middleweight Or Light-heavyweight?	80
Round Eight	1939: New York, New York – Beating The Best	92
Round Nine	World Champion	105
Round Ten	1940: Challenging The Heavies	128
Round 11	1941: Preparing For Joe Louis And Greenfield Jimmy	138
Round 12	The Fight Of The Century	153
Round Thirteen	Private Billy Conn	169
Round Fourteen	1946: Another Shot At Louis	178
Round Fifteen	Retirement Years: Pittsburgh Icon	190
Epilogue	Billy Conn's Legacy	201
Appendix A	The Fight Record Of Billy Conn	205
Appendix B	Billy Conn's Awards And Honors	209
Bibliography		211

PROLOGUE

Fifty-five thousand fans at the Polo Grounds were on their feet screaming for Billy Conn and Joe Louis in one of the greatest fights in boxing history. Conn, the "Pittsburgh Kid," had come to symbolize the city of his birth, that archetypal heartland furnace, city of smoke and grime. Pittsburgh, like America, had endured twelve years of the heartbreaking Great Depression, but its hero Billy Conn was a shining beacon of hope. He was handsome – beautiful even – with looks that put movie stars to shame. He found fame and fortune in New York, but he always came home, and he always would. He had beaten everyone they threw at him. Time after time the experts said he wasn't ready, that he was in over his head. Time after time he had proven them wrong. At age 19 and 20 he beat all of the best middleweights in their prime. At 21 he won the world light-heavyweight championship, and dominated the division so thoroughly that he had to fight heavyweights to find a challenge. Though barely 170 pounds, he had beaten the heavyweight contenders with ease. He was still only 23. They said he could never beat Joe Louis, perhaps the greatest heavyweight champ of all time. He was proving them wrong again. He had taken the fight to Louis for twelve thrilling rounds, baffling him with speed, beating him up inside, taking the big man's punches, even staggering him in the previous round. Billy had scaled just 169 that morning to 200 for Louis, yet it was Louis who was hurt, and losing.

At her home in Pittsburgh Billy's mother Maggie lay in bed dying of cancer, praying hard for him. Four miles away in a Manhattan hotel his beloved Mary Louise, whose family wouldn't let her marry him, stood in the bathroom with the shower turned on because she could no longer bear to listen. At Forbes Field they stopped the Pittsburgh Pirates game to broadcast the fight over the Public Address system.

In the corner before the thirteenth round Johnny Ray, his trainer and manager, told him to stay away, to sit on his lead – three more rounds and the heavyweight title, the "greatest prize in sports" – was his. Ray, a grizzled and scarred veteran of many ring wars, had found him in the streets of East Liberty and taught him to box. But the kid had inborn talent that couldn't be taught – speed, toughness, the will to win, and overwhelming confidence.

The bell rang for the thirteenth round. "Stay away from him!" "Stick and move!" "Play it safe!" his corner men yelled. Play it safe? That's one thing the cocky Irisher had never done. He put in his mouthpiece and declared, "I'm gonna knock him out!"

ROUND ONE

Pittsburgh and "Sliberty"

Pittsburgh dates its beginning to November 25, 1758, when British General John Forbes viewed the smoldering ruins of Fort Duquesne and proclaimed the place "Pittsborough," after Prime Minister William Pitt. The name was later shortened to Pittsburgh. Forbes had led a 7,000-man army across Pennsylvania to drive the French from their Fort Duquesne stronghold once and for all. The badly outnumbered French burned the fort and fled before the British army arrived. Accompanying Forbes was Colonel George Washington, who was familiar with the area. He had passed through in 1753 with scout Christopher Gist, nearly drowning in the icy Allegheny River. He had led troops in defeat at Fort Necessity in 1754, and participated in General Edward Braddock's disastrous attempt to conquer Fort Duquesne in 1755. It must have felt good to finally be on the winning side.

The Allegheny and Monongahela rivers meet at the "Point" to form the Ohio. In 1753 Washington described the confluence as "…well-situated for a fort." A year later the British began construction of Fort Pitt, the largest British fort ever built in North America at that time. No enemy ever penetrated the massive structure. It repelled a spirited siege in 1763 during Pontiac's Rebellion and several attacks during the

Revolutionary War. It was the first undefeated champion in what would later be known as the "City of Champions."

Pittsburgh, with its plentiful rivers and natural resources, became an industrial center for iron, glass, and armaments. The place seemed to attract nicknames, being known at various times as the "Gateway to the West," "the Iron City," "the Hearth of the Nation," "the Forge of the Universe," and the "Steel City." Originally the "Scots-Irish" from northern Ireland provided much of the population base. They had been the most numerous of the early settlers in western Pennsylvania. Many Irish Catholic and German immigrants found their way to Pittsburgh to work in the booming factories. After the Irish potato famine of the late 1840's, Irish Catholic immigration flooded the northeastern United States. By the start of the Civil War, one of every five Pittsburghers was an Irish Catholic immigrant.

Pittsburgh's factories produced the armaments that sustained the Union Army during the Civil War. After the war, steel mills and other heavy industry boomed. With its factories and laboring population, the area became famous for strikes and labor violence. The railroad strike of 1877 culminated in a riot in the Strip District with hundreds of casualties, and ended only when put down by the National Guard. The Homestead Steel Strike of 1892 saw pitched battles between strikers and Pinkerton guards, and also produced many casualties.

European immigration continued in the late nineteenth century, but drew increasingly from southern and eastern areas. Italians, Poles, Croatians, Slovaks, Ukrainians, Serbs, Russians, Hungarians, and others poured into Pittsburgh to work. Irish immigration continued, but now formed only one stream of many. By 1880 one of three Pittsburghers was foreign-born. Ethnic communities sprang up, with their own churches or synagogues, and their own businesses and social clubs. The area's hilly terrain fostered the development of tight-knit, insular neighborhoods.

Joseph Conn, a Protestant from Magilligan Parish in County Derry, Northern Ireland, came to New York in the 1880's. He was over six feet tall and powerfully built. He met an Irish Catholic woman named Jane

McTigue in New York and married her. He converted to Catholicism. They moved to Pittsburgh, where they had four children: William Robert, Rachel, Joseph, and Annie. William Robert, the father of Billy Conn, was born in the East Liberty section of Pittsburgh in 1898.

Joseph Conn claimed descent from "Conn of the Hundred Battles," a legendary Ard Ri (High King) of Ireland in the second century A.D. Conn ruled over half of Ireland until his treacherous assassination in 173 A.D. by 50 enemies disguised as women. His descendants ruled much of Ireland for the next 600 years. The name "Conn" is derived from the word "dog," the warrior-king being named for the speed of greyhounds and the pugnacity of sea dogs. The "Hundred Battles" part comes from his constant warring with provincial kings.

The migratory patterns of his descendants illustrate the history of the Gaelic people. The massive migration from Ireland to the Scottish highlands in the fifth and sixth centuries included many Conns. Some returned to Ireland with the Ulster plantation settlement in the seventeenth century, and some of these joined the large movement of northern Irish to America in the eighteenth century. To this day Conns are plentiful in Magilligan Parish and in County Down.

Peter McParland was born in County Cork, Ireland, in the 1860s. He married a woman named Annie and emigrated to England in search of better opportunity. In England they had six children: David, Mary, Kitty, Margaret (the mother of Billy Conn), Annie, and Philip. The family left England for the United States around 1907 and arrived in Pittsburgh. The immigration officials wrote the name as "McFarland," and it has remained that ever since. They settled in East Liberty, on the city's eastern end. A seventh child, Rose, was born in Pittsburgh. Peter found work as a laborer for the streetcar company. Despite being born in England, Peter and Annie's children always considered themselves as Irish, from County Cork. As a proverbial Irish woman once asked, "If a cat gave birth to kittens in an oven, would they be scones?"

The Pittsburgh neighborhood of East Liberty is in the eastern end of the city, about midway between the Allegheny River to the north and the Monongahela River to the south. The word "liberty" meant a grazing land outside the business and residential areas of a city. Pittsburgh once had a north and west "liberty" also. The Mellon family, whose financial fame extended beyond Pittsburgh, once owned the land on which East Liberty was built. With Mellon influence, the area was connected to downtown Pittsburgh through the Oakland and Lawrenceville areas, first by a paved road for horse-drawn carriages, and later by electric trolley lines. A Mellon mansion once stood on what is now Mellon Park, a rolling green playground with ball fields, basketball courts, and tennis courts.

East Liberty was opened for housing in the 1870's, as Pittsburgh's quick population growth swelled demand to house the immigrant factory workers. It became an important retail center for the eastern part of the city. The Mellons built Motor Square Garden in 1900 as a shopping market and sports arena. The Nabisco Bakery plant on Penn Avenue, across the street from Mellon Park, was the largest area employer. Worship centers reflected the backgrounds of the new residents: Sacred Heart parish was started by Irish Catholic immigrants in 1872, Saints Peter and Paul by German Catholics in 1890, Our Lady Help of Christians by Italian Catholics from Calabria in 1892, and B'nai Israel synagogue by Jews in 1923.

East Liberty's population had many residents of Irish descent, along with Italians, Germans, Blacks, Jews, and Poles. To the north, Homewood was mostly Irish, German, Italian, and Black, and respectably working class. To the south Shadyside and Squirrel Hill were upscale, where managers and professionals lived. To the west was Garfield, poor and working class like East Liberty. Less than a mile to the east of the Conn home, on Penn Avenue in the Point Breeze area, was "Millionaire's Row," one of the wealthiest neighborhoods in the United States. Out there the homes themselves had names. Henry Clay Frick's "Clayton" still stands. Henry J. Heinz's estate was called "Greenlawn;" George Westinghouse's "Solitude." Other captains of industry, fabulously wealthy, lived nearby. Carnegies, Mellons, and Thaws lived there. The estates lasted into the 1920's, when they were sold and opened up for normal housing.

The Conns and McFarlands belonged to Sacred Heart parish, and lived in the same part of East Liberty. William Robert Conn was about a year older than Margaret McFarland. They met each other and were married at Sacred Heart in 1916. He was 17, she was 16. Their first child, William David, was born October 8, 1917.

In the year Billy Conn was born, two thirds of Pittsburgh's population was made up of immigrants and their children. The city was known for its dirty, grimy air. Scores of factories lined the rivers. Blast furnaces spewed grit into the air. Pittsburgh was often dark, even on a sunny day. British writer James Parton had called it "hell with the lid off." Most Americans saw the "Smoky City" as a place where foreign hordes labored to produce steel, iron, glass, and heavy machinery in a filthy atmosphere.

In April of that year the United States had entered the Great War, the "war to end all wars." Millions of British, French, and German boys had already been killed and maimed in gruesome trench warfare. Patriotism ran high in Pittsburgh and the rest of the United States, as Americans hoped our entry would tip the balance in favor of the Allies. The first American to die in the war was an East Liberty lad of Irish descent, Thomas F. Enright.

The Pirates finished in last place that year, although Max Carey led the league in stolen bases with 46. Their new ballpark, Forbes Field, was built in 1909 in picturesque Schenley Park in the Oakland district, less than two miles from the Conn home. It was named after the general who had named Pittsburgh. The University of Pittsburgh was located in Oakland, as was Duquesne Gardens, an arena that hosted hockey games, ice capades, prizefights, basketball games, rodeos, and dance marathons. Across the street from Duquesne Gardens was St. Paul's Cathedral, the headquarters of the Catholic Diocese of Pittsburgh. The infant William David Conn would one day headline many big boxing cards at Forbes Field and Duquesne Gardens.

The New York Giants won the National League pennant in 1917. Pittsburgh native "Greenfield Jimmy" Smith was a utility infielder on that team, which played its home games at the Polo Grounds, built in 1911. Smith would become the father-in-law of Conn. Conn would one day participate in of one of boxing's most famous bouts at the Polo Grounds.

The Pittsburgh area produced plenty of good boxers at that time. Frank Klaus of East Pittsburgh and George Chip of New Castle were middleweight champs in 1912 and 1913. North Sider Frank Moran, a former University of Pittsburgh football player, fought for the heavyweight title twice, losing decisions in 1914 to Jack Johnson and in 1916 to Jess Willard. Scores of other competent pros provided frequent boxing cards at area arenas like Duquesne Gardens in Oakland and Motor Square Garden in East Liberty. The best of all was Harry Greb of 138 South Millvale Avenue in the Garfield section, about one mile from the Conn home. Middleweight Greb was establishing himself as one of the best fighters in the country, defeating top-notch and usually heavier opponents. Greb won 31 fights in 1917 against one draw. Greb's stable mates Cuddy DeMarco and Johnny Ray were contenders in the lightweight and featherweight divisions.

The war ended on November 11, 1918. In 1919 Congress passed the Volstead Act, banning the sale of alcoholic beverages in the United States. Pittsburgh had yet another nickname based on its alcohol consumption: "the wettest spot in America." Hundreds of taverns served the workingmen of the mills. Nearly all of them converted to "speakeasies," or illegal taverns, in 1919. Payoffs to the right government officials kept them open, and the city maintained its "wet" reputation. About 500 speakeasies operated within the city limits during the 1920's. Over 10,000 stills produced alcohol in Allegheny County at the same time.

The old Pittsburgh of the great tycoons, called "robber barons" by some, was passing. Andrew Carnegie, Henry Clay Frick, and Henry J. Heinz all died in 1919. A steel strike of the same year was fueled by the new wave of immigrants from eastern and southern Europe. The mills of western Pennsylvania were shut down for three months.

The year 1919 cast a dark shadow over the entire sports world. The World Series was fixed. Chicago White Sox players took money to throw games and lose the Series. America was devastated by the revelation. The sport's reputation would only be saved by the emergence of the great Babe Ruth in the 1920's. But boxing provided an immediate tonic. Jack Dempsey, who only a few years ago had been a hobo out west begging and fighting for meals, emerged as the top contender for Jess Willard's crown after an impressive string of first-round knockouts. Willard was a huge man, about 6'6" and 260 pounds. Jack Johnson, who had lost his title to Willard, proclaimed him "too big and strong to be knocked out." On July 4, 1919, in Toledo, Ohio, Dempsey knocked Willard down seven times, fracturing his cheekbone in 13 places. Mercifully, the fight was stopped after the third round. America had found a sorely needed new hero. Once again the heavyweight champion was an Irish-American, after a 22-year hiatus since Gentleman Jim Corbett lost to Cornishman Bob Fitzsimmons in 1897.

On May 4, 1919, Margaret McFarland Conn gave birth to her second child, Frank. She would have three more: Mary Jane in 1921, Jackie in 1922, and Peggy in 1924. The Conns lived at 6395 Aurelia Street in a row house. Joseph and Jane Conn lived two doors away at 6399. Peter and Annie McFarland lived in the same block at 6377.

Tall and strong, with black hair and a thin moustache, William R. Conn worked as a city policeman. He liked to drink and fight, fulfilling the Irish stereotype of the times. He was called "Wild Bill." But he worked hard and supported his family. He adored his kids. His wife Margaret ran the house in a loving, not-too-strict fashion. The kids, especially Billy, adored her. Billy's siblings all remembered his uninhibited love for his mother. The tough street kid was unusually attached to her, and not afraid to show it. He called her "Maggie." She spoke in the County Cork brogue of her parents. She had dark, curly hair, like Billy, with pale porcelain skin and pretty blue eyes. She and her sisters, who all lived nearby, sang beautifully together. They preferred Irish songs like "I'll Take You Home Again Kathleen" and "When Irish

Eyes Are Smiling." Margaret had a beautiful voice, and Billy loved to hear her sing.

Joseph Conn, Billy's grandfather, worked as a watchman in an icehouse. His son Joseph, Billy's uncle, worked at the Nabisco plant. Pete McFarland worked as a laborer for the streetcar company. Two of his sons, also Billy's uncles, worked at Nabisco.

In 1920 four of the eight national boxing champions were residents of the city of Pittsburgh. Brothers Pete and Jack Zivic, the sons of a Croatian immigrant, won the 112 and 126 pound classes. Jack Burke won the heavyweight title. The Zivics and Burke were all from the Willow Club in Lawrenceville. The fourth champ, in the 135-pound class, was Art Rooney, son of a saloon owner from the North Side. Rooney would later achieve fame as the owner of the Pittsburgh Steelers of the NFL. The Zivics fought for the 1920 Olympic team in Antwerp, Belgium, and were the first brothers ever to do so. Leon and Michael Spinks in 1976 are the only other pair of brothers to fight on the same U.S. Olympic team.

Pittsburgh underwent a building boom in the 1920's. The Liberty Bridge and Liberty Tubes opened in 1924, connecting downtown to southern parts of the city. Pitt Stadium, seating 55,000, opened in Oakland in 1925. That same year construction began on the "Cathedral of Learning," a skyscraper that would come to symbolize the University of Pittsburgh. Detractors called it "The Height of Ignorance." Thousands of homes were built in new suburbs.

In the "Roaring Twenties" the war-weary nation celebrated peace and prosperity. The stock market soared. Women wore shorter skirts and bobbed their hair. Prohibition enriched bootleggers, who drove flashy cars and wore expensive suits. It did not inhibit drinking in Pittsburgh, where cultural affinity for it ran deep. The immigrant and laboring classes merely moved it under the table in "speakeasies." East Liberty in the 1920's, where Billy Conn grew up, bustled with retail stores, restaurants, and six movie theaters. Red trolleys crackled constantly along the steel tracks of Penn Avenue, carrying shoppers from all over the eastern part of the city. The six theaters (Liberty, Sheridan Square, Enright, Cameraphone, Regent, and Harris) featured movies, newsreels, cartoons, and stage shows. The master of ceremonies at the Enright was a handsome, gifted young singer named Dick Powell, who would go on to Hollywood fame. Most Pittsburghers didn't own cars at that time, but Gulf Oil, owned by the Mellons, served those who did. The Gulf station at Penn and Baum, built in 1913, was one of the first drive-in gasoline stations in the country. The Nabisco plant on Penn Avenue produced cakes, cookies, and crackers, and gave off a pleasant, sweet smell in late afternoon. An enterprising kid could steal from an unattended truck, or buy day-old goodies at half price at the plant's retail discount store. One could hear Yiddish or southern Italian dialects spoken on the streets, or the accented English of people from Ireland, southern Italy, Germany, or Eastern Europe. African-Americans, many of whom were born in southern states like Virginia or the Carolinas, added an additional accent.

As a boy Billy Conn heard the harsh, quasi-Scottish accent of his grandfather Joseph Conn from County Down in northern Ireland, and the lilting County Cork brogue of his mother and her family. But those born in Pittsburgh and their descendants spoke their own version of English, "Pittsburghese." Its peculiarities originated from the Scots-Irish accent of the eighteenth century, when so many of them came from northern Ireland to western Pennsylvania. Pittsburghers leave the "hahse" (house) to shop "dahntahn" (downtown), or to go "aht" (out) to "Sliberty." (East Liberty) Many of the men at that time worked in a still (steel) mill on the "Mawn" (Mon – short for Monongahela) River. Some of the luckier ones got to go to "cahl-weedge." (college) People "redd up" their rooms (clean or tidy up), which is the same in past or present tense. In Pittsburgh "tahr" (tire) rhymes with "pahr" (power) and is pronounced exactly like "tahr." (tower) The plural of you is "you'ons," a contraction of you-ones, which usually comes out sounding like "yins." Something broken doesn't "need to be fixed." It "needs fixed." Dirty clothes "need worshed." Billy "Cawn" (Conn) and most of his contemporaries spoke this colorful dialect, which is exclusive to southwestern Pennsylvania.

At Forbes Field, within easy walking distance of East Liberty, the Pirates had a great year in 1925, winning the World Series four games to three over the Washington Senators. A kid could sneak in without paying, winked at by security guards in the late innings. The Pirates won the National League pennant in 1927 and faced the New York Yankees, led by Babe Ruth and Lou Gehrig. The Yanks swept the Bucs four straight.

It was an age of heroes, the foremost of whom was Babe Ruth. Charles Lindberg flew solo across the Atlantic Ocean in 1927 and became an instant icon. Jack Dempsey dominated boxing, knocking out most of his opponents with unprecedented punching power. The sport of boxing was outlawed in many jurisdictions prior to 1920, and was not considered respectable. This changed in the 1920s, as the Dempsey-Tunney heavyweight bouts drew crowds of over 100,000 and held a national radio audience spellbound.

The section of East Liberty where the Conns and McFarlands lived was south of Penn Avenue. Penn, Shakespeare, and Aurelia streets were roughly parallel, and made up of modest row houses. The Conns lived on all three streets at one time or another, but Billy grew up mostly on Aurelia Street. The Conns attended Sacred Heart Elementary School, only a few blocks away on Centre Avenue. The Sisters of Charity, who were founded by Mother Elizabeth Seton, (now Saint Elizabeth Seton) provided a strict Catholic education. Classrooms were crowded, but well controlled by strong-willed nuns. To the basic academic skills they added Catholic doctrine as explained by the Baltimore Catechism. Uniforms were not required, but girls wore dresses and boys wore collared shirts. Steam locomotives rumbled by on the Pennsylvania Railroad tracks next to the schoolyard throughout the day, spewing smoke that added to the air pollution already present from the factories. At times teachers had to wait for a train to pass so that they could be heard. At recess the boys played ball and shot marbles in the schoolyard, while the girls jumped rope and played hopscotch.

Father Thomas Coakley was appointed pastor of Sacred Heart in 1924, and remained in that position until 1957. Sources of the time describe him as "outspoken." He spoke out strongly against Communist influence in labor unions. Also, in 1924, the parish built a new church on Walnut Street, which still stands. The beautiful, massive Gothic structure boasted the longest aisle in Pittsburgh, over 200 feet long.

Mary Jane Conn, four years younger than brother Billy, suffered severe burns to her right arm in an accident at age four. Her clothes caught on fire while playing with a candle, and she was rushed to Pittsburgh Hospital. She had residual damage to the arm, and doctors recommended exercise to build up her strength. Her father built her an iron trapeze in the back yard. A few years later he bought two pairs of boxing gloves, mainly to help Mary Jane. The boys used the gloves to spar with each other, conducting vigorous sessions which Billy, the oldest, dominated. Billy found that he enjoyed boxing with the gloves.

His father "Wild Bill" Conn liked boxing and followed the professional game. The senior Conn liked to hang out with boxers and attended fights often. Boxing was a much more popular sport at that time than it is today. Baseball was the national pastime, but boxing was second in popularity. College football drew large crowds, but the pro game was in its infancy and not widely followed. Basketball was an urban game with a limited following. Pittsburgh had weekly professional boxing shows during the 1920's, 30's, and 40's at several popular venues: Duquesne Gardens in Oakland, Exposition Hall on the North Side, the Market House on the South Side, Power Auditorium in Lawrenceville, and Motor Square Garden in East Liberty, among others. Big fights were held at Forbes Field in the summer. Outlying towns like McKeesport, Uniontown, Braddock, and Washington staged frequent bouts. A boxing "card" usually consisted of a main event and five to ten preliminary bouts. Less experienced boxers fought first, in four or six round bouts. Intermediate fighters followed in six to eight round bouts. The main event was last, consisting of well-known fighters in a ten or twelve round fight. A championship fight could be fifteen rounds. Sometimes a "walk out" fight followed the main event, consisting of inexperienced fighters in a four or six rounder.

Pittsburgh had plenty of boxers to supply all types of bouts, and fighters from around the country often came here to fight. A local fighter usually headed the card against an out of town fighter or another local. But often enough the main event consisted of two well-known fighters from other areas. The town had a good fan base that supported and knew the fight game. Promoters sought ethnic and neighborhood rivalries to increase interest. With its multi-ethnic population and proud, tight-knit neighborhoods, Pittsburgh's intensely partisan fans kept the fight game thriving.

Garfield's Harry Greb, son of a German immigrant father and Irish mother, dominated the Pittsburgh boxing scene. He was called "The Iron City Express." Young Billy Conn worshipped him. Greb was a dashing figure of the Roaring Twenties who dressed in expensive suits of the latest fashion, and always had a beautiful woman or two on his arm. His record is almost too amazing to believe. He routinely and often easily defeated the best middleweights, light-heavyweights, and heavyweights in the world. He defeated the reigning champions many times in non-title bouts, while never losing to any of them. The champs fought Greb to make money, but made sure to be over the weight so that it would not risk the title. He fought 20 or more bouts a year, always against top-notch fighters. From 1916 to 1923 he had 178 consecutive bouts without a loss. Also known as "The Pittsburgh Windmill," and "The Human Windmill," he had inhuman stamina, speed, and ring smarts. After suffering a knockout in his sixth pro bout in 1913, he was never knocked out, and seemed able to take even the best punch of any heavyweight without being hurt. He finally got a shot at the American light-heavyweight title in 1922, and defeated Gene Tunney, a man who outweighed him by 15 pounds. It was the only fight Tunney would ever lose. Public outcry gained him a shot at the world middleweight title in 1923. He won 13 of 15 rounds from Johnny Wilson at the Polo Grounds in New York, capturing the title. He defended it successfully six times over the next two years.

Greb lost three hotly disputed split decisions to Tunney in 1923 and 1924. Greb also outboxed heavyweight champ Jack Dempsey in several sparring sessions, and was seriously considered for a shot at the heavyweight title despite his small size. Tunney won the title from Dempsey in 1926, as Greb predicted he would. Bill Brennan, a 200-pound heavyweight contender who lost four times to Greb and twice to Dempsey, said of Greb, "If I had to pick between Dempsey and that little buzzsaw, I'd pick Greb."

Unknown to the public, Greb had lost vision in one eye and was losing it in the other. His career of nearly 300 bouts against mostly larger men had taken its toll. At age 32, his skills were slipping. He lost badly to Tunney, now a full-fledged heavyweight, in their fifth and final bout in 1925. He lost his middleweight title to Tiger Flowers in a split decision in February of 1926, and lost again to him in another split decision in August. Although Tunney and Flowers were both great fighters destined for the Hall of Fame, Greb felt that he was no longer at the top of his game, and feared total blindness. He decided to retire. Still the dapper ladies' man, he arranged to have surgery in Atlantic City to fix his battered nose and restore his good looks.. On the operating table, he hemorrhaged and died on October 22, 1926. The Pittsburgh Windmill churned no more.

The city of Pittsburgh was stunned. Few of his many friends even knew he had gone for surgery. Nine-year-old Billy Conn had lost his hero, the world famous boxer who lived just a mile away, right off of Penn Avenue in Garfield. Greb's parents belonged to St. Joseph's, the German Catholic parish in Bloomfield. But the funeral was held at nearby Sacred Heart, Billy Conn's church, because it was much larger and could accommodate the crowd. The boxing world came to Billy Conn's neighborhood and home parish to honor his hero. One of Greb's pallbearers was Gene Tunney, who had just won the heavyweight title from Jack Dempsey a month earlier.

During the 1920s Wild Bill Conn got a better paying job as a pipe fitter at Westinghouse Electric Corporation's big plant in East Pittsburgh on the Monongahela River, an easy streetcar ride from East Liberty. Pete McFarland also found employment there as a machinist. Westinghouse, headquartered in Pittsburgh, manufactured industrial machinery and electrical products, and was expanding its operations. It was physical work in a hot, dirty factory, but paid well enough to support a family. Bill's kids were growing up, and the boys could eat like a stable of horses. He still drank and got into brawls in East Liberty saloons, but made it to work regularly and established himself as a reliable employee. He often battled the Pittsburgh Police, some of them former co-workers, who were called to break up brawls that had gotten out of hand.

Billy and the other neighborhood boys spent a lot of time on Mellon Park's excellent fields, playing baseball and football. Billy wasn't very good at baseball, but loved to run the football. With his quick feet and blazing speed, he could outrun any kid in the neighborhood. He could also outfight them all. Although quiet at home and reasonably well behaved at school, he developed a reputation as someone not to mess with, a kid who fought too seriously and didn't know when to quit. He had grown into a tall, slim, handsome teenager with a thick shock of curly black hair, dimples, and sparkling eyes and teeth. He had a quick wit and endearing smile.

The Conns, like other neighborhood kids, attended movies weekly, with six theater choices in East Liberty alone. Every Saturday meant newsreels, cartoons feature movies, and sometimes even stage shows. Theaters in Oakland, Lawrenceville, and the downtown area were just a short streetcar ride away. When he was a little older, Billy liked to play pool in local parlors and "loaf" (Pittsburghese for "hang out") with friends on street corners in "Sliberty."

In 1929 the stock market crashed, and the national economy took a nosedive. Jobs were tough to find or to hold. Bill Conn stayed on at Westinghouse, as he would for many years. (Later, as an adult, Billy called his dad "Westinghouse" because of his long years with the company.)

Billy was a fair student, but not too serious about academics. He could draw very well. He exhibited talent as a sketch artist at an early age. When Knute Rockne died in a plane crash in 1931, Billy sketched a striking portrait of the famous Notre Dame coach, which his teacher sent on to Seton Hill College. He declined her encouragement to make a career of art.

Billy spent an extra year in eighth grade, unsure of what he wanted to do. He and several other large, aging boys sat together in the back of the class. One of the nuns recommended to them that they leave crowded Sacred Heart, perhaps get some vocational training, and open up spots for other children. Billy took her advice to heart and enrolled in Connelley Vocational School in the Uptown district. He attended classes for a few days, found out he didn't like it, and dropped out.

Billy's father, concerned that he had quit Connelley and had no job prospects, took him to the Westinghouse plant one day to offer him guidance. Wild Bill stressed that this was what life held for a man in Pittsburgh, unless you bettered yourself with some kind of education or training. Billy was horrified. The grimy, smelly air, the noisy grinding of machinery – he took an instant dislike to it. He saw soiled, worn-out men coming and going to and from shifts that began and ended at all hours of the day and night. He wasn't sure what he wanted in life, but he knew that factory work was definitely not it. Connelley offered training for better jobs, but just a small step higher in the same dirty, stifling type of mill. He could draw – quite well, in fact. He could be an artist. But that meant at best a struggling life among bearded weirdos in a dingy studio somewhere. That was no life for a tough kid from the streets of Sliberty. With the brimming confidence that would always be his trademark, Billy knew in his heart that he was destined for something better. But what? Where in Pittsburgh could a guy with a grade school education make it big?

ROUND TWO

Moonie And Junior:

"I Can Lick Any Kid In The Neighborhood"

Johnny Ray had a small gym above a saloon and pool hall on Penn Avenue in East Liberty, near the Enright Theater. It contained a ring, heavy bags, speed bags, and mirrors for shadow boxing. He had five or six journeyman pros training there, plus a few amateurs at any given time. He also sold moonshine whiskey in milk bottles to make a few extra bucks.

Ray was born Harry Pitler in 1896 in the lower Hill District, at that time the heart of Pittsburgh's Jewish community, to Russian Jewish parents in a typically large immigrant family of seven children. The boys were athletic: his older brother Jake played second base for the Pirates in 1917-18, managed in the minor leagues, and coached with the Brooklyn Dodgers. His younger brother Dave was a backup quarterback at Pitt under Jock Sutherland. He had four sisters.

Pitler started fighting pro in 1913 out of the stable managed by Red Mason, which included outstanding pros Cuddy DeMarco, Buck Crouse, and the incomparable Harry Greb. Mason called him "Johnny Ray" after a stage comedian. At that time a majority of professional fighters were Irish. "Johnny Ray" sounded Irish and was a more salable name than Harry Pitler. Ray kept the name throughout his boxing and managing careers. Ray was a top lightweight contender from 1917 to 1921, but never won a title. He participated in the first radio broadcast of a prizefight, at Motor Square Garden in East Liberty. He was known as a superb defensive stylist. Even good fighters had a hard time landing a solid punch against him. And he was tough: in 138 professional bouts, he was never knocked out. The last fight of his career was in 1924 against Jack Zivic, a welterweight contender at the time. The larger and more powerful Zivic battered Ray for ten brutal rounds. Hurt, bleeding, and outgunned, the brave little Ray refused to quit. His valiant stand became a Pittsburgh boxing legend.

Billy Conn often shot pool downstairs with his buddies, and occasionally walked upstairs to watch a sparring session. Ray noticed that his young amateur boxers from the neighborhood were afraid of the tall, rangy kid with the baby face, and asked them why. They told him that Billy fought like it was life and death, and didn't know when to quit.

One day Billy and some friends were watching the boxers train, and Billy made a nasty wisecrack when one of them slipped. Irritated, Ray challenged him to put on the gloves and get in there if he thought he was so tough. Expecting an apology, Ray was surprised when the tall kid looked down at him and said "Sure." Ray laced up the gloves on himself and Billy. He figured he'd teach the kid a lesson. As the session progressed, Ray was astonished. The kid, who had never had any boxing training, was as gifted with natural ability as anyone he had ever seen. Although lanky with long arms and legs, he had silk-smooth coordination. He was fast with his hands and feet, and had quick, natural reflexes. He had courage: Ray belted him a few good ones, but the kid was unphased. He could take punches without flinching or showing any signs of fear or pain. When they finished, Ray told him that if he ever wanted to train as a boxer, he was welcome. He asked him his name. The kid told him, "Billy Conn… I can lick any kid in the neighborhood."

Months later Billy's father approached Ray about having his son take boxing lessons. He told him that the boy was having trouble with some older kids in the neighborhood, and he wanted him to know how to defend himself. Ray didn't make the connection at the time, but when Billy showed up alone he remembered the smart aleck kid who had shown so much promise in the ring. Ray teased Billy that he was probably one of those bad kids in the neighborhood looking for something to steal. Billy looked around the gym and cracked, "There's nothing here worth stealing."

Ray started Billy with elementary boxing techniques, careful that the kid learned no bad habits. Billy was an all-around assistant at the gym, sweeping up, running errands, and doing whatever Ray needed. Ray sent him to buy and deliver moonshine whiskey. Ray drank a good bit of the illicit beverage himself. Because he knew Billy's father, Ray called the younger Conn "Junior." (Billy always insisted that he was not a junior, because he and his father had different middle names.) Billy called Ray "Moonie" because of his love for the homemade whiskey. Their exclusive pet names for each other would persist for the remainder of their lives. Thus began a father-son type of relationship that would take both to the pinnacle of the boxing world. Ray knew this kid was something special and wanted to make sure he brought him along right.

Billy started getting up early every day to run through the streets of East Liberty and the fields of Mellon Park. He worked hard at the gym, spending hours at a time on one little nuance of how to deliver or avoid a specific punch. He showed a promising left jab. He hit the heavy bag to develop power. He worked the speed bag to develop his timing and reflexes. He jumped rope to develop stamina and improve his foot coordination. He sparred with the pros at Johnny Ray's gym, learning their techniques and picking up whatever ring wisdom he could. He refrained from smoking or drinking, and tried to eat a healthy diet. Friends and family were amazed at his dedication – even fanaticism – and wondered how long it would last.

Ray decided that Billy would not fight as an amateur. He felt that a fighter only learned from training with or fighting more experienced foes. He didn't want Billy wasting his time in the three-round, free-swinging amateur bouts against crude kids who couldn't teach him anything. In Ray's view, this was no flash-in-the-pan kid trying to win a tournament, but a potential big-time star who was in it for the long haul.

Ray kept Billy in training for nearly two years before involving him in any official bout. During that time, he closed his own dilapidated gym in East Liberty and affiliated with the Pittsburgh Lyceum in the Uptown section of Pittsburgh. Most of the professional trainers and boxers in Pittsburgh at that time trained at the Lyceum. Billy took the streetcar from East Liberty through Oakland into Uptown nearly every day, after he had finished his morning run.

At the Lyceum Billy met and worked with lots of good professional fighters and trainers. Local stars like Fritzie and Eddie Zivic, John Henry Lewis, Jackie Wilson, Al Quaill, and Teddy Yarosz trained there. Headline fighters who came into Pittsburgh to fight trained there, including top names in the game like Mickey Walker, Joe Louis, Tony Canzoneri, Freddie Miller, Solly Krieger, Babe Risko, and Oscar Rankins. Billy questioned the great fighters about their techniques and training methods, picking up a wealth of knowledge.

Billy developed an excellent left jab, and made progress with the left hook and right cross. He was learning to punch in combinations. He had natural defensive skills, honed by sparring with experienced partners. He developed stamina with his running, rope skipping and long sparring sessions. Young, skinny and baby-faced, he didn't look like a fighter – until he put on the gloves and sparred. He had marvelous skills, but was still physically immature compared to other professional fighters. Nevertheless, in 1934, at age 16, Ray thought his prospect was ready for his first professional fight.

Ray talked to Billy's father, telling him that he believed the kid could make money as a professional fighter. They worked out a deal involving Johnny McGarvey, a veteran local fight manager. Ray would train Billy, and Ray and McGarvey would co-manage him. Billy would keep 50%

of his earnings. Johnny Ray's 16-year-old protégé was about to emerge from the obscurity of training and sparring to fight for money before paying customers.

By 1934, the year Billy Conn began boxing professionally, the "Great Depression" was in full swing. The happy, carefree days of the Roaring Twenties were gone. Unemployment had risen to frightening levels. Democrat Franklin Delano Roosevelt was elected President in 1932, and began implementing his "New Deal," a vast bureaucracy of government programs designed to help alleviate rapidly growing poverty and joblessness. The Volstead Act was repealed in 1933, legalizing the sale of alcoholic beverages once again. Speakeasies converted back to legal taverns.

Pittsburgh was hit hard by the depression. Its many factories cut production, and thousands of workers lost their jobs. Those who kept their jobs took huge pay cuts, often 50 per cent or more. Long lines formed for "soup kitchens" that dispensed free food. Poor children ran and played in ragged clothing and shoes that their parents could not afford to replace. In January of 1932 Father James Cox of Old St. Patrick's in the Strip District led an estimated 15 to 20 thousand unemployed men to Washington by train to demand some form of government relief for their desperate situation. Many were veterans of World War I and the Spanish-American War. President Herbert Hoover met with them, but promised nothing. That November Pittsburgh, a traditional Republican town, voted overwhelmingly for Roosevelt against Hoover. The city has remained a solid Democratic bastion ever since.

Overseas, unknown to the outside world, millions of Ukrainians were perishing under the forced starvation policies of Communist ruler Josef Stalin. Germany elected Adolph Hitler and his National Socialist party to power in 1933. The Empire of Japan was beginning a massive military buildup.

In America, more young men took up boxing to earn some extra cash. The tough sport of boxing draws its participants from the poorer classes; most American boxers were immigrants, children of immigrants, or African-Americans. Among whites Italian, Jewish, Slavic, and Irish names predominated. The Irish, who had been the most prominent ethnic group in the sport since the bare-knuckle days of the late nineteenth century, now had to share the glory with many others. Print media and pundits described the decline of "The Fighting Race" in the sport it had once dominated.

Billy Conn began his career as a lightweight, weighing about 135 pounds. Boxing's champs in early 1934 included lightweight Barney Ross, born in the Lower East Side of New York City to Jewish immigrant parents, welterweight Jimmy "Babyface" McLarnin, born in Belfast, Ireland, middleweight Vince Dundee, born Vincenzo Lazzaro, light-heavyweight "Slapsie Maxie" Rosenbloom of New York, and heavyweight Primo Carnera, the "Ambling Alp" from Sequals, Italy. Dundee lost his title in September at Forbes Field to Teddy Yarosz, a son of Polish immigrants who hailed from Monaca near Pittsburgh.

Carnera stood 6'6" and fought at about 260 pounds. He was strong as an ox, but had limited boxing skills. After a string of early round KO wins in Europe, he moved to the United States to box under the management of New York Irish mobster Owney Madden, who, along with contemporaries Dutch Schultz and Lucky Luciano, ran the rackets in New York City. Madden owned the Cotton Club in Harlem, where black entertainers performed for all-white audiences. Madden was played by Bob Hoskins in the movie *The Cotton Club*. He orchestrated the career of Primo Carnera behind the scenes. Some of Carnera's fights were fixed to facilitate his rise to prominence and win betting money for mobsters who were in on it. Carnera won the title from Jack Sharkey in a fight that many assumed was fixed. On June 14, 1934, Carnera defended his title against number one contender Max Baer, a 6'2" 210 pounder (big for that time) from northern California with terrific punching power. Baer was born in Nebraska and reared in Livermore, California. He wasn't called the "Livermore Larruper" for nothing - he could hit with more power than anyone since Dempsey. Supposedly, Carnera had no idea that his rise was tainted and entered the fight with confidence. Baer battered the overmatched but courageous giant for eleven brutal rounds, after which he could no longer continue, and captured the heavyweight title. Carnera hit the canvas eleven times before he was finally unable to get up. Budd Schulberg's novel *The Harder They Fall* and the movie of the same name are thinly veiled accounts of the Carnera saga.

Max Baer is a curious part of the Billy Conn legend. At some point in 1934 or 1935 Johnny Ray took some of his fighters to the San Francisco-Oakland area for a few bouts.

He took young Conn along as a sparring partner. With a twinkle in his eye, Ray proposed that his skinny 16-year-old prospect work with the powerful heavyweight champ, Max Baer. Conn jumped fearlessly into the ring with him. The youngster danced, ducked, and parried, his fast feet and quick moves saving him time after time. After several frustrating rounds Baer gave up trying to hit him, and told the kid, "I'll bet you wish you had my strength." Conn shot back, "I'll bet you wish you had my guts."

Just two hours earlier the skinny kid had astounded waitresses at an Oakland diner by eating eleven fried eggs, a pound of bacon, three orders of hot cakes, peaches and cream, and three cups of coffee. It didn't slow him down.

On Thursday, June 28, 1934, Johnny Ray drove Billy through the rolling hills of Pennsylvania and northern West Virginia to Fairmont, a small town about 50 miles south of the Mason-Dixon line. For his first professional fight Billy was matched against Dick Woodward, a 21-year-old West Virginian, in a four-rounder. Billy had sparred with many professional fighters, of a wide range of experience and ability. He had seen amateur kids with nowhere near his talent fight three-round bouts against real opponents. Finally, it was his time. Trainers and corner men tell a nervous fighter in his debut that it's just like another sparring session, something you've done hundreds of times in the gym. But it isn't. No headgear is worn. No one stops the bout to point out a mistake or give a tiring or hurt fighter a break. It's not a stablemate buddy coming at you; it's an opponent you may have never seen who wants to make you look bad and hopes to knock you out - a tough, hungry kid desperate to make a name for himself at your expense. A referee in an official outfit warns you to "protect yourself at all times."

The Fairmont crowd that night saw a pale, thin, undeveloped teen lose a decision to a 21-year-old man of lesser skill. No Pittsburgh newspaper carried an account of the fight. Billy's one eye was nearly swollen shut. His purse was two dollars and fifty cents, of which Ray took his half. Ray also deducted 75 cents for food, so Billy ended up with a swollen eye, a decision loss, and 50 cents. It was an inauspicious start. But he had shown courage, never backing up to the stronger, older man. Billy Conn would become an artist in a different venue, one with a canvas floor and four roped poles. Dick Woodward would become the answer to a trivia question. After the fight Johnny Ray asked him if he still wanted to be a fighter. "Sure – why not!" he answered with characteristic bravado. Moonie and Junior were on their way.

ROUND THREE

No Easy Road

Billy Conn was now a professional fighter. He and Ray made the long drive to Charleston, West Virginia, for his second fight, scheduled for four rounds on Friday, July 20, against Johnny Lewis. Billy chalked up his first professional win by a third round knockout. His next fight was Thursday, August 30th, in Parkersburg, West Virginia, scheduled for six rounds against Bob Dronan. Also on the card was Harry Krause of Pittsburgh, who trained with Billy at the Lyceum and had become a good friend. Billy won a six round decision over Dronan, and Krause won his eight round decision over Young Terry.

Pittsburgh was one of the best fight towns in the country at that time, but it had not produced a champion since Harry Greb eight years ago. Teddy Yarosz of Monaca, just north of Pittsburgh, earned a shot at Vince Dundee's middleweight crown by whipping several top contenders. They fought at Forbes Field on September 9, 1934, before an enthusiastic crowd of over 20,000, the largest ever to see a fight in Pittsburgh up to that time. Yarosz, a tough, clever boxer, won a fifteen round decision, bringing the middleweight crown once again to Pittsburgh. It was a morale booster for local young fighters like Conn, and a portent of things to come. Young Billy Conn and several buddies snuck into the bout without paying, scaling a wall at Forbes Field.

Billy was scheduled to make his Pittsburgh debut on Thursday, September 27, at the North Side Arena on the undercard of the Fritzie Zivic-Harry Carlton main event. Zivic was a young welterweight prospect from the city's Lawrenceville section who was starting to attract national attention. He came from a famous fighting family, the youngest of five brothers who were all professional fighters. The oldest two, Pete and Jack, won national amateur championships in their respective weight divisions in 1920, and became the first pair of brothers ever to fight on a U.S. Olympic team. Both became good pros who were highly ranked in the 1920's, Pete as a flyweight and Jack as a welterweight. Neither ever got a title shot, but both fought the best of their era and made a good living at it. Pete opened a saloon on Butler Street in Lawrenceville after he retired. A third brother, Joe, suffered an arm injury that curtailed his career. The fourth, Eddie, was currently a good journeyman lightweight who fought top contenders, although he had yet to beat one and break into the rankings. Fritzie, 21 years old, was showing great promise. He had excellent boxing skills, good power, and a strong chin. He was a rugged kid from the tough streets of Lawrenceville who would do anything to win. He was the type of fighter Billy could learn a lot from.

Billy, weighing 137 ½, decisioned Paddy Gray of Greensburg, 139 ½, in a four-rounder. Zivic also won his ten-round main event by decision.

Billy was now 3 and 1, and gaining confidence. Johnny Ray wanted good opponents for him, ones who could give him a battle and teach him something. He viewed these early fights as a way to learn how to fight and to overcome adversity. He did not believe in building up an impressive won-lost record against easy opponents. He took Billy to Wheeling, West Virginia, on Monday, November 12th to fight the older, more experienced Petie Leone of Akron, Ohio in a six-rounder. Billy ate a big steak dinner an hour or two before the bout. The cocky kid didn't think it would affect him in a short bout. After the third round he vomited in his corner. Johnny Ray threw in the towel – Billy lost by technical knockout. He was learning all phases of the game.

Billy went back to the gym to work harder, his confidence never flagging. He was filling out, a little. His weight inched into the 140s. Shortly after the Leone fight Mickey Walker, a legendary boxer in the twilight of his career, came to the Pittsburgh Lyceum to train for a November 26th bout against Tait Littman. Walker had formerly held the world welterweight and middleweight crowns. He had fought Billy's idol, Harry Greb, in 1925.

Edward Patrick "Mickey" Walker, now 33, was a tough New Jerseyan who was nicknamed "The Toy Bulldog" because of his rugged, pug-nosed Irish face. He won the world welterweight title in 1922 at age 21, and defended it successfully six times. In 1925, while still holding the welterweight title, he took on Greb for the middleweight title at the Polo Grounds before over 50,000 fans. He lost the decision to Greb, but allegedly bested him in a speakeasy brawl later that night. After Greb lost his title to Tiger Flowers and retired, Walker beat Flowers to win the middleweight title. After three successful defenses, he fought slick boxer Tommy Loughran for the light-heavyweight title, losing in a decision. Though only five feet, seven inches tall, Walker's power and granite chin enabled him to slug with and sometimes defeat much bigger men. He was ranked as high as fifth in the heavyweight division at one point in 1931. Boxing historians consider him one of the very best pound for pound fighters ever.

When Walker came to Pittsburgh in 1934, age and the cumulative effects of over 150 bouts had caused his skills to decline. He would retire the following year. But to young Billy Conn he was a living legend, a man who had fought the best of his era, including Harry Greb. Walker took a liking to the kid and paid him ten dollars to work out with him. Johnny Ray, ever the businessman, took half the money. Walker won by a ten round decision.

ROUND FOUR

1935: Learning And Growing

In 1935, Congress passed the Social Security Act. The FDR administration instituted massive public works programs to counter persistently high unemployment. Italy, under fascist leader Benito Mussolini, invaded Ethiopia. Popular songs included "I'm in the Mood for Love," "Lullaby of Broadway," and Cole Porter's "Begin the Beguine." "Mutiny on the Bounty" won the Oscar for best picture. Former heavyweight boxing contender Victor McLaglen won best actor for *The Informer*.

On May 25th 40-year-old Babe Ruth, released by the Yankees in the previous off- season and now with the Boston Braves, hit home runs number 712, 713, and 714 of his career at Forbes Field. His last homer was the first ball ever to clear the towering right field roof. Pirate outfielder Paul Waner said it was still rising as it cleared the roof. The Pirates finished fourth that year, although shortstop Arky Vaughan won the batting title with a .385 average.

Early in January, 1935, a hot young heavyweight prospect from Detroit came to Pittsburgh to train for a January 11th bout at Duquesne Gardens against Hans Birkie of Germany. The Detroiter was a light-skinned African-American (referred to as a "Negro" in the media language of the time) who had speed, skill, and one-punch knockout power in either hand, a rare combination. Joe Louis had won all of his 13 bouts, 10 by knockout. Conn met Louis in training and worked Louis' corner for the bout, handing him the spit bottle between rounds. Louis could hardly imagine that the skinny 17-year-old welterweight would one day challenge him for the heavyweight title.

The national press was fascinated by the explosive power of Joe Louis, and Pittsburgh was no different. This bout was his eastern debut; all of his previous bouts had been in Detroit or Chicago. Birkie was an experienced heavyweight with a reputation as a tough guy to knock out. He had fought a lot of good heavyweights and beaten a few, and had only suffered one knockout in his career. The crowd of 4387 watched Louis dominate the fight through the early rounds, but he produced no knockdowns. Some fans began to boo – they had come to see the knockout power of the new sensation. By the end of the ninth round Birkie had two swollen eyes and was way behind in the scoring. But the fans wanted a knockout, and the booing increased. In the tenth and final round Louis landed five fast and hard left hooks in a row. Birkie was helpless on the ropes, his arms dangling at his sides. The referee stopped it with just over a minute to go in the fight. Louis had his fourteenth victory and 11th knockout.

The next day's *Pittsburgh Press* sports headlines shouted "Brown Bomber Explodes! Boom! Goes Birkie." Columnist Chester L. Smith wrote: "In the ring he has an insolent confidence that cannot but be disconcerting. He doesn't change expression once in a half dozen rounds and if you watch the mere suggestion of a mustache stuck somewhat precariously on his lip you will detect no movement there. Last night his mummified face wore its mask until the final round. Only then did the corners of his mouth curl ever so slightly. It was bad news for Hans when it did."

Although he was impressed with the "…frigid-faced colored boy…" Smith pronounced him not quite ready for Max Baer.

Louis was managed by John Roxborough and Julian Black, and trained by Jack Blackburn. All three were black. Blackburn, a well-respected trainer in the Detroit area, preferred to work with white fighters because he felt it was more lucrative. White fans were less likely to pay their hard-earned money to see a black fighter than a white one. He would only train a black fighter who he felt had great potential. He saw that kind of ability in young Joe Louis.

The first and only black heavyweight champion had been Jack Johnson, who held the title from 1908 to 1915. Johnson openly taunted his white opponents and appeared with white women in public, enraging white America. He defeated all of the "white hopes" that challenged him until 1915, when massive Jess Willard finally took the title from the 37-year-old Johnson. Because of Johnson, a "color line" prevented any black from fighting for the heavyweight title. No law prevented it, but it became a custom so as to prevent another Jack Johnson from holding the crown. Several black contenders were denied a legitimate shot in the 1920's. Blacks were permitted to fight for titles in all other weight classes. But the heavyweight title was considered so important to the national image that the powerful interests of the time took no chances. The all-black management team of Joe Louis laid down rules for him to avoid antagonizing the white public. He was never to taunt opponents or appear in public with white women. He was to be well-behaved at all times and display good sportsmanship. He had to convince white America that he was anything but Jack Johnson. The restrictions were not difficult for Louis, a naturally humble and polite young man.

Billy's next fight was a six-rounder against Johnny Birek, scheduled for January 29th at Motor Square Garden, just a few blocks from home. The main event featured John Henry Lewis, a top light-heavyweight contender. A native of Los Angeles, Lewis was managed by Pittsburgh numbers kingpin Gus Greenlee, and had moved to the area. Greenlee was a colorful character from the Hill District, the center of Pittsburgh's black community. Besides managing several prizefighters, he owned the Crawford Grille, which regularly featured big names like Duke Ellington, Lena Horne, and Ella Fitzgerald, and the Pittsburgh Crawfords, a baseball team of the Negro National League whose players included Josh Gibson and Satchel Paige.

Billy's neighbors and friends packed the local venue to cheer him on in the opener of five bouts. Weighing 143 ½, he outboxed Birek, 144, to win a six round decision and bring his record to 4 and 2. In the main event Lewis knocked out Don Petrin of Newark in the third. Only 20 years old, Lewis was one of the top-ranked light heavyweights in the world. He appeared to be headed for a title shot.

Billy's next fight was Monday, February 25th at the Moose Temple in downtown Pittsburgh. Again in the opening bout, he lost a six-round decision to Ray Eberle. Both boys weighed 143. Two weeks later on March 13th he won a four round decision in Wheeling over Stanley Nagy. In that bout he was staggered in the first round, and came back to his corner groggy. He sucked it up and won the remaining three rounds. He fought again in a Monday night bout at the Moose Temple on April 8th, knocking out George Schlee of the North Side at 1:30 of the first round. In the main event that night Fritzie Zivic stopped Dominic Mancini of the North Side in the 11th round due to a cut over Mancini's right eye. In an eight round semi-final, two good young middleweights battled it out. Al Quaill of Brookline won a close decision over Honeyboy Jones, a native of Massilon, Ohio who had moved to Pittsburgh to join Gus Greenlee's stable.

Billy was scheduled for his fourth fight in two months on April 25th at Motor Square Garden against Ralph Gizzy of Donora. In the main event former lightweight champ Tony Canzoneri took on Eddie Zivic. Billy had worked with Canzoneri, a master boxer, and picked up a few tips. Nevertheless, before a capacity crowd in his own neighborhood, Billy lost by decision in the four round opener. Canzoneri stopped Zivic in the seventh round. Two weeks later Canzoneri recaptured the lightweight title with a fifteen round decision over Lou Ambers.

Billy had had ten pro fights in less than ten months, with a record of six wins and four losses. He was coming along nicely, but still lacked physical maturity. He was now nearly six feet tall, but his weight still hovered in the mid-140s. Johnny Ray had put him in against tough opponents, and would continue to do so. He insisted that it was the best way to develop.

Jake Mintz owned and operated Hickey Park, an outdoor arena in Millvale, just across the Allegheny River from Pittsburgh. He promoted pro boxing cards there on Monday nights in the summer months. It was good exposure for local pugs, with a seating capacity of about 5,000. In the opening of the June 3rd card Billy took on Ray Eberle, who had defeated him in February. This time Billy won a unanimous six round decision, and impressed local fight fans. He was getting a reputation as a kid who had skill, fought aggressively, and put on a good show. In the main event John Henry Lewis needed only 1:39 of the first round to knock out Tom Patrick, a husky California Irishman.

On the following Monday, June 10th, Billy took on Ralph Gizzy again, hoping to avenge his earlier defeat like he did with Eberle. In a fast-paced, entertaining six round opener, Gizzy again got the decision.

Meanwhile, things were stirring in the heavyweight division. On June 13, 1935, Max Baer defended his title against James Braddock, an Irish-American who was born in Hell's Kitchen in New York City and grew up in New Jersey. Braddock started boxing professionally as a welterweight, but quickly grew into a light heavyweight. At 6'3" tall, he had good reach, good boxing skills, and a powerful right hand. In 1929 he earned a shot at Tommy Loughran's light heavyweight crown, losing a 15 round decision to the highly respected champion. Braddock suffered hand injuries in subsequent fights that plagued him for years. With jobs scarce in the 1930's and a wife and three kids, he went on relief and performed whatever odd jobs he could get. Although unable to train full time and suffering pain in his hands, he continued to box. He lost 18 of his next 30 fights after Loughran. Because he had a name, he was served up as a sacrificial lamb for young heavyweight prospect Corn Griffin on the undercard of the Baer-Carnera title tilt at the Long Island Bowl in June of 1934. Braddock took the fight on two days notice, and was a 5 to 1 underdog against Griffin. He knew that this was his last chance to redeem his once-promising career. He shocked the boxing world with an impressive third round knockout of Griffin. His reputation somewhat rehabilitated, he was matched against John Henry Lewis, who was being groomed for a shot at the light heavyweight crown. He was again a heavy underdog. Lewis had beaten him easily a year earlier. But not this time: Braddock again won an upset victory, this time by decision. He was matched against number one heavyweight contender Art Lasky in March of 1935, with the winner promised a shot at Baer's title. He was considered a steppingstone for Lasky, who was favored 5 to 1. For the third straight time Braddock pulled off a shocking upset, outboxing Lasky in 15 rounds. Damon Runyan dubbed Braddock "The Cinderella Man" for his rags to riches story.

The title fight with Baer was scheduled for June 13, 1935, at the Long island Bowl. Just one year earlier Braddock had been a used up fighter designated as an "opponent" for Corn Griffin. Now he was fighting for the heavyweight championship of the world, the greatest prize in sports. Baer was installed as a huge 10 to 1 favorite, as unsentimental bettors expected the Cinderella Man to meet midnight. Braddock had 22 losses, which would be unprecedented for a heavyweight champion. Baer foolishly took him lightly, and was not in top shape, expecting to knock him out. Braddock outboxed Baer easily over 15 rounds, to become the new champ with a record of 43-22-5. The Irish again had a heavyweight champion, the first since Gene Tunney retired in 1928.

Joe Louis took on former champ Primo Carnera on June 25th before over 60,000 fans at Yankee Stadium. Authorities considered postponing the fight because tension was high between the Italian and black communities over Italy's invasion of Ethiopia. But the fight went on. It was the first big name opponent for Joe Louis. Louis outboxed and outslugged Carnera, battering him to a sixth round TKO. Although not a skilled boxer, the 260 - pound Carnera possessed great strength. He was shocked at the way Louis not only beat him to the punch, but also manhandled him about the ring. Louis was now 23 and 0, with 19 knockouts. He proved that he was a force within the heavyweight division. An eventual title shot seemed inevitable.

With a record of seven wins and five losses, Billy continued to take on the best local kids. He battled Teddy Movan of McKeesport on Tuesday, July 9th at Hickey Park. The show had been postponed from its usual Monday due to rain. In a six round opener Movan, 147 ½, won the decision over Conn at 145 ¾. Less than three weeks later, Billy again bested Ray Eberle in a four round opening bout at Hickey. In that night's main event Fritzie Zivic won 11 of 12 rounds from Mike Barto of New Kensington. On August 19th at Hickey, Billy lost a close, fast-paced four round decision to Movan.

Billy was now 8 and 7 after 14 months of professional fighting. His record wasn't impressive, but his game was starting to come together. His quick left jab was difficult to stop. His defensive skills were improving. He felt stronger, too, fighting at about 147. He had held his own with good local pros, despite his youth and inexperience. But he needed to take it to the next level, to start winning. That was the way to get noticed and move on to the big money fights. He didn't want to be a four and six round fighter forever. Johnny Ray assured him that he wouldn't be, and Billy believed him.

On September 9, 1935, Billy fought George Liggins of McDonald in a four-rounder at Duquesne Gardens on the undercard of a non-title bout between featherweight champ Freddie Miller and Eddie Zivic. Billy questioned Miller about his techniques. Miller worked with him in the gym and showed him a few tricks, adding valuable information to Billy's fistic knowledge. Miller, a German-American from Cincinnati, was a world champion who had fought all over the United States as well as in London, Barcelona, Paris, Madrid, Liverpool, Glasgow, Brussels, and Belfast. He outboxed the heavier Zivic, inflicting gashes on his forehead and above his right eye. Billy also won impressively, showing speed and skill before the large crowd. The following night, Billy won a six round decision in Washington, Pa., over Johnny Yurcini. He had boxed ten rounds in two consecutive nights without difficulty. He had the stamina to do that and more. He beat Yurcini again on October 7th in Johnstown in a six round decision. The following day he turned 18.

Billy had put three good wins together in less than a month. He was matched with Movan again for October 14th at Motor Square Garden on the undercard of middleweights Al Quaill and Ken Overlin. Before a packed house he and Movan battled to a draw in what by all accounts was a great fight. Pittsburgh Press sportswriter Les Biederman offered some nice comments: "Billy Conn, 147 ½, and Teddy Movan, 150, put up one of the best fights in months in the six-rounder, with the judges splitting wide open and the referee balloting a draw. Conn appeared to have the edge. Billy has a promising future ahead and soon he's going to be a main-bouter. Swell fighter."

Overlin, the seventh ranked middleweight contender, won a narrow decision over Quaill in what was also described as a great fight. Overlin would go on to defeat Quaill three more times and eventually win the world middleweight title in 1940.

Five weeks later, in another Monday night card at the North Side Arena, Billy used his quick stiff jab to win a six round decision over Steve Walters. Billy weighed 150, the heaviest he had ever been. He felt stronger. The pre-fight hype described him as "Billy Conn, a prelim kid with a world of promise." He wouldn't remain a prelim kid for long.

Elsewhere in the boxing world, Teddy Yarosz lost his title in a September 15th bout at Forbes Field. His conqueror was a rugged Pole from Syracuse, born Henry Pylkowski, who fought under the name "Babe Risko." On October 31st John Henry Lewis won the world light-heavyweight title in St. Louis by outpointing Bob Olin in 15 rounds. In the heavyweight division Joe Louis continued on a tear. After his June destruction of Carnera, he fought King Levinsky on August 7th at Comiskey Park in Chicago before over 50,000 fans. The starting time was moved up 30 minutes because Levinsky became so terrified of Joe Louis that promoter Mike Jacobs feared he would back out. Louis knocked him down four times in the first round before the referee stopped it. On September 24th Louis and Max Baer met at Yankee Stadium in a highly publicized fight. The huge crowd of over 80,000 included thousands of blacks from nearby Harlem. Busloads of black fans from out of town, and not just from Detroit, poured into the venerable "House that Ruth built." Louis had touched a nerve around the country. Black America had a new hero in the midst of the Depression's hard times. Baer was hoping to earn a chance to win his title back with a victory against the upstart. Louis was looking to become the number one contender for the crown. Fans expected a slugfest between the two best heavyweight punchers. The fight was one-sided all the way. Louis knocked Baer down twice in the third round and finished him off with a volley of devastating punches in the fourth. Black fans celebrated all night long in Harlem, joyfully singing "...the bear goes over the mountain."

Louis fought contender Paolino Uzcudun of Spain on December 13th before a sold-out crowd at New York's Madison Square Garden. The Spaniard had never been knocked out or even knocked down in a long career against top competition, including fights with former champs Max Schmeling, Primo Carnera, and Max Baer. Uzcudun fought Louis defensively, trying to survive. In the fourth round Louis ended the fight with one punch, a right described by matchmaker Harry Markson as the hardest punch he had ever seen. It drove two of the Spaniard's teeth through his lower lip and knocked him out cold.

At the end of 1935, Billy had a record of twelve wins, seven losses, and one draw after a year and a half of professional boxing. He felt he had won his last five fights impressively, despite the fact that the Movan bout had been ruled a draw. He knew he could beat Movan, also considered an excellent prospect, and itched for another shot at him. He was stronger at 150, and still growing. Local fans had singled him out as someone they would pay to watch. Jake Mintz had planned some big Monday cards for the upcoming year, and looked for Billy to be part of the draw.

ROUND FIVE

1936: Winning All The Way

In 1936 the Spanish Civil War began. Nazi Germany staged the Olympics in Berlin as a propaganda tool to publicize its growing power. Despite a spectacular track and field performance by African-American Jesse Owens, Germany garnered the most medals and claimed that it had "won" the Olympics. FDR defeated Alf Landon by a landslide to win a second term. Popular songs included "I've Got You Under My Skin" and "Pennies From Heaven." Margaret Mitchell's novel *Gone With the Wind* soared to the top of the best seller charts. *The Great Ziegfeld* won best picture. The New York Yankees defeated the New York Giants four games to two to win the World Series. The Pirates finished fourth, but Paul Waner won his fourth batting title with a .373 average.

Billy's first fight in 1936 was Monday, January 27th at a Jake Mintz North Side Arena card against Johnny Yurcini, whom he had defeated twice by decision. In the six round opener, Billy battered Yurcini so badly for three rounds that he couldn't answer the bell for the fourth. The bout was officially scored a fourth round TKO. A week later, February 3rd, he took on veteran Louis Kid Cook in a six rounder. Billy outboxed him to win a decision. The bout was described as the best one of the night. Billy weighed 152. He was matched again with Cook on February 17th at the same arena in an eight round semi-final, his first time at that distance and in a bout of that prominence. In the first round, perhaps overconfident, Billy was knocked down for a count of eight. He won all of the remaining rounds to capture another decision win.

Four weeks later on March 16th, again at the North Side Arena, he whipped Steve Nicklish of Oil City in a six round decision. Billy opened a cut over Nicklish's left eye with a hard right hand in the first round. He was in a groove, showing outstanding skills both offensively and defensively the entire bout. Billy weighed 152 again. Nicklish was 155, nearly a full-fledged middleweight. In the main event light-heavyweight contender Al Gainer of Pittsburgh battered heavyweight Red Barry with three knockdowns and a fifth round TKO. Despite the presence of the talented and experienced Gainer, press reports described Billy Conn as the smoothest boxer on the card.

Three of the four bouts that night ended in knockouts, sending the crowd home early at 9:30. That was fortunate, because the heavy rains brought on one of the worst natural disasters in Pittsburgh history, the St. Patrick's Day flood of 1936.

The winter of 1935-36 was unusually cold and snowy. Vast reserves of snow and ice had built up in the western Pennsylvania mountains. On February 26th an ice gorge formed on the Allegheny, upriver from Pittsburgh. Heavy rain (5.45 inches) fell in the first two weeks of March, aggravating an already dangerous situation. On March, the water began rising at the confluence of the rivers downtown. Flood stage (25 feet) was surpassed early on March 17th, St. Patrick's Day. The water kept rising fast. Downtown workers were sent home. The public transportation system could not handle the volume. A mass exodus on foot ensued. Those heading south walked across the Liberty Bridge and through the Liberty Tunnels. Bigelow Boulevard was jammed with pedestrians heading east.

From March 16th to March 18th an additional four inches of rain fell in the area. By March 18th the downtown streets were waterways. The water crested at an astounding 46 feet, 21 feet above flood stage. Some streets were under 20 feet of water. By March 19th the water had receded to 32 feet, still well above flood stage.

Damage was extensive. Power and telephone lines were down. There was no drinking water. Fear of disease and looting gripped the city. Mayor William McNair requested help from the National Guard and state police, which was quickly granted. The downtown area was roped off at Grant Street and placed under martial law. The city's factories and schools shut down, and would remain closed for the next two weeks. Radio stations went off the air. Sporting events, including boxing, were cancelled. In addition to the downtown area, the communities of Lawrenceville, the Strip, the North Side, Etna, Millvale, and Sharpsburg along the Allegheny River were devastated. East Liberty was too far from the rivers to receive any direct damage, but experienced the city-wide loss of drinking water and the shutdown of most city businesses and schools.

Tens of thousands of Pittsburghers found themselves suddenly homeless. Thousands were seriously injured; many were missing. Desperate shouts for help filled the air in the ravaged communities along the river, as terrified residents waited for rescue from the upper floors and rooftops of their homes. Explosions and fires caused further damage and loss of life. Incessant fire alarms overwhelmed the city fire department.

Red Cross workers brought in truckloads of food and drinking water from outside the area, and set up emergency sites throughout the city. The dreaded typhoid epidemic was averted. Looting and vandalism were minimal.

Not until March 23rd were downtown streets visible. Water and electricity were gradually restored. The National Guard withdrew on March 30th.

The final toll of the St. Patrick's Day Flood was more than 200 dead, 3,000 injured and 110,000 homeless. Property damage was extensive. It was a severe blow to a city struggling through the hard economic times of the 1930's.

Billy's next fight was at the Moose Temple downtown on April 13th. Water damage had been repaired for the most part, and Pittsburghers were eager to resume normal activity. He took on Steve Nicklish again in a six rounder on the undercard of Al Quaill and Gene Dundee. He won easily, decking Nicklish twice. The *Pittsburgh Press* complimented him again: "Billy Conn, fast growing into a middleweight, and the best of the preliminary fighters in this district, polished off Steve Nicklich (sic) in a six-rounder. Nicklich was down twice. Conn now scales 155 pounds and one of these days is going to make trouble for a lot of good fighters."

On April 27th, again at the Moose, Billy used his quick jab in combination with strong right crosses to win a six round decision over General Burrows. After a slow start, he dominated from the third round on. The Press report referred to him as "Eddie Conn." They would soon enough get his name right. In the main event he watched Solly Krieger of New York, a top-ranked power punching middleweight contender, batter Anson Green of Homestead with an eighth round TKO. Krieger closed Green's one eye and nearly closed the other. Billy and his trainer Johnny Ray studied fighters like Teddy Yarosz and Krieger, who fought often in Pittsburgh, knowing that Billy would have to beat that caliber of fighter to become a contender and earn big money.

On May 19th Billy won a six round decision over Dick Ambrose of Bloomfield on the undercard of Teddy Yarosz versus Bob Turner at Forbes Field. The *Press* described it as a dull fight: "Conn has looked much better in the past." But he had beaten a full-fledged, experienced middleweight, who weighed 161 for the bout. Yarosz, on a campaign to recapture the middleweight crown, won eight of ten rounds from Turner.

Billy was matched with one of Gus Greenlee's fighters, Honeyboy Jones, for an eight round semifinal May 27th at Greenlee Field. Greenlee was a colorful character who controlled the numbers racket in Pittsburgh's predominantly black Hill District. Six feet, two inches tall and weighing well in excess of 200 pounds, he dressed in flamboyant clothing and chewed on a big cigar. He owned a nightclub, the Crawford Grille, a professional Negro League baseball team, and a thriving liquor business. His nightclub featured big time performers like Duke Ellington, Cab Calloway, and Lena Horne, whose father Teddy Horne was one of Greenlee's top business associates. It was a gathering place for gangsters, politicians, athletes, and jazz fans both white and black. In 1932 he built Greenlee Field on Bedford Avenue in the heart of the Hill District. It had a solid brick grandstand covered by an awning, a lush, spacious outfield, and excellent locker room facilities. Seating capacity was about 7500. His Pittsburgh Crawfords used it as their home from 1932 to 1938, when it was torn down. Negro League Hall-of-Famers Satchel Paige, Josh Gibson, Kool Papa Bell, and Oscar Charleston played there regularly.

Greenlee managed John Henry Lewis, the light heavyweight champion of the world, and several other good prospects, including middleweight Honeyboy Jones. The Pittsburgh area was loaded with middleweight talent. Monaca's Teddy Yarosz had been recently champion, lost his crown, and aimed to get it back. Al Quaill of Brookline was breaking into the rankings and fighting top middleweights from around the country. Three young prospects, Billy Conn, Honeyboy Jones, and Teddy Movan, showed great potential and were developing nicely. Local fans looked forward to Conn and Jones squaring off as the top undercard bout of the John Henry Lewis-Charlie Massera fight. Massera was a small heavyweight from Monongahela, just south of Pittsburgh. He had been good enough to fight good heavyweights, and suffered a third round knockout to Joe Louis a year and a half ago.

Legions of raucous Conn fans from East Liberty and elsewhere poured into Greenlee Field in the heart of Pittsburgh's black community at that time, and black fans turned out to support Jones and Lewis. The media hyped Conn's winning streak of 12 fights in a row. (Interestingly, the press reported his win streak as 12, which counted the draw with Movan as a win. Billy and most of the fans felt that he had won that fight, and the media seemed to go along with that sentiment.) Conn's skills had blossomed under the tutelage of Johnny Ray. Conn had offers to go to New York with better-connected management teams and train there, but decided to stay in Pittsburgh with the man who had birthed his career.

Jones had speed, skill, and power, and had beaten several good middleweights. He sparred regularly with a world champion, John Henry Lewis. The crowd expected a good fight, and they got it. Conn won a narrow victory in a bout described as three minutes of action every round. The *Press* reported: "Conn's superior boxing skill gave him the bulge although he didn't take a back seat when the slugging sign went up. That kid's got it." The fans cheered both boys' efforts. Lewis won eight of ten rounds from Massera, who nevertheless put up a competitive, entertaining fight.

The Conn-Jones fight created such a stir that the two were booked for a rematch one week later as the ten round main event, again at Greenlee Field. It would be Billy's first time at that distance. The *Pittsburgh Press* carried a feature story on Billy the day of the fight, with a large sketch that he had drawn of himself. Les Biederman wrote: "Billy hasn't yet come into the big money in boxing, but even now turns over almost all of his purses to his mother. His mother has never seen him fight, but his father never misses. He has two sisters and two brothers. Billy has ice water in his veins and before a fight you can usually see him reading a paper or a magazine."

Billy told Biederman that he was a fan of Notre Dame football. His favorite foods were ice cream and milk shakes. Other favorites were actor Paul Muni, actress Dolores Del Rio, radio broadcaster Father Coughlin, bandleader Kay Kyser, and boxer Freddie Miller, the featherweight champ who had worked with him in the gym. He said he attended Sacred Heart Church and went to bed early. He sounded like a perfectly polite, Catholic boy. His opponents would see a different side of him in the ring.

The fight was all everyone had hoped for, described well by the *Pittsburgh Press*: "The first ten-rounder was the fight of the night. Fight of the night? Fight of the year. Billy Conn, the baby-faced assassin from East Liberty, repeated an earlier victory over Honeyboy Jones, tough

Hill District colored boy, in a battle that marked Conn's debut as a main bouter… Last evening he paced himself well, slowing down just a trifle in the 7th and 8th, then going full steam in the 9th and 10th. Conn and Jones wasted little time getting underway. In the 1st round they stood with heads buried on each other's chests and fired away for fully a minute. Conn rattled several swell left hooks and right crosses of Jones' head and ribs and Jones retaliated in kind. They had the fans standing in the 10th, yelling and applauding as the two boys gave their very all to pull the fight out of the fire. Jones was pretty well used up at the finish."

At the announcement of the decision in Conn's favor, the fans rose in a standing ovation for both boys. Billy had won his 14th straight and the allegiance of a growing number of fans. Having beaten Jones twice, he felt sure he could whip Movan, and wanted a rematch.

Movan would have to wait. Billy's next fight was an eight round rematch against General Burrows at Hickey Park on Monday, June 15th. In the main event middleweight contender Solly Krieger of New York took on Joe Spiegal of Uniontown. It was Krieger's third straight fight in Pittsburgh. He had built a local following with his power punching style. The *Press* lavished more praise on Billy: "Conn, as good looking a prospect as has turned up here in years, meets General Burrows in a return 8-rounder. Billy has 14 straight victories to his credit and there isn't a fan in the city who doesn't enjoy watching him in the ring."

Perhaps overconfident, perhaps tired from the two grueling fights with Jones, Billy started slowly. His accuracy seemed to be off. Burrows knocked him down for a count of nine in the second round, and the celebrated winning streak was in jeopardy. But he fought back furiously, knocking Burrows down in the third and winning all of the remaining rounds decisively. It was his "fifteenth" win in a row, moving his overall record to 22 wins, 7 losses, and 1 draw. He had exhibited a pattern in several fights of starting slowly, then working his way into a groove and coming on strong in the middle and late rounds. After three tough fights of 26 rounds in 12 days, he needed a rest. He took off for Conneaut Lake in northwestern Pennsylvania for a vacation.

The following Friday, June 19th, Joe Louis and former champ Max Schmeling squared off in Yankee Stadium, with the winner promised a shot at Braddock's title. Louis was a heavy favorite. Max had been champ in 1933, but was now considered over the hill. Louis was considered invincible. Max studied films of Louis, and observed several of his fights in person. Louis pulverized all of the opponents, but Max noticed an amateurish mistake the youngster made. Joe did not bring his left hand back after throwing a left jab, leaving him vulnerable to an overhand right. When asked about his chances, Max told the press "I think I see something." He would not reveal what the "something" was. The media made fun of his accent, reporting that Max said "I tink I see some-ting." Max prepared to counter Joe with overhand rights.

Unlike most Louis opponents, Max Schmeling was not afraid. He saw himself as a professional with a job to do. Max took heavy punishment from Joe early in the bout, trying to get close enough to land a big right with the required perfect timing. In the fifth round the opening came, and he knocked Joe down. For the next six rounds, he landed many big rights, scoring several more knockdowns. Louis was puzzled. In the eleventh, Louis was hurt and groggy, but still showed remarkable courage and persistence. Finally Max landed a big right that put Joe down for a count of ten, registering one of the biggest upsets in ring history.

Max never got his shot at Braddock. The boxing powers in the United States feared losing control of the lucrative heavyweight title to a foreign country if Schmeling beat Braddock, which they believed he would do if given the chance. They conspired to get Louis the title shot instead. Schmeling was out in the cold.

Billy didn't get much time off before learning he would have the rematch he wanted, Teddy Movan. Promoters Jake Mintz and Ellwood Rigby combined to stage a big show at Forbes Field on July 30th. In the main event, John Henry Lewis took on top contender Al Gainer, the hardest puncher in the division, in a 12 round non-title bout. The undercard featured Honeyboy Jones versus Bill Schwerin, Billy Conn versus Teddy Movan, and Fritzie Zivic versus Laddie Tonielli of Chicago. Zivic was now a top contender in the welterweight division, and had won six in a row against stiff competition. The Press reported that Jake Mintz had offered champion Barney Ross a $10,000 guarantee to defend his title against Zivic at Forbes Field in September.

In those days many local managers sent promising young fighters to New York, where the boxing game was centered. They could receive better training there, and book frequent fights against good competition. Some would sign with big time trainers and further their careers. Conn had been offered such a deal, but had turned it down to remain in Pittsburgh with Johnny Ray. Teddy Movan took such an offer and continued his career in New York, moving there in early 1936. He won seven of eight fights against good young middleweights. Upon returning to Pittsburgh that summer, he heard nothing but how good Billy Conn was. Having beaten Conn twice and drawn with him once, Movan wanted to show Pittsburgh that he was its best young middleweight. Brimming with confidence from his success in New York, Movan told the *Press*, "Get me this guy Conn. I whipped him twice and I'll whip him again."

The bout was billed as a grudge match, with both fighters feeling that they were vastly improved in the past year, and eager to renew their series.

Over 17,000 fans showed up, the second largest crowd to see a fight in Pittsburgh up until that time. Teddy Yarosz's 1934 title bout with Dundee still held the record, having drawn over 20,000. Movan came at Billy hard in the early rounds, but couldn't connect much. Billy's superb defense made him miss and look bad. Billy methodically landed his quick jabs and rights, winning easily. As the Press said, Conn "…wound up giving the McKeesporter a fairly good beating."

In other bouts, Honeyboy Jones TKO'd Schwerin in the seventh, Zivic TKO'd Tonielli in the sixth, and Lewis won by decision over Gainer.

Movan was sorely disappointed by his loss to Conn, and campaigned for another chance. After all, he owned two victories over Billy and felt he deserved another shot. He got his wish eleven days later, as the main event on a card of four local eight-rounders at Hickey Park. Conn and Movan started slowly in the first round, feeling each other out. Teddy was determined not to rush wildly and let Billy make him miss so badly as in their last fight. In the second round Billy turned it on, landing repeated left jabs and left hooks, with an occasional hard right thrown to keep Movan off balance. His speed of hand and foot made Movan look clumsy, and Movan landed very few punches. The fight became progressively more one-sided as Conn battered Movan, who bled freely from the nose from the second round on. In the latter rounds Billy landed more hard rights. Near the end of the eighth and final round Movan was helpless against the ropes. Referee Red Robinson moved in to stop the bout just as the final bell rang. Robinson ruled that the bell proceeded his stoppage, and the bout was officially ruled a decision win for Conn. Afterward doctors discovered that Movan had broken his right thumb during the bout.

Billy had looked strong and sharp against Movan's game effort. He had shown no letup in eight rounds, nearly as fresh at the end of the fight as he was at the start. He had improved more than Movan over the past year, despite the latter's New York experience. He was booked for another main event at Hickey Park four weeks later against Honeyboy Jones, whom he had beaten in two close fights. Jake Mintz knew that the fans would come out for this one between two crowd pleasers, even though they had fought twice just three months ago. This one was scheduled for ten rounds.

Billy started slowly in the bout, as was his tendency at times. Perhaps having already beaten Jones twice, it was hard to get himself up for it. Jones had no such problem. He ached to beat Conn, and had come close twice. Conn's victories over Movan had established him as the best young prospect. Jones had been winning also, and a victory here could be a huge boost to his career. Jones started fast, outboxing and outpunching Billy the first four rounds as Conn fans watched in disbelief. Billy was consistently missing with the left hook; Jones had figured out a way to avoid it. In the fifth round Billy changed tactics, landing frequent right hands and outboxing Jones on the inside. He forced the action in all six remaining rounds, winning all of them on some cards. The verdict was a split decision. Judge Jap Williams and referee Red Robinson voted for Conn, while Judge Columbus voted for Jones. The *Pittsburgh Press* had it 6-4 for Conn.

It was a close but impressive win for Conn. He had shown the ability to change tactics during a fight against a good fighter. Once again, he came on strong at the end to win. He was ready for bigger names, and bigger purses.

Ellwood Rigby promoted another show at Forbes Field on September 21st. Babe Risko, who had just lost the middleweight title to Freddie Steele, agreed to fight Teddy Yarosz in Pittsburgh. Both were former champs and the winner stood a good chance of getting another title shot. The top prelims were also middleweights. Solly Krieger of New York and Frankie Battaglia of Winnipeg were also rated near the top of the division. Another prelim matched Billy Conn against Roscoe Manning, described as a "Newark Negro" with much more experience than Conn. Manning, who had a reputation as a good body puncher, weighed in at a surprising 166, nearly ten pounds heavier than Conn.

Billy was much too fast for Manning. He opened a cut over Manning's eye in the second round, and had the eye closed by the fifth. Unable to see out of his left eye and already thoroughly beaten, Manning refused to come out for the sixth round, giving Billy a TKO win. After the bout Manning's manager claimed that his fighter wasn't in top shape. Billy purse was $750 for beating Manning, the most he had ever been paid for a fight.

Slugging Solly Krieger easily beat the favored Battalino, and Yarosz beat Risko for the first time in three tries, winning by decision.

Billy was on the march to middleweight contention as he neared his nineteenth birthday. The division was the most talented in boxing, with Freddie Steele, Teddy Yarosz, Babe Risko, Solly Krieger, Oscar Rankins, Al Hostak, Lou Brouillard, Marcel Thil, Vince Dundee, and

Fred Apostoli. All but Rankins would hold the title at some point in the 1930's.

Billy's next bout was October 19th at Islam Grotto on the North Side against Charlie Weise, a tough, experienced Brooklyn middleweight who could punch and take a punch. Weise was considered a "trial horse," which is a fighter who is a step below the top contenders and is a good test for young prospects. A kid who could beat a guy like Charlie Weise would have to be considered a "comer," a prospect with a bright future. It was scheduled for ten rounds. Billy was a ten round fighter now, advanced forever beyond the four, six and eight round preliminary status. Billy surprised the fans by abandoning his usual slick style and attacking Weise aggressively. He outboxed Weise on the inside and battered him about the ring with a vengeance in nearly every round. He kept up a furious pace, making Weise miss repeatedly and making him pay with lefts and rights. He won an easy ten round decision. The following Thursday, just three days later, he faced Ralph Chong, another trial horse, in the semi-final of the Solly Krieger-Oscar Rankins bout at Duquesne Gardens. The *Pittsburgh Press* questioned the legality of fighting again so soon in ten round bouts, but the fight went on. Chong was a rarity, a Chinese-American professional boxer. Thick-legged and sturdy, he could take a punch and deliver one. The *Press* referred to him as a "piano-legged Oriental." Billy won the decision, but looked sloppy. Two ten round bouts in four days may have been a little too much.

Krieger, called a "New York Jewish boy" and Rankins, called a "West Coast Negro" by the *Press*, put on a terrific fight. (The sports media in those days played up ethnic differences and stereotypes, as shown by the references to Chong, Krieger, and Rankins. A battle between an Italian and black fighter might be touted as a rerun of the Italy-Ethiopia war; an Irish fighter might be accused of having an "Irish temper.") Both were renowned sluggers. Rankins was cut over both eyes and went down in the tenth, but landed some shots that made Krieger wince, and made the crowd wonder how he stayed upright. Krieger won a 12 round decision and put himself in line for a possible title shot. Conn later described the Krieger-Rankins fight of that night as one of the best he had ever seen.

It was appropriate that a great fight be staged in Pittsburgh on October 22, 1936, the tenth anniversary of the death of Harry Greb.

Billy Conn, just turned 19, had emerged as the best young middleweight prospect in Pittsburgh, but there was another young Pittsburgh fighter who had done even more than Conn. Fritzie Zivic, 23, had won 12 fights in a row against good competition and was ranked near the top of the welterweight division. Pittsburgh promoters had thus far been unsuccessful in getting him a title shot. Despite Jake Mintz's offer to champ Barney Ross, Ross gave the title shot to Izzy Janozzo, ranked below Zivic. Zivic had begun his career in 1931 at age 18, and already had over 50 professional fights. Both Conn and Zivic were skillful, crowd-pleasing fighters who gave their all. Both had large local followings. They lived barely a mile apart, one in East Liberty and one in Lawrenceville.

Conn's emergence throughout 1936 generated a lot of positive publicity. The Zivic camp felt that Conn was getting more ink than their fighter, who had accomplished more. Zivic manager Luke Carney issued a challenge to the Conn camp. Ray and McGarvey initially ignored it, but Carney repeated it several times, prompting the Conn camp to take offense. McGarvey had harsh words with Carney, explaining that Conn wasn't yet experienced enough for Zivic and that it wasn't proper at this point to be issuing challenges. Ray and Carney almost came to blows in a heated confrontation. Each camp knew that they had a hot property with a world of fistic and financial potential, and were jealous of the other's reputation.

After all of the bad blood and verbal taunts, Johnny Ray thought long and hard about his Junior fighting Fritzie Zivic. Havey (not Harvey) Boyle of the *Pittsburgh Post-Gazette* reported that Ray felt Conn's reputation could suffer by refusing to fight a welterweight. Ray, a master strategist, had studied Zivic and decided that Junior just might have the style to beat Fritzie, even at this early stage in his career. Ray offered this opinion publicly. At that point the Zivic camp seemed to back off somewhat, realizing what they had to lose by fighting Conn. At the Dapper Dan awards dinner McGarvey told reporter Regis Welsh, "Carney's acting like he's afraid of something and it must be Conn."

At the same dinner Conn told Welsh: "Get me Zivic. I think it would be a great fight."

Welsh reported in the same article that Billy Conn looked "as dapper as anyone" at the dinner. Billy had become a strikingly handsome young man and a snappy dresser.

The fighters themselves knew and liked each other. They had sparred often in the gym. Both were courageous kids willing to fight anybody. The posturing and ill feeling was between their handlers, not between Billy and Fritzie.

Promoters Ellwood Rigby and Jules Beck both saw a bout between the two as a natural, a potential moneymaker. Zivic's edge in experience was countered by Conn's edge in size, about four inches and ten pounds. The fight could be sold as a competitive one. Rigby signed Conn to a contract to fight Zivic on Christmas Day at Duquesne Gardens. Beck signed Zivic to a contract to fight Conn on Christmas Day at an undetermined site. But a fight can only happen when both parties sign, and neither promoter could get both fighters on the same piece of paper.

Both fighters were booked to headline a December 2nd card at Motor Square Garden in Conn's neighborhood to drum up publicity for their eventual meeting. Conn was matched with Jimmy Brown of Canton, Ohio. Zivic drew a tougher assignment with welterweight contender Harry Dublinsky of Chicago. Both youngsters, well aware of the other's reputation, fought like they had something to prove. Conn boxed beautifully, his long quick lefts and hard rights taking their toll on Brown. He put on a defensive show, blocking nearly everything that Brown threw. In the sixth round he tore into Brown, knocking him down three times. He knocked him down again in the seventh, and in the eighth. The "game Negro" kept coming, suffering a sixth knockdown in the ninth round, when the referee finally stopped it.

Zivic came out winging, as was his style, decking Dublinsky three times in the first round, once in the second, twice in the fourth and once more in the sixth before the towel came flying into the ring, signaling surrender.

Regis Welsh of the *Pittsburgh Press* wrote:

"It was a great night for these two kids, each envious of the other's reputation, and each more eager to fight one another than the promoters seem willing to match them. They are decidedly opposite stylists, Zivic the rough, swinging, punching, mauling type; Conn, a boxer, willing to take risks that he can eventually nail him with a right hand about as potent as Zivic's. They'd make a swell match here – and the sooner the better, even at the expense of killing one of them off."

A bidding war between Rigby and Beck ensued. Rigby won by offering the boxers an unprecedented 65% of the gate, which was expected to gross eight to twelve thousand. Zivic was to receive 35% and Conn was to receive 30%. In boxing promotions at that time 55% was the maximum ever offered to the fighters. The remainder of the money was needed for expenses such as building costs and pay for prelim fighters and referees, and to allow for the promoter to make a profit. Rigby was willing to risk making minimal profit to be associated with the event. Both fighters signed with Rigby in a media-staged event at the Pittsburgher Hotel downtown. The new date was Monday, December 28th.

On December 18th, just ten days before the fight, the Pittsburgh Press reported that state boxing commissioner William McClelland had shocked the parties involved by calling off the fight. McClelland declared the contract invalid because of the high percentage guaranteed to the fighters and the weight differential. He said that the 65% for the fighters was excessive, since the maximum in any previous bout was 55%. He also had problems with the weights of the participants. The contract called for Conn to weigh 159 or less, with no weight stipulated for Zivic. Since Zivic usually fought at 146 or 147, Conn could outweigh him by twelve or more pounds. McClelland said that the law prohibited a weight disparity of over ten pounds. (Heavyweights exempted, of course.)

Promoter Rigby and the Conn and Zivic camps, including the fighters, met in McClelland's office on December 21st, just one week before the scheduled date of the bout, which was already nearly a sellout. McClelland put Conn and Zivic on a scale in street clothes. Conn weighed 167 1/2, Zivic 157 ½. The contract was revised to reduce Zivic's take from 35 to 30 percent, and Conn's from 30 to 25 percent, meeting the 55% maximum. Conn was required to weight 157 or less, while Zivic was required to weigh 147 or more. With the new stipulations, McClelland sanctioned the bout. Ellwood Rigby breathed a sigh of relief.

All of the negotiations were settled. The posturing and accusations were over. Christmas was over. Monday, December 28th was fight night at Duquesne Gardens. The place sold out despite the economic distress. The press buildup was feverish: Lawrenceville versus East Liberty, Croatian versus Irish, tough KO puncher versus classic boxer. The records spoke for themselves: Zivic had won 12 of his last 13 fights, eight by KO. Conn had not lost in his last 23 fights, dating back to August of 1935. Zivic, ranked the number four welterweight in the world by Ring Magazine, was a two to one favorite based on his superior opposition.

Havey Boyle wrote in the *Post-Gazette*: "The situation has not left tempers calm or feelings unruffled and all this will be reflected in the attitude of the fighters when they square off Monday night. Neither is a kitten in the ring under normal circumstances and each, now knowing that their respective backers have a score to settle, will put on a little extra steam."

Boyle reiterated his feeling that despite Ray's posturing about being forced to fight to avoid damage to Conn's reputation, Ray wouldn't take the fight if he didn't think Conn would win. Boyle quoted Conn as saying: "I think I can lick anyone that Johnny Ray tells me I can lick. I know if I do what Ray tells me that I will be all right against anyone he picks."

The kid obviously had supreme trust in his mentor, who had moved him along against tougher competition than a young prospect usually faced. Ray's reputation was on the line in this one as much as Conn's.

Welsh wrote that the "inside dope" favored Zivic because of his experience. He described Conn as talented but "immature" in the ring compared to Zivic. Local experts expected Zivic to start fast and rattle the youngster with his punching power, but cautioned that if Conn survived into the late rounds his superior size and boxing ability could cause trouble for Zivic.

On fight day Conn weighed in at 156 ¾; Zivic weighed 149 ½. The difference was just seven pounds, easily satisfying McClelland's mandate. Duquesne Gardens sold out, with 5,163 paying customers in a time of severe economic distress. Hundreds of partisans were turned away, unable to purchase tickets. Rowdy youths, especially those from East Liberty and Lawrenceville, threatened to storm the gate and were only held in check by a strong police presence. The battle between these two local kids had captivated Pittsburgh. Both had touched the struggling city's pride in a special way, and would for many years to come, even after their careers had ended and they were revered as Hall of Fame legends. As Havey Boyle eloquently put it: "Two nicer kids in boxing (outside of the ring) it would be difficult to find. Two tougher kids (in the ring)... it would be even more difficult to find."

In the top prelims Jackie Wilson and Harry Krause won impressively, both defeating opponents from Cleveland. Tension built as the boisterous crowd awaited the main event. Conn and Zivic and their cohorts marched into the ring to the wild cheers of their backers. Both had much to lose, but Zivic had more. For Conn a loss to a welterweight, even though a top ranked one, would delay his rise to a middleweight ranking. For Zivic, a loss to a greenhorn like Conn, even though he was bigger and locally respected, could jeopardize his quest for a world title shot. In the corners Carney and Ray prepared their star pupils, rubbing the Vaseline jelly on their faces and giving last minute instructions. The bell rang; the crowd's eyes were riveted on the center of the brightly lit ring. Billy Conn moved toward Fritzie Zivic, his first name opponent. Zivic, as expected, came after him hard. Zivic tore into the youngster, battering him about the ring with left hooks and right uppercuts that had felled many a foe. Conn looked rattled. Only his superb reflexes prevented a knockout. As the bell ended the first round, both boys kept fighting and had to be separated by referee Al Grayber. All three judges gave Zivic the round. Conn looked like he was in over his head, as many had said. The second round started much the same way. Billy bled from the mouth and a cut on his left cheek. Late in the round Billy's quick left jab started to land, keeping Zivic at bay. The third round went back and fourth, Zivic getting in good shots at times, Conn outboxing him at times. Zivic was warned for butting. Near the end of the round Conn landed a tremendous right to the heart, making Zivic wince. Zivic dominated the fourth and fifth rounds, building a big lead at the halfway point, and apparently headed for victory. But Conn had taken Zivic's best and survived, never losing his confidence or poise. In the sixth Billy used his long jab and quick feet to keep Zivic away while peppering him repeatedly. The seventh and eighth went much the same way. Zivic, unable to land to the head, attacked the body. He landed some punches, but couldn't slow down the dancing, jabbing Conn. With two rounds to go, it was very close. Conn needed the last two rounds. He danced and jabbed, his long left penetrating Zivic's defense through the ninth. Zivic kept firing his vicious left hook, which had broken Lou Ambers' jaw a year earlier, just missing the quick youngster most of the time. The fight appeared to be up for grabs as they touched gloves for the tenth and final round. Zivic stormed out like he had in the first round. Billy stood toe to toe with him. They slugged it out, neither backing away, with the screaming crowd on its feet. Zivic landed two good rights, backing Conn up to the ropes. But Billy fought back hard, landing a flurry of punches. Then Billy danced away, and stuck his jab into Zivic's face for the remainder of the round. Zivic frantically fired punches, missing his elusive foe with most of them. The standing crowd cheered wildly as the bell rang, ending an epic battle between two superb local talents. Both fighters had earned each other's respect. The left side of Conn's face and his lips were swollen. Zivic had a small cut on the left cheek. Silence fell over the arena as the verdict was announced. Judge Jap Williams scored it 6-3-1 for Conn, giving him the last five rounds.

Referee Al Grayber scored it 5-4-1 for Zivic, to whom he had given the last round. Judge William McBeth had it 5-4-1 for the winner by split decision, Billy Conn. Conn supporters exploded in cheers, but all of the fans applauded both fighters. Conn and Zivic shook hands in a heartfelt show of sportsmanship.

Regis Welsh of the *Pittsburgh Press* scored it 5-3-2 for Conn. Welsh wrote:

"There was plenty of controversy over the verdict. Enough, maybe, to call for a rematch. But let's not have it. There was glory enough for both last night. Conn was superb in his operations once he got underway. Zivic, thwarted of a kayo by nothing but Billy's gameness, has other fields to conquer. For a match that should never have been made, it was a grand fight between two good fighters. But once was enough. Even the most rabid partisan should agree on that. It still leaves these two swell kids to entertain without tarnish to either's reputation. Let it be so."

The *Pittsburgh Press* lauded Conn in its headlines: "CONN'S GAME COMEBACK OVERCOMES RUGGED ZIVIC: Billy's Boxing Style Baffles Fritzie in Season's Biggest Upset." The *Post-Gazette* was kinder to Zivic in its headline: "CONN SURPRISES BY VICTORY OVER ZIVIC: Billy Awarded Verdict in Hair-raising Battle."

Zivic's purse was $2502.60. Conn's was $2085.50, by far the most he had ever received for a fight. Billy asked for his money in five-dollar bills, so that it looked like more. Half of it went to his management team, who had earned it. Johnny Ray had moved him along nicely, silencing the critics who claimed he was pushing Billy too fast. Billy had learned a lot about fighting in two and a half years.

Billy Conn was a fighter on the fast track as 1936 ended. Still sore from Zivic-inflicted cuts on his cheek and mouth, he looked forward to bigger fights with bigger purses in 1937. He had won all nineteen of his fights in 1936, progressing from an unknown welterweight to a main event middleweight. He had whipped veterans Louis Kid Cook, Steve Nicklish, and General Burrows twice apiece, even coming back strong from knockdowns against Cook and Burrows. He had beaten the very talented Honeyboy Jones three times, the second time in his first main event. He had avenged his losses to Teddy Movan, the second time in one-sided, convincing fashion. He had forced Roscoe Manning to quit and knocked out Jimmy Brown; both were competent journeyman middleweights. And he had beaten Fritzie Zivic, top-ranked welterweight contender, in a highly publicized main event fight. He had trailed badly in the third Jones fight and against Zivic, but had come back strong to win in the end.

It had all come together, just like Johnny Ray said it would. He had the long quick left jab that he could land almost at will, enabling him to follow up with combinations of left hooks, rights, and uppercuts. His quick feet and reflexes saved him from punishment. He had filled out and now had the physical strength to battle strong middleweights. He had proven that he could take a punch and had the heart and stamina to come back from adversity and win tough fights. At age 19, his future seemed as bright as Pittsburgh's dirty skies were dark.

ROUND SIX

1937: Hitting The Big Time

On January 1st, 1937, the Pitt Panthers capped an outstanding football season by defeating Washington 21-0 in the Rose Bowl. The Duquesne Dukes did the same by beating Mississippi State 18-12 in the Orange Bowl. Popular songs included "In the Still of the Night" and "Johnny One Note." *The Life of Emile Zola* won best picture. German dirigible "The Hindenberg" exploded in flames over New Jersey. Famed female aviator Amelia Earhart was missing in the Pacific. The Pirates finished third. Paul Waner batted .354, but fell short in his attempt at a fourth batting title.

Ray and McGarvey wasted no time in landing a big name opponent for their hot young fighter. Babe Risko had recently been world middleweight champion, winning the title from Teddy Yarosz at Forbes Field in September, 1935. He lost it to Freddie Steele by 15 round decision in July, 1936, and lost again in a return bout on February 19, 1937, held at New York's Madison Square Garden. Eager to get back on the winning track and pursue another title shot, Risko agreed to fight the young, inexperienced Conn at Duquesne Gardens on March 11th. Risko was a rugged, full-sized, top-ranked middleweight. Conn had barely gotten by welterweight Fritzie Zivic. The fight seemed a sure bet for Risko: teach the kid a boxing lesson, make some good dough, and move on. Local press critics ridiculed Conn's management team for throwing him in with such a top middleweight at this point. They said the kid needed to mature and beat some good fighters before taking on Risko. They pointed out that a recent promising middleweight prospect from Pittsburgh, Al Quaill, had been hurt badly by being matched with opponents for whom he was not yet ready. Risko, a rugged Pole from Syracuse, could box, punch, and had a world of experience. Besides his two fifteen round battles with Steele, he had beaten Teddy Yarosz in two of three fights, and had knocked him out in the first one. Johnny Ray felt that Conn was ready for such a big step. Observers who had criticized him for matching the kid with Zivic thought he was really crazy now, and perhaps sacrificing the kid's future to make a quick killing. Young Billy Conn, questioned by the *Pittsburgh Press* if he was rushing things, gave them the controversial answer they wanted: "They said the same thing when I fought Zivic, and I beat him, didn't I? Risko's reputation is not going to scare me. Yarosz beat him by boxing his ears off. I'll do the same thing and give him a few right-handers just to keep him from getting too fresh."

Of course the media and promoters loved it, because it helped sell tickets and papers. But this brash kid didn't know what he was getting into. He had never taken on a fighter with the strength and power of Risko. Even Zivic, with all his experience, had not fought at anywhere near the levels Risko had: four middleweight title bouts in the last two years, winning two and losing two. He had also fought many top contenders, and was definitely in his prime at age 25. Conn's record stood at 33 wins, 7 losses, and 1 draw. Much was made of his streak of 24 bouts without a loss. But Risko's record of 37 wins, 12 losses, and 5 draws was against vastly superior competition.

Both fighters weighed in at 160. Risko was 5'10", three inches shorter than Conn. Risko was ruggedly handsome, with dark hair and a solid build. Conn's curly-haired, boyish looks had made him a local heartthrob.

Just before the fight began, Johnny Ray collapsed in pain in the lobby of the arena. He refused to go to a hospital. After receiving first aid in the locker room, he gave "Junior" final instructions. Unable to stand, Ray was helped to a seat near Conn's corner. Johnny McGarvey took his place in the ring. Seated near Ray were Teddy Yarosz and his manager Ray Foutts. They had come to scout Risko, who had beaten Teddy in two of three fights, and perhaps to see how the Conn kid was coming along.

So Billy Conn awaited the bell for the biggest fight of his life without his mentor who had been right there with him for every fight of his career. Ray could barely speak, and could not yell instructions above the crowd noise. All he could do was watch. But Conn wasn't rattled. The nineteen year old remained supremely confident, too naïve to understand what he was up against; or maybe he knew something no one else knew.

Risko started quickly, like Zivic had, using his strength and powerful shoulders to bull Conn around the ring. But Conn battled back, landing effectively to the body. Both fighters attacked the body in the early rounds, Risko landing mostly rights and Conn mostly left hooks. Despite Risko's reputation as a puncher, Conn stood up well to the attack, and seemed fresher than Risko at the halfway point. Risko was unable to land his big right hand to Conn's head. Conn appeared to have the edge in the sixth, and perhaps a slight lead with four rounds to go. In the seventh Conn fired his long jab with authority, snapping Risko's head back repeatedly and opening a cut over his left eye. Conn was in a groove, dancing, jabbing, and hooking, and Risko was unable to land much of anything. To the shock of the crowd, the experts, and Babe Risko, Conn had taken command of the fight. In the eighth Conn attacked, staggering Risko with a left hook to the jaw and following it up with a good battering of rights and lefts. The packed house, now more sure that their boy Billy was going to pull off the upset, erupted in wild, raucous cheering. Could this be the former champ who had just battled Steele for 15 tough rounds? In the ninth Conn jabbed and danced, easily outboxing Risko, who began to swing and miss wildly. Toward the end of the round Conn attacked again, driving Risko into the ropes with a barrage of hard rights and left hooks. As they touched gloves for the tenth and final round, a knockout did not seem out of the question. But Conn, on the advice of his handlers, was content to box, and avoid a slugfest with the dangerous Risko. Conn landed jabs while Risko landed very little. The bout ended in a surprisingly easy victory for Conn, who had won at least seven of the ten rounds on the judges' and most observers' cards. He had been too fast for Risko, and, most shockingly, had ultimately outpunched him. Risko's handsome face, bruised and cut, testified to the accuracy of Conn's punching.

After the decision was announced, Conn left the ring and went immediately to the stricken Johnny Ray, kissing him on the lips. He repeated the gesture in the locker room as they celebrated.

Conn had whipped Risko more decisively than champion Freddie Steele had in two title bouts. His stock rose enormously – big money awaited. "JUVENILE BOXING MASTER GIVES FORMER CHAMPION SOUND LACING" crowed the *Pittsburgh Press*. He had inserted himself into the crowded middleweight picture, although in those days a lot more than one victory against a top contender was needed to attain contender status. Local media began pushing for the inevitable Conn-Yarosz match-up.

The next day *Pittsburgh Press* sports editor Chester Smith publicly repudiated his own pre-fight statement that Conn was overmatched with Risko, and wrote: "To the surprise of a great many and the apparent delight of all, Billy took Babe Risko apart in Duquesne Gardens last night..."

Smith also referred to Conn's father, stating that the elder Conn "...will sling a punch himself if somebody says something about the boy that isn't up the right alley."

Billy had spoken to his father about several brawls his father had engaged in during Billy's fights. Billy explained that he had enough to worry about with his own fight, and would appreciate not having to worry about his father fighting also. "Wild Bill" Conn, still young at age 38 and with a well-earned reputation as a brawler, did not heed Billy's request. After repeated incidents, Billy asked his father to stop attending his bouts, a request the elder Conn ignored.

Conn's victory made the world take notice, and also made Zivic and the other Pittsburgh fighters look better. But he was only one new good prospect in the talent-rich middleweight division. Two champions claimed the world title: Freddie Steele of Seattle and Marcel Thil of France. Throughout the 1920s there was only one champion: first Johnny Wilson, then Harry Greb, then Tiger Flowers, then Mickey Walker. When Walker relinquished the crown in 1931, jurisdictional disputes gave way to a divided title.

The local media clamored for a Conn-Yarosz showdown. Yarosz had beaten tough Solly Krieger in his hometown of New York in January, and hoped for another title shot. Conn's victory over Risko showed that Billy could compete in the big leagues, and made the bout a natural. But the handlers decided it would be better to have the principals take on other opponents and let the buildup result in a big-money bout at Forbes Field in the summer.

A week after the Conn-Risko fight Solly Krieger and Oscar Rankins clashed again at Duquesne Gardens. Ray wanted Krieger for Conn's next fight. Krieger was well known and popular in Pittsburgh, and a victory over him would boost Billy's stock even higher. It would be a risky fight – Krieger was a dangerous puncher who could knock out anyone who got careless. Rankins beat Krieger in a close decision this time, in another brutal battle. Krieger suffered a broken bone in his left hand, and would be unable to fight for at least several months. Rankins, however, was available. Like Krieger, he was a dangerous puncher and highly respected in the middleweight division. Also like Krieger, he had fought often in Pittsburgh and was known to local fans as a crowd pleaser. A bout was scheduled for April 1st at Duquesne Gardens, just two weeks away.

While training for Rankins, Conn aggravated an old ear injury in sparring. He had had problems with the ear in the past, and had re-injured it in the victory over Risko. Dr. Grover Weil examined him and recommended a minor surgical procedure before Billy did any more boxing. Billy went to Mercy Hospital for the surgery. He showed his frustration when reporters interviewed him there. "I can't stand being in here," he told them. "I got to beat a lot of other fellows before summer comes and I can't beat them in this place."

Bouts with either Krieger or Rankins were out for now. Billy's ear had to heal from the surgery.

For Conn's next fight, his team booked Vince Dundee of Baltimore, former middleweight champion who had won the title in 1933 and lost it in 1934 to Teddy Yarosz. Born Vincenzo Lazzaro in Italy in 1904, Dundee had a reputation as a tricky boxer, but appeared to be a little past his prime at age 33. He had suffered a third round knockout to Freddie Steele in 1936, but had come back with four straight wins in 1937 against lesser opposition. He would be a good name to add to Billy's resume, although his skill and experience could be trouble. The bout was set for May 3rd at Duquesne Gardens. Yarosz was matched with Lou Brouillard in his hometown of Boston for May 7th.

Rankins manager George Trafton, angered that his fighter was not matched with Conn in what would be a lucrative bout, accused Ray of avoiding Rankins. He complained that Ray wanted a bout with Rankins right after the Krieger bout because Rankins had suffered cuts in that bout that had not fully healed. Now that his fighter was healthy, Trafton stated, Ray wanted to avoid him.

Conn, often called the "teenage sensation" by the media, found himself in the unprecedented position of favorite against a big name opponent. His dismantling of Risko had raised expectations. Although Dundee's skills had declined somewhat, he was still known as a masterful boxer. One of his many tactics was the "rope trick" in which he would bounce off the ropes and make his opponent miss, then take advantage of the opening to nail the opponent. A full-length picture of Conn in the *Pittsburgh Sun-Telegraph* on May 2nd carried the caption: "Billy Conn, East Liberty middleweight, who returns to the fistic wars tomorrow night at Duquesne Garden when he opposes Vince Dundee, former world's middleweight champion. Conn is meeting one of the craftiest boxers the ring has ever known and one who may surprise the surprising young East Ender."

Conn weighed in at 161, Dundee at 157 ¾. Unlike his behavior with Risko, Conn showed great respect for Dundee, addressing him as "Mr. Dundee."

With Johnny Ray back in his corner, Billy came out jabbing, easily outboxing the shorter ex-champ in the first two rounds. Near the end of the second round, he landed a big right that buckled Dundee's knees. Dundee had to find a way to neutralize the youngster's speed and reach. In the third round Dundee came to life, showing the skill that had made him a champion. Conn's aggressive attack missed frequently against Dundee's tricky head movement and rope trick. Dundee landed a lot of jabs and a big right that had Conn bleeding from the mouth. It would be the only clear-cut winning round for Dundee. In the fourth round Billy caught on to the rope trick, following Dundee to the ropes and attacking the body, too smart to try to nail his elusive head. Billy won the fourth and fifth rounds. In the sixth Dundee came on strong, slugging it out with Billy up close. Billy got the better of it, battering him with lefts and rights to the head and body. The seventh and eighth rounds were close, but the edge went to Conn. Near the end of the eighth Billy landed a left hook that hurt Dundee. The ninth and tenth rounds were action-packed slugfests that brought the crowd to its feet. Billy's relentless attack showered hard lefts and rights on Dundee for two whole rounds, but the ex-champ fought back hard, and survived on grit and experience. At the final bell Billy respectfully shook hands with "Mr. Dundee" and thanked him for imparting some of his valuable ring wisdom. The decision wasn't close. Billy won at least eight of the ten rounds on all cards, but most of the rounds were competitive. The Pittsburgh crowd enthusiastically cheered the loser as he left the ring. Both fighters gushed respect for each other in post-fight interviews. Conn said: "I guess I missed more punches tonight than I ever did… He's the best I ever fought."

Dundee was touched by the youngster's respect: "Imagine that – calling me Mr. Dundee. I must be somebody. Say, that kid's all right. I hope he goes a long way. He's a little bit green right now, but he's all right. He keeps popping you with a left hand. His right is not as dangerous as it looks. He throws it too far. But he'll shorten it up. Yes sir, he's a great prospect."

Regis Welsh praised Conn for his boxing and punching skills, but criticized him for lack of a killer instinct when he had Dundee in trouble. Havey Boyle agreed that Conn was a great prospect, but one who still needed more experience and more power in his right hand. He pointed out that Steele had knocked Dundee out in the third round a year ago. He cautioned not to expect too much at such an early stage in Conn's career.

In the walkout bout after the main event, lightweight Harry Krause decisioned Pete Leone. Four days after Conn's win, Teddy Yarosz decisioned Lou Brouillard in Boston. Yarosz had two big wins in a row, and ached for another title shot. On May 11th Steele retained his title with a third round knockout of Frankie Battaglia in Seattle, his third straight successful title defense.

At age 19, Conn had beaten two former world champions, showing unusual ring intelligence for one so young and inexperienced. Dundee's rope trick had baffled many opponents, but Conn adjusted to it and neutralized it. He was ready to take on Teddy Yarosz, another crafty boxer. Yarosz was one of the top middleweights in the world, but Conn wanted to prove that he wasn't even the best middleweight in Pittsburgh.

Offended by Oscar Rankins manager George Trafton's accusations, Ray agreed to a bout with Rankins for May 27 at Duquesne Gardens, promoted by Ellwood Rigby. Rankins was known throughout the boxing world as one of its hardest punchers. He was a dangerous test for young Conn. He trained for the bout in Chicago, sparring with Joe Louis, who was preparing for a heavyweight title bout against James Braddock on June 22 at Chicago's Comiskey Park. Trafton continued his pre-fight hype, predicting that Oscar would knock out Conn. On fight day Conn weighed in at 161 ½; Rankins tipped the scales at 162 ¼.

Rigby requested extra police to escort the fighters into the ring, lest the feud between Trafton and Ray get out of hand. The fighters entered the ring before a packed house without incident. In the first round Billy repeatedly landed his stabbing left jab to Oscar's face. Oscar bored in, but Billy tied him up when he got too close. His confidence growing, Billy got more aggressive in the second round, closing in to slug with the feared Rankins. Rankins landed a terrific short right to Conn's jaw. Billy hit the canvas nose first, and then rolled over. At the count of four, he was still on his back. It did not look like he would make it. Summoning all of his youthful determination, he stirred at the count of five, and quickly rose to one knee by seven. He rose at nine, still groggy, but had beaten the count. Rankins tore into him, landing powerful lefts and rights to the body. Billy showed good instincts by protecting his head and holding on to the charging Oscar when he could. He survived the round, and walked back to his corner still a little wobbly. In the corner they dumped the water bucket over his head to help him shake off the effects of the punches. He came out better for the third, but still had to face the two-barrelled cannon that was Oscar Rankins. Rankins charged again, trying to finish the job. Billy backpedaled and jabbed. Oscar landed some good body shots, but could not land square on Billy's elusive head. Billy survived again. But he was well behind, and had as yet mounted no offense. In the fourth Billy came right to him, and they slugged it out toe-to-toe. Surprisingly, Conn more than held his own, landing damaging short rights and left hooks, while using his defensive skills to prevent Rankins from landing solidly. In the fifth Billy got his jab going again, keeping Oscar off balance and landing a few left hooks and right crosses. He staggered Oscar with a perfect left hook to the body late in the round. In the sixth Billy continued to force the action, stabbing with the jab and opening a cut over Oscar's left eye. He staggered Oscar again with a hard right to the jaw. Both the fifth and sixth were extremely fast-paced rounds. In the seventh Oscar backed up Billy with a powerful body attack and forced the action for most of the round. In the eighth they continued to slug it out, with Oscar landing hard to the body and Billy backing him up several times with retaliatory shots. The ninth went back and forth, with each fighter aggressive and landing good shots. Billy scored with three good left hooks and a lot of jabs. As they touched gloves for the tenth and final round, both fighters had taken quite a beating, but were too strong-willed and too talented to let the other dominate. Oscar landed good body shots in the tenth as Billy scored mostly with jabs. Billy Conn had shown that he could take prolonged hard punching from the most powerful slugger in the middleweight division, and had actually backed up the vaunted Rankins with his own power. The decision would be close, as were many of the rounds.

Judge George McBeth voting for Rankins, while Judge George Kutzbauer and referee Red Robinson voted for Conn, giving Billy a split decision win. Local reporters saw the fight differently. Havey Boyle felt that Rankins deserved the nod, while Regis Welsh had Conn winning all but the second, third, and eighth rounds.

In the locker room after the fight, Conn apologized to Johnny Ray for getting knocked out. When a puzzled Ray explained that he had won by decision, Billy told him that he remembered nothing after the second round knockdown, and assumed that he had been knocked out at that point.

Billy had come back from his worst adversity and won, showing great ring instincts and a champion's heart. All observers marveled at the ring intelligence of one so young and inexperienced. At 19 he had beaten three of the top middleweights in the world.

The local media continued the drumbeat for Conn-Yarosz at Forbes Field. Yarosz was in line for a title shot against Steele or Thil due to his big recent victories, but couldn't get it just yet. He agreed to a Conn fight because it would be so lucrative, even though a loss would jeopardize his lofty middleweight ranking. He felt he could beat young Conn, and the money was too good to pass up.

Promoters Ellwood Rigby and Barney McGinley signed Conn and Yarosz to a 12 round bout for June 30, 1937, at Forbes Field. The Pennsylvania state middleweight title, held by Yarosz, would be at stake.

The contract called for Yarosz to receive 30% of the net receipts and Conn 25%. Both fighters had to weigh 161 or less. Rigby predicted a crowd of 15 to 20 thousand, and a gate of up to 40 thousand dollars.

Teddy Yarosz had been the premier boxer in Pittsburgh since the early 1930's. Born in 1910 on Pittsburgh's North Side, he had grown up mostly in Monaca, a few miles northwest of Pittsburgh. He reached early prominence as a welterweight, earning a top ten ranking in 1930. He reached number six in *The Ring* magazine's rankings by 1932, but by 1933 he could no longer make 147 pounds, and campaigned as a middleweight. He beat number one middleweight contender Vince Dundee by decision twice, in August and September of 1933. The following month, Dundee won the title from Lou Brouillard. Meanwhile, Yarosz lost a tough decision to fellow contender Young Terry, only Teddy's second loss in over 60 fights. After his loss to Young Terry, Yarosz reeled off nine straight wins, including victories over former champs Ben Jeby and Pete Latzo. Yarosz and Vince Dundee met for the middleweight title at Forbes Field on Septembet 11, 1934, with Yarosz winning a 15 round decision. On New Year's Day, 1935, hampered by a knee injury, champion Yarosz suffered his first knockout loss in over 70 bouts, to Babe Risko in the seventh round of a non-title bout. Risko had earned a shot at Teddy's title. They fought at Forbes Field again on September 19, 1935, and this time Risko won a 15 round decision and the title. Teddy stated that his knee was fine and was not the cause of his loss. Risko lost the title to Freddie Steele in his second defense, in July of 1936. In the meantime, Yarosz avenged his loss to Young Terry by knockout, and then finally beat Risko in another Forbes Field bout in September of 1936. He followed his Risko victory with wins over top contenders Ken Overlin and Solly Krieger, both future champs, and over Lou Brouillard, former world welter and middleweight champ. Teddy had certainly earned his number one ranking; Steele had all but promised him a title shot if he beat Conn.

Going into the Conn bout Yarosz' record stood at 80 wins, 4 losses, and 2 draws. The losses were to top fighters, all of whom Teddy had also beaten. He claimed victories over five former world champs, and two future world champs. There are more than a few boxers in the Hall of Fame with records less impressive than that of Teddy Yarosz.

Yarosz was a slick, clever boxer, difficult to hit. He was a tough Polish kid who had suffered but one knockout in a long career. Conn was fast and tough, but had only beaten four big names. Conn was 19; a year ago he was just a preliminary kid. Yarosz was in his prime at 27 and had been through big fight pressure many times. The early betting favored Yarosz two to one.

Pittsburgh was excited about the upcoming Conn-Yarosz fight, but the entire world paused on June 22nd for a big heavyweight championship bout. Hard-hitting Joe Louis was expected to take the title from James Braddock at Chicago's Comiskey Park. Louis was the first black man to fight for the title since Jack Johnson, who had last fought over 25 years ago. Over 50,000 fans crowded into the baseball park to watch. Experts felt that Braddock was overmatched and would be easy prey for the young slugger. But the "Cinderella Man" had come up the hard way, and had proven his heart and courage. While many contenders of the era trembled in fear of Louis' painful onslaught, Braddock was fearless. He took the attack right to Louis, and knocked him down with a big right uppercut in the first round. Louis was stunned briefly, but recovered quickly. Stone-faced, he attacked methodically, battering Braddock through round after round. By the end of the seventh round, Braddock was cut over both eyes, which were nearly swollen shut. His manager wanted to stop the bout. Braddock promised to never speak to the man again if he did so. In the eighth Braddock, bleeding badly and barely able to see, went out *his* way, hitting the canvas face first and unconscious following a vicious Louis attack. Midnight had finally come for the Cinderella Man. But instead of a glass slipper, he took home a $300,000 check.

The Braddock-Louis bout signified an ethnic change in the heavyweight championship of boxing. Braddock was the latest of a colorful menagerie of Irish-American champions that included characters like Paddy Ryan, John L. Sullivan (The Boston Strong Boy), "Gentleman"

Jim Corbett, Jack Dempsey (The Manassa Mauler), and Gene Tunney (The Fighting Marine). Since Joe Louis, most heavyweight champs have been African-American, including greats Jersey Joe Walcott, Sonny Liston, Muhammad Ali, Joe Frazier, George Foreman, Larry Holmes, Mike Tyson, and Evander Holyfield.

Yarosz and Conn were both quick, skilled boxers, with great stamina and strong chins. Yarosz had trainer Ray Arcel working with him now. Arcel had trained lightweight great Benny Leonard in the 1920's, and had worked with several other top fighters. He was a master strategist, and is now in boxing's Hall of Fame. Johnny Ray was new to the big time. Conn was by far his most successful fighter. He had previously worked with only journeyman pugs, yet was well-respected.

Conn's other manager, Johnny McGarvey, had long suffered from liver disease. Prior to the Yarosz fight he suffered a mild heart attack, and was under doctor's orders not to attend. The Conn team set up training at the Eagle's Rest camp on Babcock Boulevard north of Pittsburgh, while Yarosz went to Summit, N.J. Conn trained in secret. His management barred all reporters and the public. Conn sparred mostly with Al Quaill and Mickey O'Brien and reportedly looked good in training. On Sunday, June 27th, Conn's workout session was open to the public. Over 1,000 fans showed up to watch him spar 12 rounds at the North Hills site, four each against three different opponents. His left was lightning fast and deadly accurate, even against Al Quaill, a skilled middleweight who was fighting in the top preliminary bout. After 12 rounds of sparring Billy hit the heavy bag for three rounds and the speed bag for two rounds, showing no signs of fatigue. He weighed 162 pounds after his workout. The newspapers reported that Yarosz also sparred 12 rounds that day and looked good.

Wednesday, June 30th dawned gray and ominous, and not just due to air pollution from Pittsburgh's mills. Rain was in the forecast. The fighters met for the weigh-in at Commissioner McClelland's office in the Law and Finance Building downtown. A huge throng of fight fans, well-wishers, and onlookers crowded around the building to watch the fighters enter. Ray Foutts and Ray Arcel accompanied Yarosz; Johnny Ray and the ailing Johnny McGarvey accompanied Conn. Both fighters stripped to their underwear in McClelland's office. Both appeared to be in great shape, and both weighed exactly 161. McClelland told them: "You two boys have been a credit to the fight game, not only in Pittsburgh but in a national sense." He warned them that no fouling would be tolerated.

Ticket sales had been good, but the rain threatened to hold down attendance. Rigby insisted to reporters that the gate would reach his original prediction of 40 thousand, despite the threatening weather.

Lots of bettors liked Conn as a two to one underdog. By fight time the odds narrowed to ten to eight, still in favor of Yarosz. Boxing celebrities in attendance included world champion Freddie Steele, and former champs Babe Risko and Vince Dundee. Dundee predicted that Conn would win because of his superior left, longer reach, and youth. Retired former champs Frank Klaus and George Chip, both of the Pittsburgh area, also attended. Labor leader Phil Murray and scores of judges and politicians attended. The crowd exceeded 14,000, but did not reach the 20,000 Rigby had hoped for. Nevertheless, it was nearly three times a capacity Duquesne Garden crowd, and Billy Conn would receive his biggest purse to date by far. Steele's manager Dave Miller promised Rigby that the winner would receive the next shot at Freddie's title.

Press hype reached fever pitch, dominating the sports headlines for days leading up to the fight. Chas "Brute" Kramer of the *Sports Journal* called it "Pittsburgh's greatest ring natural," and wrote: "Billy Conn is the greatest figure to come upon the boxing scene in Pittsburgh since the halcyon days of Harry Greb."

The skies still threatened, but the rain held off. The Conn team, minus McGarvey, walked through the Forbes Field crowd to the ring near second base. Almost three years ago to the day, Billy had his first pro fight, a loss to Dick Woodward. (Yarosz won the middleweight title that year.) Just one year ago he was but a promising preliminary kid. Since that time he had rocketed into national prominence at age 19. His rooters cheered him on as he entered the ring. Yarosz had legions from the Beaver Valley, along with many fans of Polish extraction to cheer him on. Conn had his Irish and East Liberty fans, along with many others who had jumped on his bandwagon. The crowd was animated, watching two local stars finally clash. Both fighters were brightly adorned, Teddy in red trunks with black trim, Billy in purple with black trim. It was bigger than the Zivic fight; Conn was better known now, and Yarosz had long been a boxer of national and world prominence. Pittsburgh had two middleweights worth watching.

Billy typically started slow in the early rounds, and this fight was no different. Yarosz outboxed him in the first round, and again in the second. After Yarosz won the third round on all cards, Conn fans grew impatient. Billy had to get going – or was he just too inexperienced for a fighter of Teddy's caliber at this point?

Early in the fourth Conn shook Yarosz with a hard left hook to the head. Conn forced the action for the remainder of the round, while Yarosz held and grabbed him. Conn continued his attack in the fifth, battering Yarosz about the ring. A hard right to the head in the middle of the round hurt Yarosz again. Conn had battled back from his early deficit and had Yarosz hurt and holding on. But Teddy had a champion's heart and a world of experience. He battled back in the sixth, as both fighters put on classy displays of slugging and boxing. Through the sixth, seventh, and eighth, neither had an edge, as both fought at a furious pace with skill and determination. In the ninth Conn unleashed a ferocious body attack with both hands. Teddy covered and held, while Billy shifted to a two-handed head attack. It was Conn's round all the way. Teddy attacked hard in the tenth, but Billy outfought him inside and outside, at times snapping his celebrated jab from long distance. After the tenth round, Referee Al Grayber warned Conn in his corner for "rabbit punching" on the break. With two rounds to go it was very close. Both fighters fought hard in the eleventh, with Yarosz appearing to have an edge. In the twelfth they stood toe to toe and slugged it out as the fans rose to their feet and cheered wildly throughout the round. The bell ended one of the best fights in Pittsburgh's memory.

The charged up, highly partisan crowd awaited the decision. Judge Williams had Conn winning six rounds to four, with two even. Judge McBeth saw it much differently, with Yarosz winning eight rounds to three, and one even. Referee Al Grayber had Conn winning five rounds, Yarosz three, and four even. Conn had won a split decision. Yarosz backers and others who believed he had been robbed booed the decision, and threw seat cushions into the ring as Conn backers cheered. The Quaill-Duca bout was held up for ten minutes until the furor died down.

Billy visited Teddy in his dressing room immediately afterward to congratulate him on a great fight. Both fighters shook hands and agreed that they had no hard feelings. Back in Conn's dressing room a jubilant Johnny Ray clowned around, smoking a cigarette in the shower and sticking one in his ear.

Yarosz was surprised by the physical strength of the skinny youngster, and complimented him: "He's a good fighter. He's game and he's strong. He didn't hurt me at all. I tired during part of the fight, why, I can't explain."

Conn said of the fight: "Teddy's punches lacked steam, and although I was hit with several solid punches, I never was hurt. He's a hard fellow to fight. Going into the last part of the fight, I knew I was ahead. I started slowly, but I caught on quickly. I thought my best punches were a right to the jaw and a left hook to the stomach. Yarosz held me a lot, too."

Yarosz had lost his chance for another title bout for now. Dave Miller, Freddie Steele's manager, said that they were not considering Conn for a title bout at this time either. He had promised the winner a title shot with the expectation that it would be Yarosz. Conn was not yet a big enough name nationally to draw the kind of crowd they wanted. Johnny Ray told reporters that he wanted about another year of experience for Billy before he fought for a championship.

The fight netted $24,869. Yarosz received $7,461, Conn $6,217. Rigby and McGinley made an acceptable profit of around $5,000. Conn had earned his biggest purse by far, at a time when the average steelworker made about $500 a year if he was lucky enough to have a job.

Billy had now beaten three former world champions in four months, the last of whom was the number one middleweight contender. Paul Beeler wrote a feature article about him in *The Ring* magazine entitled "Pittsburgh Fistic Star." *The Ring*, founded in 1926 by Nat Fleisher, was dubbed "The Bible of Boxing." It had a large national circulation among boxing fans. The article would certainly bring attention to the new middleweight sensation.

Beeler stressed the Pittsburgh tradition of great middleweights and predicted that Conn would be the fifth world middleweight champ from the area, succeeding Frank Klaus, George Chip, Harry Greb, and Teddy Yarosz. He stressed Conn's Irish heritage ("…a true, dyed-in-the-wool, fighting Irishman.") He described Johnny Ray's meeting with the young boy from the streets of East Liberty and turning him into a top professional fighter. He praised Ray and McGarvey for their boxing and financial expertise: "Billy Conn is the best managed fighter in the game."

Beeler lauded Conn's recent victories, pointing out that he had beaten Risko and Dundee by making them fight his fight. He praised the comeback from the Oscar Rankins knockdown as proof that the kid could "take it." He wrote that Yarosz was in the best shape of his life and trained by the great Ray Arcel, yet Conn still beat him. He praised Conn's assets: "His left jab and hook are beautiful to watch, his right to the body carries plenty of authority, and he is that rare combination, a great boxer who is, at the same time, aggressive."

Beeler saw Conn, with his youth and frame, as growing into a light heavyweight and possibly heavyweight after winning a middleweight title. The article brought national attention to Conn and Ray, who were now in a position to demand big money against top opponents.

Johnny Ray wanted to match Conn next with Fred Apostoli, a Californian who had also made a big recent splash in the middleweight division. Apostoli, 24, was a power puncher who had put together a string of knockouts that included top contender Solly Krieger. Apostoli was awarded a title shot against Marcel Thil in September in New York's Polo Grounds, so Ray had to find another opponent. He wanted more exposure for his star, and agreed to an August 13th bout in San Francisco against Young Corbett III, former welterweight champion and current middleweight contender. Conn's big fights had all been in Pittsburgh. It would be good for him to experience a hostile crowd against a hometown boy. Corbett was from Fresno, but fought mostly in San Francisco and had a large following there.

Young Corbett III was born Raffaele Capabianca Giordano in Naples, Italy, in 1905. His ring name was a tribute to boxing legend "Gentleman Jim" Corbett, a native of San Francisco. He was the third professional boxer to use the name "Young Corbett." Young Corbett III won the world welterweight title in 1933, and lost it later that year. He now campaigned as a middleweight, and had attained a number 5 ranking from Ring Magazine in the talent-rich division. It was another risky fight for Conn. Corbett was a cagey veteran before a partisan crowd and local officials. He also fought as a lefthander, which could be a difficult adjustment for a young fighter. But Ray felt his star could handle it, as he had handled everything thrown against him so far.

Before the Corbett fight, Conn took on Ralph Chong again in a tuneup in Youngstown, Ohio, on August 3. Conn won in a 6th round TKO.

The Conn team made the long trip to San Francisco by car. Johnny McGarvey was still recovering from his heart attack earlier in the year, and also suffered from a liver ailment. But he had recovered enough to make the transcontinental trip.

San Francisco had just completed the Golden Gate Bridge, the longest bridge in the world at that time. In its harbor stood the island of Alcatraz. A maximum - security federal prison had opened there in 1934, which housed the notorious criminal Al Capone. The quaint city had cable cars traversing its steep hills, and a bustling Chinatown. It had been a center of Irish immigration in earlier years, and later one of Italian immigration.

Corbett weighed 157 to Conn's 160 in the bout at San Francisco's Dreamland Auditorium. Local promoters hyped it as a battle between two top contenders, and as youth versus experience. Age and experience were a contrast, with Conn age 19 and Corbett 32. Corbett had been in many more big bouts.

While training for Corbett at Duffy's Gym in Oakland, Conn encountered ex-champ Max Baer, still a formidable contender and nearly 220 pounds. According to Eddie Muller of the *San Francisco Examiner*, Baer asked Conn to spar, expecting little difficulty from a middleweight. Baer clowned around, as he often did. Conn landed a beautiful combination, a left hook to the body followed by a right to the jaw. Baer's knees buckled, and he held on, grabbing and wrestling Conn until the bell sounded. That ended the sparring session.

In the first round Corbett's southpaw stance was a little puzzling for Billy, who attacked to the body. When a righthander ("orthodox" style) fights a southpaw, his opponent has a different foot forward, which can be confusing in the heat of battle. Both fighters are more open to a power shot, the left from a southpaw and the right from an orthodox fighter. Corbett was used to this arrangement, as he usually fought righthanders. Southpaw professionals were rare. Many trainers made natural lefthanders fight in the orthodox style, because it could be difficult to get fights if one fought southpaw. In the second round Billy continued on the attack, but the fighters clashed heads hard. Billy staggered back with a three inch gash above his left eye, which gushed blood. The veteran Corbett jumped on the startled youngster, raining punches and landing a big left that toppled Billy to the floor. He rose at the count of three. Corbett attacked again, but the round ended shortly thereafter. Between rounds Conn's corner was unable to stop the flow of blood. Corbett fought cautiously in the third, conserving his strength. Conn did too, still adjusting to the southpaw stance and to the blood that continued to flow from his forehead. In the fourth

Billy attacked with both hands to the body, stalking Corbett relentlessly despite blood-impaired vision. The fifth round was virtually the same, with Conn scoring to the body. In the sixth, Billy attacked the head, landing long rights that hurt Corbett. He continued to force the action in the seventh, landing a big left hook to the stomach that made Corbett gasp and hold on. In the eighth and ninth Billy landed to the body while Corbett landed lefts to the head. Conn's cut bled freely throughout the entire fight. In the tenth Corbett landed more lefts to the head and looked fresher than he had in the middle rounds.

Referee Jack Downey, the only judge of the fight, ruled Corbett the winner. The Conn team felt that they had been robbed by a hometown decision and wanted a rematch. Dick Friendlich of the *San Francisco Chronicle* had the fight a draw, and conceded that many of the local fans felt that Conn had won. Friendlich wrote: "Certainly, Conn would have emerged victor if he hadn't run afoul of the butting match, because from the fourth to the ninth he gave Corbett a fine body punching."

The cut had bled freely and affected Conn's vision, yet he had fought valiantly and made it a close fight, a disputed decision in the other man's home base. But the decision stood, ending Billy's win streak, which had extended back to August of 1935. After three split decision wins versus Zivic, Rankins, and Yarosz, he came out on the short end of this one.

On the return trip Johnny McGarvey took ill again. He died of liver complications shortly after arriving home. Pittsburgh businessman Milton Jaffe took over his duties as business manager.

With the Freddie Steele-Ken Overlin and Marcel Thil-Fred Apostoli title bouts scheduled for September, Conn and Yarosz were shut out for now. They agreed to a lucrative rematch for September 30th at Duquesne Garden. The winner would be back on track, but the loser would drop out of any current title hopes.

Steele defended his crown successfully for the fourth time in less than a year with a fourth round knockout of Ken Overlin on September 11th. On September 23rd, at the Polo Grounds before a large outdoor crowd, Apostoli battered Frenchman Thil for a tenth round TKO and captured that version of the middleweight crown. Both middleweight champs now resided in the United States.

Promoters Rigby and McGinley billed the Conn-Yarosz rematch as the "East Liberty Flash" versus the "Monaca Mauler." Conn, cocky as ever, predicted that he would knock Yarosz out this time. It would be a fifteen round bout for the Pennsylvania state middleweight championship. Yarosz had gone the fifteen round distance three times previously. Conn had never gone fifteen, and had only gone twelve once, but with his youth and stamina it did not figure to be a problem. Again, they agreed to a weight of 161, with the added provision "give or take a pound." Conn weighed in a 162 ¾ the day of the fight, and had to sweat off three quarters of a pound to weigh in at 162. Yarosz weighed 161.

Ray Arcel had Teddy ready for Billy this time. The early rounds were all Yarosz. Again, Billy took a while to get going. The old master seemed to have the young upstart's number this time. Teddy, perhaps bitter over his previous close loss to the youngster, engaged in some questionable tactics. Regis Welsh reported "Yarosz butted, heeled, and gouged even when way ahead." By the end of the eleventh round Teddy had a big lead and appeared to be on the verge of avenging one of the few losses in his long career.

Even while trailing badly, Billy's confidence never waned. Perhaps Teddy's unsavory tactics got Billy's "Irish" up. Perhaps the stamina of youth came into play. But beginning in the twelfth round the tide turned dramatically. Conn forced the action, landing heavily with lefts and rights, winning the twelfth and thirteenth easily. In the fourteenth he dominated even more, battering Yarosz around the ring for the entire round. In the fifteenth Conn continued his barrage as Yarosz held on to him, barely returning any punches at all. Conn battered him without letup. At the bell Yarosz collapsed to the canvas and had to be helped to his corner.

It was a difficult fight to score. Yarosz had dominated through eleven rounds, yet Conn had won the last four big, and was fresh and strong at the end as Yarosz collapsed. The judges' vote revealed another narrow split decision win for Conn. Teddy's title hopes faded as Billy's revived.

Johnny Ray got the rematch he wanted for Billy's next fight: Young Corbett III at Duquesne Gardens for November 8th, promoted by Barney McGinley and Jake Mintz. Ray boasted that the southpaw style would not bother Billy this time. Both he and Conn felt that Corbett's win over Conn was a fluke, aided by Billy's nasty cut from a head butt that bled throughout the fight. But Corbett was still a wily veteran with much more experience than Conn. Fight day weights were Conn 163 ½, Corbett 158 ¼. The Conn team, troubled by Billy's frequent tendency to lose early rounds, had him warm up with three fast rounds of shadow boxing just prior to the fight.

This fight was quite different from the first one with Corbett. Billy used his footwork and reach advantage to outmaneuver Corbett from the start. Corbett hung tough and boxed well early, but had difficulty reaching the taller youngster. In the fourth he made his bid, coming out aggressively and finally landing good lefts to the jaw and body. While he won the round, his punches appeared to have little effect on Conn. In the fifth both fighters boxed well, Billy landing jabs and hooks, Corbett getting in some long lefts. In the sixth they battled toe-to-toe until Corbett had to back off. Billy stayed aggressive, and the round ended with Billy pounding away as Corbett held on. In the seventh Billy dominated, landing some big rights in addition to his lefts, and staggering the Californian. Billy continued to dominate in the eighth and ninth, landing almost at will as Corbett appeared tired and tried to hold him. Billy outboxed him easily in the tenth; the fight ended with Billy winning by a wide margin. He had avenged his only defeat since he started fighting the big names. He had defeated his fourth former world champion of the current year. (Corbett was inducted into the International Boxing Hall of Fame in 2004.)

In the prelims Honeyboy Jones won by a split decision over Al Quaill, and Billy's pal Harry Krause won by fifth round knockout over Tommy Daniels.

Billy's purse for the fight was nearly $3,000. Corbett got a $4,000 guarantee from a total gate of about $9,000, leaving little profit for McGinley and Mintz.

Billy had made a lot of money, and decided to take up residence in a nice hotel. He drove a black Cadillac and wore expensive clothes. On Thanksgiving, Wild Bill chided him for thinking he was better than everybody else. Harsh words led to harsher, and father and son decided to settle the argument with fists. Both went outside and stripped to the waist in the cold November evening. Wild Bill, still only 39 years old, held his own briefly, until Billy landed some body shots that hurt him. Frank and Jackie, on the way home, came upon their father and brother fighting. Frank tried to help his father, who was at that point taking a beating, and Jackie jumped in to protect Billy from a two-man attack. A neighbor called the police, who broke it up. Afterward the family enjoyed Thanksgiving dinner together.

Billy's next fight was set for December 16th at Duquesne Gardens against Brooklyn's Solly Krieger, another tough middleweight who had a powerful punch and an iron jaw. Krieger had fought the best, beating top contenders Oscar Rankins, Frank Battaglia, and Walter Woods. He had lost a decision to Teddy Yarosz in January. The only man to knock him out was Fred Apostoli, now middleweight champ. Billy was favored in this one, but Solly was a dangerous puncher. Johnny Ray had booked no easy "tuneup" fights for Billy all year. Every fight was with an experienced, talented contender. This final fight of 1937 would be no different.

Conn weighed in at 163 to Krieger's 163 ½ for the twelve round bout. Billy boxed and jabbed early, but had difficulty keeping the aggressive Krieger away. Krieger landed well to the body, taking the middle rounds by forcing the action and backing Billy into the ropes repeatedly. In the eighth a short left hook to the body dropped Billy to the canvas. He was off balance and slipped, but the punch did land, causing the judges to score it as a knockdown. He got up and brawled with Krieger, but was unable to hurt him. Early in the tenth Billy landed a big right and followed with a good left hook, but Solly kept coming. Billy continued to land well, dominating the tenth and eleventh rounds and appeared to hurt Krieger for the first time in the bout, as Solly held on to him. The typical Conn late rally had begun, but it was too late. In the twelfth Krieger came out strong, winning it big with body shots and uppercuts to the head. Billy appeared to have run out of gas. The decision was not in doubt. Billy had lost his second fight of the year. He later claimed that he was not in top shape for the bout, which taught him the valuable lesson that a fighter must always be in top shape.

Krieger was gracious in victory, complimenting the youngster: "He's a good, strong kid. Knows a lot about the fight game and should be a good fighter some day. He started to bother me late in the fight, that's why I made that fast finish. I wanted to win this one and when the twelfth round came up I didn't want to let anything stand in the way. But Billy is a good fighter. He should go somewhere."

Krieger would go on to win a middleweight title within a year. His predictions about Billy would be truer than he could have imagined.

Despite the Krieger loss, 1937 was a spectacular year for Billy Conn. He came out of nowhere to beat four former champions and attain a national reputation. He won six of eight fights against former or future champs with the notable exception of Oscar Rankins, who was of championship caliber. He had gained valuable experience against the world's best middleweights. He had made a lot of money at a time of widespread poverty in the country. Johnny Ray's strategy of putting him in with the best had worked. He had survived, learned, and come out on top most of the time. His mentor had the utmost confidence in his abilities. Still only twenty years old, he was a good bet to be a world champion some day.

ROUND SEVEN

1938: Middleweight Or Light-heavyweight?

In 1938, Germany invaded Austria and threatened Czechoslovakia. Popular songs included "Beer Barrel Polka" and "God Bless America." Spencer Tracy won Best Actor for *Boys Town*. Frank Capra's *You Can't Take It With You* won Best Picture. Errol Flynn starred in *Robin Hood*. The Pirates finished second to the Cubs by two games after leading the National League for most of the summer. The Yankees beat the Cubs four straight in the World Series. On November 1st at Pimlico Racetrack in Baltimore, Seabiscuit upset Triple Crown champion War Admiral in a match race.

On January 7, 1938, the two middleweight champs, Steele and Apostoli, met in a bout that risked neither one's title. Apostoli won by a ninth round knockout, proving that he was the best middleweight in the world.

Conn kept active, taking on Honeyboy Jones for the fourth time in a twelve round bout at Motor Square Garden on January 24th. Jones was not a big name nationally, but was a tough fight nonetheless. He was fast and smart, and likely as good as some of the marquee fighters Billy had beaten. He had recently beaten Vince Dundee and Al Quaill, two quality middleweights. Billy weighed in at 165 to Honeyboy's 158.

80

Young Billy was filling out, and it was getting more difficult to make the middleweight limit. Perhaps his future lay in the light heavyweight division, currently ruled by Pittsburgh resident John Henry Lewis.

Billy boxed beautifully against Jones, landing jabs and rights to the head, and left hooks to the body. Jones fought back hard, landing jabs and an occasional right. He opened a cut over Billy's right eye, which had not completely healed since the Krieger fight, and over the left eye. Billy won the first ten rounds, despite being cut over both eyes. In the eleventh Jones threw caution to the wind, unleashing wild swinging rights throughout the round. He needed a knockout to win, and he was going all out for it. This was his only chance to beat a top contender and make a name for himself. Billy obliged him and they slugged it out head-to-head, toe-to-toe all over the ring in the eleventh and twelfth. In the end, Billy looked like the loser with cuts over both eyes, but had won all twelve rounds. Honeyboy's game effort had failed.

After the Jones fight, pundits again questioned Billy's punching power. He had battered Jones round after round, but had been unable to knock him out. They also questioned his strategic sense. Billy had the sweetest boxing skills in all of the "Sweet Science." He could throw combinations with speed and beauty rarely seen in the history of the game. His footwork dazzled like the legendary Gentleman Jim Corbett. Yet he loved to slug it out, giving up his advantage and exposing himself to a possible knockout. Some of it was due to temper, some of it to the fact that he just loved to mix it up. It made for an exciting young fighter who brought an aura of beauty and danger into the ring. With his movie star good looks and brash (at times) mouth, Billy was a real crowd pleaser.

Early in 1938 Johnny Ray and Billy decided to move into the light heavyweight division. At six feet tall, the 20-year-old youngster was filling out and growing out of the middleweight class. Billy took off for a Florida vacation, "loafing" and eating three good meals a day, trying to add weight. Ray scheduled two ten-round light heavyweight bouts: Dominic Ceccarelli on April 4th at Motor Square Garden, and Eric Seelig May 10th at Duquesne Gardens.

Ceccarelli, of Italy, was considered a good trial horse who could take a punch. He had been knocked out only once in his career, by heavyweight Gunnar Barland, and had gone the distance with powerful light heavyweight contender Al Gainer. He weighed in at 170 for the bout. Billy weighed in at 167 ½, less than he had hoped for in his light heavyweight debut. He told the press that he resented the accusations that he couldn't punch. Ceccarelli would be a good test.

Billy provided an answer in the first round. After nearly an entire round of dancing and jabbing, he let go a left hook described as "wrist deep" into the Italian's stomach. Ceccarelli froze, then fell back on his rear end, his head propped up against the ropes. The bell saved him from a first round KO. Ceccarelli recovered enough to fight defensively for the next few rounds, as Billy ripped stiff jabs to the face and left hooks to the body, and landed an occasional right uppercut to the chin. Ceccarelli landed little throughout the fight, but did get in some looping rights to Billy's chin in the sixth and seventh. Billy took them well. Billy opened a nasty cut over Ceccarelli's right eye, which swelled and closed later in the fight. Billy used superior speed to outbox him inside and outside, flooring him again in the ninth with a liver shot. Ceccarelli survived by covering up most of the fight and rarely taking chances. Afterward, he described Conn as "…a pretty good puncher."

Billy looked to be in great condition at 167 ½. He was unmarked at the end of the bout and showed not the slightest sign of fatigue.

Regis Welsh interviewed Billy for a *Pittsburgh Press* article on April 17th. Conn reviewed his fabulous year of 1937: "After I fought Fritzie Zivic I knew I could get somewhere. That's why I fought Babe Risko, Teddy Yarosz and Vince Dundee. I knew they couldn't punch. And even if I couldn't, I figured that I was younger, and while maybe not smarter, was stronger. The toughest fight I ever had was with that Oscar Rankins. Everyone had told me not to fight him. But I did. And after he knocked me down, I didn't remember anything about it until they started to tell me about it the next day. He was the hardest puncher and toughest fellow I ever fought. He even hurt me hitting me on the shoulders. Dundee was the smartest. He had a lot of tricks. So did

Yarosz. But Yarosz always tipped his hand when he got hurt. He would lose his boxing class and start rough stuff. That was right down my alley. 'Cause I can be rough, too, when I have to be. Yarosz had good legs. They saved him in our last fight."

Billy looked forward to moving up to the light heavyweight class. John Henry Lewis won the title in 1935 and had defended it successfully three times.

"I'd like to fight John Henry Lewis," said Conn, "...if only for the thrill of telling people that one time I fought for the light heavyweight championship of the world."

Conn liked his chances: "I don't think John Henry could hurt me – and I might hurt him. My left hook is developing with my increased weight. Didn't I knock a guy down a few weeks ago? Maybe I could nail John Henry, too. I always have better luck hitting big fellows."

John Henry, when told of Conn's statement, responded, "Billy would make a good fight. And it would draw plenty of people."

Welsh seemed surprised at Conn's loquaciousness, as Billy rambled on about his future: "I'd rather be a heavyweight. None of them big guys are too smart. And a fellow who knows his way around ought to be able to drive them crazy with jabs and hooks. Maybe before another year I'll be big enough. And I hope that some of the big fellows I've seen are still around then."

At the end of the interview, Billy calmed down and smiled. Welsh described his "parting remark." "Maybe I talk too much. I'd much rather fight. I know more about that. But – watch me belt those big guys."

Eight days after the interview appeared, April 25th, John Henry Lewis KO'd Emilio Martinez in Minnesota, his fourth successful title defense. Barely a week later, Lewis took on Dominic Ceccarelli in Baltimore. Despite a forceful battering, Lewis was not able to knock out the Italian either, and took a ten round decision.

Conn took on Eric Seelig of Germany on May 10th at Duquesne Gardens in another ten round bout. Seelig was the German light-heavyweight champ in 1933. He was *The Ring* magazine's number ten middleweight in 1936, but had since dropped out of the rankings. Now campaigning as a light-heavyweight again, he was another tough trial horse with a reputation as a difficult man to knock out. Billy weighed in at 169 ½ to Seelig's 165 ½.

For the first few rounds Billy pounded away, abandoning his slick boxing skills to attack Seelig with hooks and rights to the head and body. In the fifth Seelig landed a right to the chin that hurt Billy. He followed up aggressively, forcing Billy to fight defensively. Billy responded with more body blows for the next few rounds, and used his defensive skills to make Seelig miss. Billy won the decision. Both judges voted for him, while referee Red Robinson scored the bout a draw. Regis Welsh wrote that Billy could have won easily by boxing Seelig, but chose to slug it out, leaving himself open for that big punch in the fifth round.

Heavyweight champ Joe Louis decisioned Welshman Tommy Farr in his first title defense. In 1938 he knocked out challengers Nathan Mann and Harry Thomas. He wanted a rematch with the only man who had beaten him. "I'm not the true champion until I beat Max Schmeling," he declared.

The Louis-Schmeling title bout was arranged for June 22, 1938, at Yankee Stadium. Max was eager to take on Louis again and perhaps win back the title. At 32 years old, he was a little past his prime, but as the only man who had beaten Louis, he was the best draw out there. That fight remains the most hyped and most anticipated matchup in boxing history, exceeding the Dempsey-Tunney battles of the 1920's and the Frazier-Ali spectacle of 1971. It took on international significance, with Schmeling seen as representing the growing menace of Nazi Germany, and Louis representing the good old USA. Schmeling's reluctance to be portrayed as the Nazi superman was not known to the American or European public. His rugged face and bushy eyebrows made him the "Hun" that had caused the Great War and threatened to start another. The average American had little knowledge of his warm feelings for America and his many friends here. He had become "the enemy." Hitler's use of the 1936 Olympics to boast of German superiority had helped to politicize sports. (The Soviet Union would use the Olympics in a similar manner in the post-World War II era.) Despite the individual performance of Jesse Owens and other African-Americans, Germany amassed more medals than any other nation. For the first time a nation claimed to have "won" the Olympics. Now that same nation threatened to take the heavyweight boxing championship, nearly always held by an American since John L. Sullivan became the first champion under the Queensbury rules in 1889. American patriotism ran high, and ironically crystallized in support of a black man. The humble and likeable Joe Louis, born in rural Alabama and reared in a Detroit ghetto, became the "American hope" who fought for our way of life against the goose-stepping totalitarians of central Europe.

Millions of Americans listened to the radio broadcast of the fight. Over 70,000 fans poured into Yankee Stadium to watch. This time Joe was ready. He attacked Schmeling immediately, raining punches. Suddenly Joe landed a vicious right; Schmeling crumbled to the canvas. Max beat the count, but was still hurt. Joe drove him into the ropes, trapping him there. Joe landed a deadly accurate flurry of head and body punches. As a groggy Max turned to avoid him, Joe's last punch of the flurry landed in the lower part of the back. Max screamed in agony, and fell to the canvas again. He somehow managed to get up before the count of ten. Joe quickly put him down for the third and last time, ending the fight at 2:04 of the first round. Joe Louis became a revered American hero. To many African-Americans, he had reached godly status.

X-rays taken after the fight confirmed two fractured vertebrae in Schmeling's lower back. It was previously thought impossible for a human punch –gloved – to break the back of a large, powerful man like Max Schmeling. But the X-rays didn't lie. No one had ever punched with the power of Joe Louis – not even Jack Dempsey.

Promoters Jake Mintz and Barney McGinley put together a big Forbes Field card for July 25th, headlined by the third Conn-Yarosz meeting, this time for twelve rounds. An outstanding undercard featured Al Quaill versus Billy Soose, a promising new boxer from Farrell, and

Sammy Angott versus Leo Rodak of Chicago. Soose and Angott would become world champs in 1941, at middleweight and lightweight.

The card faced trouble when state boxing William McClelland refused to sanction it. He had suspended Yarosz manager Ray Foutts after the second Conn-Yarosz bout for allegedly taking compensation under the table in the form of free tickets. McClelland prohibited him from participating in or attending any bouts in Pennsylvania. Since he managed both Yarosz and Quaill, McClelland would not allow them to fight on the Pittsburgh card. The dispute was settled when Yarosz and Quaill submitted statements to McClelland that Foutts would not be involved in their business affairs and would not receive a percentage of their purse. Yarosz' contract with Foutts had expired on June 30th, and Teddy chose not to renew it. He and Foutts had had recent financial disputes, and the suspension gave Yarosz an added incentive to part with Foutts. Of greater concern to Yarosz was the officiating. He felt that he deserved the decision in the first two bouts with Conn. He sent a letter to McClelland asking for officials with "better judgment" for this fight.

Conn received a $3,000 guarantee, while Yarosz settled for 25% of the net gate. Conn trained at Eagle's Rest north of Pittsburgh, while Yarosz trained in his hometown of Monaca. With two popular local fighters with world championship aspirations, the Pittsburgh papers ran major stories daily in the week leading up to the fight.

Both Conn and Yarosz went into this bout without their managers. Johnny Ray was hospitalized for alcohol-related ailments. Yarosz manager Ray Foutts was under suspension by the state boxing commissioner. Conn weighed in at 168 to Yarosz's 162. A good crowd of 10,859 attended. The rough tactics used by the fighters in the first two bouts, especially the second one, had fostered bad blood between them that still simmered.

Yarosz started off holding and grabbing. Conn lost his temper and kept hitting Teddy in the back of the neck with illegal "rabbit punches." Regis Welsh reported that Conn threw 38 rabbit punches in the first round. Teddy stuck his thumbs in Conn's eyes, a vicious, dangerous foul. They kept fighting after the bell in the second and fifth rounds, both times initiated by Yarosz. Referee Freddie Mastrean did not exert his authority enough to control the fighters. He warned both several times between rounds, to no effect. With both managers missing, no one exerted any discipline. The fighters employed kidney punches, head butts, low blows, thumbing, and rabbit punches throughout the bout, as Mastrean allowed it to descend into a chaotic street brawl. The Pittsburgh Press ran a picture the next day that showed Yarosz elbowing Conn in the face. Both fighters did more than enough to be disqualified.

At the end of the bout Teddy had a huge lump on the back of his head from rabbit punches. His sides glowed red from kidney punches. Billy had swollen eyes from Teddy's thumbing, and glove string marks all over his face. The judges awarded the decision to Yarosz.

Both Conn and Yarosz had brought so much acclaim to the area by their substantial accomplishments in the ring, but nearly threw it all away in one disgraceful night. Billy had been unable to control his temper. Teddy's tactics angered him so much that he lost all sense of boxing and fought like a street brawler. Johnny Ray, unable to control his drinking, wasn't there when Billy needed him. After rising from nowhere to a brilliant national prominence at such a young age, Billy's future now looked questionable. His lofty reputation was nearly destroyed in one night. Press sports editor Chet Smith wrote: "Yarosz can't go much farther, Conn isn't going anywhere."

Regis Welsh, who had chronicled Conn's meteoric rise, took a dim view of his future: "Conn, once a great fighter, just has too much Irish in him to control his fighting ability once he gets 'burned up.'"

The writers overreacted to one bad night, but one thing was certain: Junior and Moonie both needed to get each other back on track.

Ray Actis had been ranked as one of the top light heavyweights in the world in 1936 and 1937. He was a formidable power puncher who had fought sparingly in the past year due to a hand injury. Many contenders avoided him because of his dangerous punching power. Johnny Ray booked a bout in Actis' hometown, San Francisco, for September 4th.

It was a pivotal bout for Conn, who needed an impressive win to re-establish his reputation. He weighed in at 167 to 166 for Actis.

Billy boxed the first two rounds, winning both easily. In the third he mixed it up. Actis landed a big left hook that sent Billy to the canvas for a nine count. He got up clear-headed, and outboxed Actis for the rest of the round. In the fourth Conn dominated, sending Actis to the canvas with a left hook. He continued the trend in the fifth, jabbing and hooking and winning big. Actis landed some big rights in the sixth, but Billy took them well. In the seventh Billy danced and jabbed, periodically landing some good power punches. In the eighth Billy pressed hard, firing combinations that staggered Actis. He landed about 40 unanswered punches before the ref stepped in and stopped the bout, Actis collapsing in his arms. Billy had won an impressive victory, beating a puncher at his own game.

The Actis win helped erase the effect of the Yarosz debacle. Billy again came through with a big win when he needed it. With light heavyweight victories over Ceccarelli, Seelig, and Actis, he was nationally ranked in the division. Light heavyweight champ John Henry Lewis successfully defended his title in a 15 round decision over Al Gainer in New Haven on October 25th, and talk of a lucrative title bout with Billy Conn continued.

Unbeknownst to the public, Lewis had lost vision in his left eye, and planned to retire soon before suffering damage to both eyes. He was hurting for money, and needed a big payday before retiring. His friend Joe Louis was informed of his condition, and agreed to give him a title shot with the paycheck he needed. Louis had become such a big draw that he could easily make a difference in the financial status of someone like John Henry.

Promoter Mike Jacobs saw the bout as a losing proposition. He felt that the American public would not support a heavyweight title bout between two black men – something that had never happened. After a hard sell from the Louis people, he reluctantly agreed to promote a January, 1939, bout at Madison Square Garden. His worries were unfounded. The bout sold out quickly, so formidable had become the Louis magic.

Joe Louis decided that the most compassionate way to take out John Henry would be a quick knockout. Joe pressed the action in the first round, and landed a powerful combination that sent John Henry to the canvas for a count of ten. John Henry retired after the bout and never fought again. The hoped-for title bout of John Henry Lewis and Billy Conn would not occur.

Billy took on an old nemesis, Honeyboy Jones, for the fifth time on October 27th at Duquesne Gardens. The opening bout was a four-rounder with Jackie Conn, Billy's younger brother, versus Jackie Whelan. The younger Conn had been training with Johnny Ray, and at age 16 was ready for his pro debut. He was shorter and built thicker than Billy. He didn't possess Billy's superb boxing skills or speed, but he could punch and take a punch, and he loved to fight. Jackie Conn, weighing 150, won the decision in an action-packed fight that pleased the crowd.

The top preliminary featured Fritzie Zivic versus Sal Saban of Cuba. Zivic had won 16 of his last 17 fights, ten by knockout, and had moved to number two contender for the welterweight crown held by Henry Armstrong. Zivic won a ten round decision in a brutal battering of the Cuban, who stood up bravely to last the distance.

In the main bout Billy dominated throughout. Jones grabbed frequently as Billy outscored him every round, alternating boxing and brawling styles. In the eighth and ninth Jones was hurt and held on, as Billy concentrated his attack on the ribs. Billy won an easy ten round decision.

Billy's only decisive loss since becoming a main event fighter was to Solly Krieger in December of 1937. He wanted to avenge it and establish himself as one of the top fighters in the world. Krieger had come on strong in 1938, with eight knockout victories following his big win over Conn. He received a middleweight title shot for November 1st in Seattle against Al Hostak. Hostak had won the title by knockout from Freddie Steele in July, and gave the first title shot to the surging Krieger. Krieger won a fifteen round decision, capturing that share of the world middleweight title.

Billy needed to roll the dice and take on the toughest opponent possible to regain his once lofty reputation. The Conn team offered Krieger a $3,000 guarantee to fight Billy in Pittsburgh. Krieger agreed to a 12 round bout at Duquesne Gardens on November 25th. Both fighters agreed to weigh above 160 so that Krieger's title would not be at stake.

Krieger came into Pittsburgh a week early and began daily workouts at the Pittsburgh Lyceum. He was now a world champ, and soaked up the deserved acclaim from the Pittsburgh fistic crowd. This would be his seventh Pittsburgh appearance. He had put on entertaining fights in the city and earned a good measure of popularity. It was almost as if he were a returning native son. Much more was at stake for the real local hero, Billy Conn. Solly's title wasn't on the line; Billy's reputation was. He needed a prestigious win to get back in the national picture. Krieger was a tough, skilled boxer who had beaten him soundly almost exactly a year ago. But Billy could outbox anyone. If he could keep to boxing and not lose his temper and slug it out, he might win. Krieger was a solid favorite early on, but the odds narrowed to ten-to-eight as Pittsburgh bettors liked what they saw in Conn's training. Billy looked as sharp as ever. A snowstorm on November 25th postponed the bout until Monday night, November 28th.

Solly weighed 163 to Billy's 165 ¼. Billy started boxing, and won the first three rounds with surprising ease. Johnny Ray had emphasized defense, and Solly seemed puzzled, unable to solve Billy's scheme of long jabs and quick feet. Billy stuck his jab at will, and when Solly returned punches Billy wasn't there. The first three rounds were a virtual shutout. Some observers said that Solly didn't land a single punch. In the fourth, true to form, Billy mixed it up. Solly landed a right to the chin that hurt Billy, and followed it up with a barrage of punches. But this was a different Billy Conn from a year ago: older, stronger, smarter. He recovered quickly and went back to boxing. From rounds five to ten

Billy continued to baffle Solly. With a left jab and hooks constantly landing on his face, he was off balance. When he countered, the elusive kid wasn't there. It was like fighting a ghost. In the eleventh, way ahead, Billy moved in for the kill. Solly landed a big left hook to the jaw that snapped Billy's head back. Billy recovered quickly and slugged some more. Solly had a reputation as a big puncher, but couldn't seem to hurt the youngster he had beaten up badly a year ago. Billy won the twelfth easily landing his lightning jabs and hooks at will while the middleweight champ missed again and again. It was a brilliant performance. Solly had won only the eleventh round on some cards, while a few rounds were called draws. Billy won at least eight or nine of the twelve rounds on all cards. It was a stunning thrashing of a reigning world champion. Billy had clearly recaptured his magic.

Afterward, Krieger seemed genuinely puzzled: "I don't know what was the matter," he stammered. "...I couldn't get going."

Regis Welsh waxed poetic in the *Post-Gazette* in an opening paragraph indicative of the elegant, flowery prose of the times: "The glory road, long befogged and beset with treacherous twists, today opens as a straightaway speedway for Billy Conn in his effort to reach the throne room of fistic reward. Once again, surer of himself than ever before; more accomplished in the things he can do best than he ever proved here; matured in the tricks of the business of fighting champions, the East Liberty kid, a year ago a golden prospect who tarnished slightly, burnishes brightly in the future fistic scheme of things."

Billy had taken his game to another level, one that few fighters in boxing history could match. Although he earned only $600 for the fight, one fifth of what Krieger earned, it opened the door to more lucrative matches. A few days later he was offered a contract for a bout in Madison Square Garden on January 6th versus the other reigning middleweight champ – the one considered the best in the world – Fred Apostoli. Billy would be making his debut in the fistic capital of the world: New York City. The title would not be at stake: both fighters would agree to weigh in at over the 160-pound limit.

ROUND EIGHT

1939: New York, New York – Beating The Best

In 1939, Germany invaded Czechoslovakia and Poland. Great Britain and France declared war on Germany. It was a historic year for movies: *Gone With The Wind, The Wizard of Oz, Goodbye Mr. Chips,* and *Mr. Smith Goes to Washington.* Notable books were James Joyce's *Finnegan's Wake,* John Steinbeck's *The Grapes of Wrath,* and, ominously, Adolph Hitler's *Mein Kampf.* The Yankees beat the Cincinnati Reds four straight in the World Series. The Pirates finished sixth.

Federigo Apostoli, a former bellhop from San Francisco, was the son of Italian immigrants. He won a share of the middleweight title in September, 1937. He KO'd rival champ Freddie Steele in January of 1939, proving that he was the world's best middleweight. Along with Joe Louis and welterweight champ Henry Armstrong, he was considered one of the best pound-for-pound fighters in the game. He had a record of 30 wins and three losses. He lost to Steele early in 1935 in his seventh pro fight, and to future champ Ken Overlin in January of 1937. He lost a decision in early 1938 to the tricky Young Corbett III. He gave Corbett a title shot in November of that year and knocked him out in the eighth round. His style was described as "slashing." His fast-paced attacks tended to inflict cuts. He stopped both Corbett and Krieger due to severe cuts. He could punch well to the head or body, and had great stamina. Fans expected he and Conn to put on an entertaining battle, as both fighters were known for their toughness and ability to sustain a fast pace for an entire fight. Apostoli would be making his ninth appearance in New York, his fourth at the venerable Madison Square Garden. He won the title there and had successfully defended it there several times. The Garden and the New York media pressure would all be new to Billy. Apostoli lost his New York debut, in January of 1937, but had won the next eight there, all against top opponents. He was a solid 14-5 favorite against Billy Conn.

The twenty-one-year-old from Pittsburgh was about to make his debut in glittering New York City, the "Mecca of Boxing" and the world's sports, entertainment, and financial capital. The most populous city in the world boasted Wall Street, Broadway, the Statue of Liberty, brand new Radio City Music Hall in Rockefeller Center, Yankee Stadium, the Polo Grounds, and Ebbetts Field. He would fight at the famed arena on Eighth Avenue between 49th and 50th Streets, home to all of the big fights that were not conducted in outdoor stadiums. The Garden held 18,500 for boxing. The pulse of the boxing world had sprung up around it. The area of 49th Street between Broadway and 50th was called "Jacobs Beach" because top promoter Mike Jacobs had his office and ticket agency there. In 1935 Jack Dempsey's restaurant opened at Eighth and 50th, opposite the Garden; he added an annex in 1938 at Broadway and 49th. Mickey Walker's "Toy Bulldog Tavern" also opened in 1935 at Eighth and 49th. James Braddock opened "Braddock's Corner" in 1938 at West 49th Street near Seventh Avenue. Stillman's Gym, where many pro fighters trained, was at Eighth Avenue and 54th. All of these shrines to the sport were virtually within spitting distance of each other. Writers, athletes, trainers, promoters, fans, and con men visited them and contributed to the ambiance at the center of Fistiana. The most famous hangout was Lindy's, on Broadway between 49th and 50th. Damon Runyan, creator of numerous short stories, renowned journalist for sports, show trials, and celebrity features, lived across the street in a hotel and visited Lindy's daily. One of his short stories inspired the play and movie "Guys and Dolls." In that show Lindy's was called "Mindy's," and the area's denizens sprang to fictional life. Real life underworld big shots like Frank Costello, Arnold Rothstein, Bugsy Siegel, Legs Diamond, Lucky Luciano, Meyer Lansky, Dutch Schultz, and Owney Madden were frequent visitors in the 1920's and 1930's.

Billy Conn and his handlers arrived in New York two weeks before the fight. Johnny Ray and Billy visited Freddie Fierro at the Pioneer Gym in Manhattan. Fierro had worked with many big name fighters, including Fritzie Zivic, who recommended him highly. Ray felt that an extra head, especially a wise and experienced one like Fierro, would help. It was – and is – a common practice for a fighter newly reaching the big time to seek such help. Fierro agreed to help for his usual fee. Billy called Fierro, a short, stocky man, "Fat" from the moment he met him. Annoyed at first, "Fat" Fierro came to accept the teasing nickname from a young fighter he grew to love like a son.

The New York Irish hailed Billy Conn as a potential savior. Since the dethroning of Braddock by Joe Louis, no Irish-American held a world title. The Irish greats of recent vintage – Dempsey, Tunney, Walker, Jimmy McLarnin, Jimmy Slattery, Tommy Loughran – were all retired.

Billy sparred for two weeks against local kids with Apostoli's style. He impressed local "sharps" and bettors so much with his workouts that the odds dropped from 14-5 to 2-1, still in favor of Apostoli. Conn and Apostoli had two common opponents: Young Corbett III and Solly Krieger. Both lost to the tricky Corbett the first time, but won big in the rematch, Conn by decision and Apostoli by KO. Billy lost badly to Krieger the first time, but won an easy decision in the rematch. Apostoli had two wins over Krieger, the first by decision and the second by a fifth-round knockout.

Apostoli would receive 30% of the net gate, Conn 17.5%. A crowd of nearly 11,000 paid over $25,000 to watch the middleweight champ take on the acclaimed newcomer from Pittsburgh. Chartered "Ham and Cabbage Specials" carried trainloads of Irish (and other) Pittsburghers to New York for the fight.

Billy exuded confidence at the weigh-in and told Regis Welsh: "I'll box Apostoli's ears off – and he's not going to hit me the way he hit Solly Krieger, Glenn Lee, or Young Corbett. Even if he does manage to clip me, I'm sure he can't hit any harder than Krieger, Ray Actis, or Oscar Rankins. And I beat the three of them."

Most expert observers felt that Billy didn't have the punch to stop Apostoli's slashing attacks, and expected him to cut Billy up like he had done to Krieger and Corbett. But a few disagreed. Krieger's manager Hymie Caplin and Max Schmeling's manager Joe Jacobs predicted a Conn win. Former lightweight champ Benny Leonard declared that Conn's long left jab would keep Apostoli off balance and win the fight for Billy.

At the weigh-in Billy looked lean while Apostoli looked more compact and muscular. Apostoli looked at the skinny youngster and felt that he could break him in half. But the numbers underscored a crucial fact: at 167 ¾ to 160 ½, Billy had a weight advantage of seven pounds; he was three inches taller at 6'0" to 5'9".

Pittsburgh's KDKA radio station broadcast the fight at 10 p.m. After the last prelim finished, the crowd awaited the entrance of the main event principals. Apostoli was an old hand at this, his ninth New York appearance. He was well known to the New York crowd and popular for his aggressive and winning style. Most of them had never seen Billy Conn.

As Billy strode toward the bright lights of the ring, the crowd, especially the women, gasped in oohs and aahs. His tall, svelte body towered above his handlers, and exuded youthful energy. Thick, black, curly locks spilled over his forehead and ears, bouncing as he strutted. Sparkling eyes, full lips, white teeth, dimples in his cheeks, strong jaw – this boy looked like a movie star, not a pug. The guy next to him, whispering to him, short and weather beaten, with scarred eyebrows, flattened nose, cauliflower ears – he looked like an old pug. That was Johnny Ray, the old Pittsburgh lightweight, who looked nothing like a slick, big-time New York manager. He had brought the kid along since childhood.

The crowd's response bolstered Billy, who smiled and waved, oozing confidence and ease. His green velvet robe with "Billy Conn" written in white across the back flowed with him. He ducked into the ring, dancing on the canvas. He shed his robe and shadow boxed, his lithe movements as smooth as a tiger in the wild. Female hearts fluttered. To the women, he was as pretty as a matinee idol. To the men, this was a guy who could steal your girl's heart – and kick your ass! To the Irish, here was a Celtic god from the hinterlands, come to restore Hibernian supremacy. He had to win.

After the announcements and introductions, the bell rang for the first round. New York would see if the handsome kid could fight. They knew Apostoli could – he was a proven winner, a worthy world champion, 25 years old and in his prime. He wanted to put this cocky upstart in his place. He was handsome, too. One New York sportswriter said this fight was between the two best looking men in all of boxing.

Apostoli rushed from his corner to get at Billy. Billy sidestepped, dancing and jabbing. He flicked long jabs at the shorter man, stabbing him repeatedly. The kid was very fast – both hands and feet. Apostoli landed one good left hook to the head, but Billy dominated the round. Rounds two and three continued in much the same manner, with Apostoli rushing a dancing Conn who stabbed him with long jabs, and occasionally a left hook or hard right to the body. In the fourth Apostoli got to him, as Billy willingly slugged to show his bravery. Apostoli landed a left hook to the body, and followed with another left-right combination, driving Billy into the ropes. Billy looked hurt. Apostoli landed two hooks to the head and a big one to the stomach. Billy recovered, stabbing his left jab like a piston and knocking out Apostoli's mouthpiece. Between rounds, Johnny Ray made a dramatic show of dousing Billy's face in the water bucket. In the fifth Apostoli's bobbing and weaving couldn't get him close enough to land a good shot. Billy kept him off balance with stinging jabs. As Billy danced and Apostoli followed, Billy would suddenly whirl around and catch him with a solid right. Billy danced and jabbed throughout the sixth, seventh, and eighth, knocking out Apostoli's mouthpiece in each of those rounds. Apostoli's desperate punches grew increasingly wild, but he did force the action much of the time. In the ninth Apostoli received a warning for two low punches, as he kept after the dancing, jabbing Conn. As they came out for the tenth, Apostoli knew he needed a knockout to win. After chasing Billy around the ring, he caught him on the ropes early and landed a flurry of solid punches, opening a small cut under Billy's left eye. Billy clinched and held on. Then suddenly, as he had in the fourth, he came to life, landing a big left hook to the head and a right to the chin. Billy swarmed all over Apostoli as the fight ended. It had been a torrid pace and a brilliant exhibition by Conn. Referee Billy Cavanaugh had it 5 to 2 Conn, with three rounds even. Judge George LeCron had it 6-4 Conn. Judge Billy Healey had it 5-4 Conn, with one round even.

The Apostoli camp admitted that Conn had won, but felt that a 15-round fight would be a different story. They claimed that Freddie was coming on late, winning the ninth and tenth, and demanded a rematch at 15 rounds. In the dressing room Apostoli said, "Billy's a hell of a good fighter and I want to fight him again in a fifteen rounder. I've got no alibis."

Johnny Ray countered, "Fight Apostoli at fifteen rounds? Why not? The longer a fight goes, the better Billy gets."

Billy himself dismissed Apostoli's power: "Krieger is much tougher. He hits harder than Apostoli and he keeps driving both hands to the body. Apostoli never really hurt me last night. Krieger did in Pittsburgh."

Billy was now the toast of Pittsburgh and New York. The New York fans and Jacobs Beach crowd buzzed over this stunning new talent. He had it all: speed, ring smarts, defense, courage. He was in demand: Apostoli wanted a rematch at 15 rounds; Krieger wanted a rubber match. The Garden was eager to have him against anybody. The money would keep rolling in.

Billy had just beaten the two reigning middleweight champions. But was he a middleweight or light heavyweight? His best weight was about 167 or 168. He would have difficulty in making 160, but neither champ wanted a title bout with him anyway. At only 21 years old and still growing, his future seemed to be in the light heavyweight division.

Champion John Henry Lewis had retired due to eye damage. Number one contender Tiger Jack Fox was matched with number two, Melio Bettina, to crown a new champion. Fox was favored in the Madison Square Garden bout, but Bettina knocked him out in the ninth round to capture the crown.

Billy signed for a rematch with Apostoli of 15 rounds for Friday, February 10th at Madison Square Garden. The title would not be at stake. Billy agreed to weigh 168 or less. He was promised a shot at Bettina's light heavyweight title if he won. A larger crowd was expected, and each fighter was guaranteed 25 % of the net gate. Billy was making more money than he had ever dreamed of, and much more was in store if he continued to win. The top preliminary pitted Fritzie Zivic against "San Francisco Negro" Eddie Booker, undefeated in 45 pro bouts, accentuating the "San Francisco versus Pittsburgh" theme of the night.

Despite Conn's victory over him, odds makers installed Apostoli as an early 8-5 favorite. They felt that the longer distance would help him, as Conn seemed to fade a little at the end of the first bout. Apostoli was a proven commodity. Billy was still new to the New York scene. Apostoli was expected to concentrate on the body, since he had so much difficulty hitting Conn's elusive head in the first bout. Apostoli had a history of doing better the second time he met an opponent, a sign of ring intelligence. He had knocked Corbett and Steele out in the second bout after losing to them in the first bout. He had KO'd Krieger and Glenn Lee in the rematch after winning by decision the first time. But Billy had also beaten Krieger and Corbett decisively after losing to both in the first bout. Confident as ever, he told reporter Jack Miley: "When I lick a fellow once, he stays licked. Apostoli is a cinch. Only this time I'll do a better job; I was too nervous and tense in my last start. I can fight better than that."

Billy trained at the Pioneer Gym, with "Fat" Fierro again accompanying Johnny Ray in his corner. So impressive were his workouts that word got around, and hundreds of fans jammed into the small gym to watch. Billy was working 13 to 15 rounds per day, most of it in sparring several different partners. He showed so much speed and stamina that the odds narrowed to 6-5, still in favor of Apostoli, by fight day. Apostoli, at Stillman's, did not look as sharp, and worked fewer rounds.

On Tuesday night before the fight Billy attended the Duquesne University basketball game at the Garden, sitting next to Coach Chick Davies. The Dukes lost to Long Island University.

A "Conn Special" train carried 400 Pittsburghers to New York for the fight. Several hundred more came by car. The fight sold out – and then some. Nearly 19,000 paying customers – standing room only – jammed into the Garden, boosting the gate to nearly $50,000. Billy weighed 167 for the bout, Apostoli 161.

Conn fans gave Billy a raucous sendoff from the Hotel New Yorker as he left for the Garden. He told reporters his plans for after the expected victory: "We'll probably go to Europe. Naturally, I'd like to see Ireland and meet the folks and maybe get a chance to do some fighting."

With the war situation in Europe about to explode, Billy would not be going there anytime soon.

Conn and Apostoli entered the ring to the loud cheers of supporters before one of the largest crowds in Garden history. The fight outdrew the sold out Joe Louis-John Henry Lewis bout of a month earlier. The fighters came out cautiously in the first round. Both had a well-deserved reputation for winning rematches; strategy and quick thinking would be important factors in this fight. Both landed some good hooks, but missed a lot of punches as they probed each other's defenses. In the second round they closed and fought. Conn started screaming that Apostoli had thumbed him in the eye. They battled furiously, clashing heads. Conn suffered a nasty cut under the left eye from a butt, which he claimed was intentional. They stopped and screamed at each other, hurling profanity and ethnic insults. The referee stopped the action momentarily and examined Conn's cut. He ruled that it was due to an unintentional butt. They went after each other with a vengeance when the action continued, Billy landing long left hooks to the head and Apostoli countering with an effective body attack. In the third Apostoli continued his body attack, taking that round as well as the second. Billy, handicapped by bleeding and swelling around the eyes from butting and thumbing, was off to a slow start. The fourth round was fought at a torrid pace, as Apostoli drove Billy to the ropes with vicious body punches, while Billy landed left jabs and left hooks, outboxing Fred. Billy landed a big right late in the round that staggered Fred, and took the round on all three judges' cards. Apostoli used effective body punching again to win the fifth, which was also punctuated by screaming insults. Apostoli's body attack strategy was working. He had a solid lead going into the sixth round. In the sixth Billy slipped twice near his own corner, which was soaked with water. The second time he injured his ankle, and was given a few minutes to recover. At this point Conn, behind in the fight, with impaired vision and a sore ankle, was in deep trouble. He had to get going. He danced and jabbed brilliantly, winning the round. Just when it looked like Apostoli was on his way to a convincing victory, the youthful Conn picked up the already torrid pace. Billy won the seventh, eighth, ninth, and tenth rounds by superior speed and brilliant boxing. Apostoli couldn't seem to solve him, and was penalized for a low blow in the seventh. Billy continued to outbox Fred in the eleventh, but the referee awarded the round to Apostoli when Billy hit him low. Apostoli came out for the twelfth firing rights, most of which missed. Billy outboxed him again, and had a solid lead with three rounds to go. The Apostoli camp had demanded a fifteen round fight because they believed their fighter had more stamina; they believed he had lost the first bout because it was only ten rounds. But neither man showed any signs of tiring yet. In the thirteenth Apostoli got back on track, winning the round with body punches. Billy was again penalized for a low blow. In the fourteenth they slugged with each other with no letup. Both men had fought at a killing pace for thirteen rounds, yet neither one showed any signs of fatigue or quit. The crowd roared its approval. It was a brilliant exhibition by two great fighters. Billy had a slight edge in the punching, and won the round on all three cards. The fifteenth continued at the same unbelievable pace, both men landing punches and boxing beautifully. Apostoli landed a big body blow near the end that won him the round. The fight ended with the overflow crowd on its feet, cheering in appreciation. The decision was close, but unanimous. Judges Joe Lynch and George LeCron had it 9-6 for Conn, while referee Frank Fullam had it 8-7.

It was a big win and another big payday for Conn. Each man received $10,502, which was 25% of the net gate.

Jack Singer asked Billy about the second round furor. Billy told him, "He stuck his thumb in my eye and I cussed him out. Then he cussed me out and we butted heads. That's all."

Apostoli told Singer he had no alibis, but his manager Larry White was less gracious: "I admit Conn had an edge last time. But Fred won easily tonight. Talk about burglary! From now on, we fight just middleweights."

Johnny Ray declared that Conn would fight just light-heavyweights now. Making the contract weight for this fight had drained him.

The boxing experts and scribes gushed over Conn. He had shown not only skill, but a champion's heart and brain. Many wrote that he had outwitted Apostoli, who was respected as a smart fighter of enormous talent.

Having shown a great fighting heart and charismatic glamour, Billy became extremely popular in both New York and Pittsburgh. Many prominent Pittsburghers sought his acquaintance. One such figure was James Lawrence "Greenfield Jimmy" Smith, who met Billy in New York and took a liking to the kid. Smith was the son of Irish immigrant parents and had grown up in the Greenfield neighborhood, not far from Conn's East Liberty. He had played baseball for the New York Giants, Pittsburgh Pirates, and Cincinnati Reds in a ten-year major league career. He was a prominent businessman in Pittsburgh who had his hand in a lot of lucrative activities. Through bootlegging, the coal business, and nightclub ownership he had become quite prosperous. He lived in a beautiful home on Beechwood Boulevard in the exclusive Squirrel Hill section, adjacent to Greenfield. He owned an expensive brick home in Ocean City, New Jersey, where he and his family spent the summers. When he discovered that Billy had never seen the ocean, he invited him to the Jersey shore to stay at his home there. Billy took him up on the offer. Billy's artist heart had to be impressed by the beauty of the ocean waves and the massive structure his friend owned on St. Charles Place, the only brick house in quaint Ocean City. But it would soon all pale in comparison to a more familiar type of beauty. Jimmy introduced Billy to his sixteen-year-old daughter Mary Louise, thinking it would be a thrill for the girl to meet a world famous athlete who was constantly in the news. Smith had no idea what he was starting. Billy was instantly smitten with the beautiful blonde teenager. While alone with her, he told her that he was going to marry her some day. She told him he was crazy. Although she certainly noticed his movie star looks, she was not smitten. She had her preppy school friends and lots of male suitors her own age. It did not seem possible that this older man could fit into her world. She forgot about him as soon as he left.

But Billy couldn't forget her. Back in Pittsburgh, he called her at home and asked her to go out with him. They went to Bill Green's nightclub on Route 51 south of Pittsburgh for their first date. He didn't quite fit in her world, but she found herself becoming attracted to this older man of 21. She says, "He was older, smarter, and more grounded than the boys I hung out with."

She started seeing him regularly. She didn't tell her father, but her mother knew about it. When her father found out, he forbade her to see him. He had nothing personal against Billy, but he didn't want his daughter seeing a boxer. He told her that he knew the boxing world and didn't want her in that environment.

The situation had some ironic parallels to Smith's own life. He was the son of an immigrant steelworker, an Irish Catholic, and a tough character with a reputation as a hell of a street fighter. The woman he wanted to marry was an elegant Episcopalian of English ancestry from Canada. Her family objected to her marrying a Catholic. The family ultimately relented. Jimmy now saw himself as upper crust, and rejected the idea of his daughter seeing a common prizefighter.

Mary Louise continued to see Billy on the sly, despite her father's objection. Her father found out and immediately sent her to Rosemont

College near Philadelphia, a Catholic girls school where she would be under the strict supervision of nuns. He informed the school officials his daughter was not to see Mr. Billy Conn under any circumstances.

Although Billy had plenty of other women at that time, he could not let go of the young Mary Louise. He called her and sent her presents. He called her "Matt" because of the way her hair matted when wet.

A Conn-Bettina title bout was in the works for the summer, but Bettina needed a tuneup fight before taking on so formidable an opponent as Billy Conn. He came to Pittsburgh's Duquesne Gardens May 10 for a bout with Italo Colonello, a big heavyweight.

The Conn team took on Solly Krieger at Madison Square Garden May 12th in a twelve rounder. Although Ray wanted only light heavyweight bouts, Mike Jacobs was willing to offer another lucrative deal. A weight limit of 172 rather than 168 cinched the deal. It was risky to fight such a dangerous slugger while waiting for a title fight, but the money was too good to pass up. They wanted to ride the wave of popularity in the Big Apple after three straight wins against reigning champions. Johnny Ray had never shied away from a risk, and he felt that Billy could handle Solly easily again. Krieger wanted a chance to redeem himself after his poor performance against Conn in their second bout.

Bettina knocked out Colonello in the third round, showing excellent power against a large heavyweight.

Billy was a 12-5 favorite to beat Solly Krieger again, based on his last three impressive wins. Krieger had won four fights since the Conn loss, two by KO. He still held his share of the middleweight crown, and seemed to be back on track. Billy felt much more comfortable with the limit of 172 pounds, hoping to add some weight for his upcoming light heavyweight title match. He actually weighed in at 170, compared to Krieger's 166 ½. Nearly 11,000 fans paid over $25,000.

Jackie Conn was also on the card in a four rounder versus "New York Negro" Freddie Lewis. It was Jackie's New York debut also. He had won all twelve of his pro fights – all four rounders. He had a good punch and a lot of heart, but nowhere near Billy's speed and skill. Billy often sparred with Jackie at the Pioneer Gym in preparation for this fight. Billy felt that Jackie didn't train properly and didn't have the skill to become a good fighter. He wanted to convince him to quit, and showed no mercy in sparring sessions. Even some of the tough New Yorkers winced as Billy battered his younger brother, who was usually hurt and often bleeding from the mouth and nose. But Jackie took the punishment without complaint.

Seventeen-year-old Jackie gawked at the New York sites. His brother bought him an expensive bright green suit, which he wore everywhere. Jack Miley wrote: "Jackie looked like a walking pool table." But he was able to get dates with an older professional singer who liked the suit.

Jackie confided in Billy that he worried about stage fright before such a big crowd at the famous Garden. Billy reminded him to worry about his opponent, and told him, "They're not coming to see you, they're coming to see me." Jackie won by a second round TKO.

Billy began his fight with stinging jabs, landing at will. Solly charged, but Billy's quick feet easily avoided him. Conn's huge speed advantage was obvious from start to finish. He continued to pepper Solly with jabs. Despite Solly's reputation as a tough infighter, Billy moved in on him at times and landed left and right uppercuts repeatedly. Even at close range, Solly could barely land a punch. The fight continued in the same pattern until the seventh round, when Billy landed hard rights to the chin off of jabs, staggering Solly. With his newfound strength and maturity, Billy could not only outbox Solly, but outslug him as well. The fight was less competitive than the previous one, and ended in a virtual shutout. Billy had his fourth straight victory over reigning middleweight champs, this one a mismatch. He was ready for Melio Bettina and the light heavyweight title.

ROUND NINE

World Champion

After Billy Conn's spectacular string at Madison Square Garden, Mike Jacobs wanted him to take on Melio Bettina there for the light-heavyweight title. Billy was the hottest thing in boxing that summer of 1939. Joe Louis had beaten all contenders and appeared to be invincible. Welterweight champ Henry Armstrong was a great fighter who had held the featherweight, lightweight, and now welterweight titles, but the lower weight classes never generated as much excitement as the larger men did. Conn was handsome, white, charismatic, and gifted in the ring. He was already being talked about as a potential challenger for Louis in the not-too-distant future.

Prior to 1903, any man weighing over the 160-pound middleweight limit was a heavyweight. Because of the large weight differential between a man in the 160s or 170s and the larger heavyweights, some weighing over 200 pounds, a new "light-heavyweight" class was created with a limit of 175 pounds. George Gardner defeated Jack Root on July 4, 1903, to become the first light-heavyweight champ. Bob Fitzsimmons, who won the heavyweight title while weighing only 170 pounds, lost it to 220 pound Jim Jeffries. Since he weighed under 175, Fitzsimmons was eligible for the light-heavyweight title. He defeated Gardner in November of 1903 to win it. Later champs in the division included

105

Jack Dillon, Battling Levinsky, Philadelphia Jack O'Brien, and Georges Carpentier. Slick-boxing Tommy Loughran held the title from 1927 until he retired in 1930. Slapsie Maxie Rosenbloom held it from 1930 until 1934, losing to Bob Olin, who in turn lost to Pittsburgh "adopted son" John Henry Lewis. When Lewis retired in 1939 due to vision problems, the top two contenders, Tiger Jack Fox and Melio Bettina, met at Madison Square Garden on February 3, 1939, to crown a new champ. Although Fox was favored to win, Bettina KO'd him in the ninth round.

Bettina's first defense would be against the new sensation, Billy Conn, which assured him a big payday. Bettina was 23 years old and from nearby Beacon, New York. He was swarthy, hairy-chested, and muscular. Though only 5-8 ½" he had a phenomenal 74" reach due to his broad shoulders and long arms. He was a rugged fighter with excellent punching power in either hand. He fought from a left-handed stance, like Young Corbett III. He threw punches from all angles with adequate speed, and his unorthodox stance caused difficulty for opponents. He was not fast on his feet like Billy Conn. He had won his last 17 fights, 11 by knockout. He decisioned Dom Ceccarelli, whom Conn and John Henry Lewis had both decisioned. He had the power and toughness to beat good heavyweights, decisioning 194 pound Henry Cooper. His last loss was nearly three years ago to Buck Everett, which he avenged by a first round knockout in a rematch. On May 3rd he gave Pittsburgh fans a close-up preview of their hero Conn's opponent, knocking out heavyweight Italo Colonello in the third round.

No Pittsburgher had held a world title for three years, since Yarosz lost the middleweight crown to Babe Risko in 1936. The city had an impressive history in the middleweight division, with four world champs: Frank Klaus, George Chip, Harry Greb, and Teddy Yarosz. Scores of area natives had been contenders in all divisions, but none had ever won the light-heavyweight or heavyweight titles. Greb held the "American" light-heavyweight title after beating Gene Tunney in 1922. Frank Moran lost in two heavyweight title attempts, to Jack Johnson in 1914 and Jess Willard in 1916.

Some interesting parallels were developing between Conn and his idol Greb. Both fought at middleweight and light-heavyweight, switching back and forth to take on the best fighters available. Greb had defeated reigning light-heavyweight champs Dillon and Levinsky several times each in non-title bouts, as Conn had done to Apostoli and Krieger. Both were skillful and tough enough to take on any fighter at any weight. Greb had beaten lots of good heavyweights, as Conn would do in the future.

Conn and Bettina signed for a July 13th bout at Madison Square Garden. As champion, Bettina would receive the larger share of the gate. The contract guaranteed a return bout within four months for the champion Bettina if he lost. Conn was installed as a 12 to 5 favorite, an unusually strong show of support for a challenger. The experts felt that Conn was much too fast for Bettina. But they had thought that about Fox, and Bettina had knocked him out.

Over 1500 Pittsburghers made the trip to New York by train and car. Bettina's Beacon, New York contingent numbered over 5,000, about one-third of the 15,000 plus that packed Madison Square Garden.

In training for the fight, Billy worked hard at improving his right hand power. His left jab and hook were superb and needed no improvement, but his right, though quick and accurate, lacked knockout power. He was now slightly over six feet tall and weighed about 170 pounds. Now 21 years old, he was getting stronger as he matured. Despite an overall slim build, he had a thick, solid neck and strong, muscular legs. He could take a punch better now. Solly Krieger had found that out. Fat Fierro worked with Billy on the right hand, trying different angles and positions to get more of his body into it. Billy also worked alone for hours on the heavy bag, experimenting with throwing the right different ways. He noticed more power in sparring, stunning several opponents with rights, and knocking out a large heavyweight with a clean right under the heart. "He was like a kid with a new toy," according to Fierro. But Fierro warned him that he was primarily a boxer, and should not get into a slugging match if he could control the bout by boxing.

Billy was often labeled a hot-tempered Irishman by the press, who loved to play up the ethnic rivalries and stereotypes in boxing. The day before the fight he told Lester Bromberg of the *New York World-Telegram* that his father would be at the fight, and rambled on about his father's fighting Irish spirit. "Aw, the old man is a fighting Mick himself. He's the best fighter in the family. Up till a year ago I used to fight with him out in the backyard. I'm getting too good for him now. After all, he's forty-one years old. There are plenty of guys he can still fight – for fun, that is. He knows where to find his fights around Pittsburgh. I don't know about here. Give him a day or two, I guess, and he'll get guys to slug it out with."

He told Bromberg of the time his dad and Johnny Ray got into it on a trip to Erie. Wild Bill got a broken nose and Ray lost a tooth. Afterward, they were the best of friends.

Billy continued, "That old man of mine goes around Pittsburgh telling everybody I'm a cinch to beat Joe Louis right now. I figure I can beat Louis, but it ain't nice to go talking about it. My old man don't stop at just saying that. He steps right out onto the floor and shows them how I'll do it – a hook, a jab, a feint, you know. Some day I figure I have to go over to Ireland and find out what made my old man's family like this. My old man says he comes from a family of fighting kings and that they used to chase all over the country winning battles, then fighting among themselves when there wasn't anything else doing. He says he does his best to live up to the old custom."

New York's boxing fans, especially the Irish, ate it up.

Just prior to the fight, Bettina's throng of backers paraded outside the Garden with signs and a marching band. The boisterous Beaconites had caused quite a scene in the big city, marching from Grand Central Station to the Garden blaring their musical instruments. The *Post-Gazette's* Jimmy Miller reported that an onlooker told him "It's gonna take more than a band to lick that Irishman."

It was a sweltering July night in New York, and even hotter inside the Garden, packed with fans. The favored challenger weighed 170 ¼ to 173 ¼ for Bettina. In a prelim bout, Jackie Conn took on New Yorker Lou

Vallante in a four-rounder. The Beacon crowd booed Jackie as he was introduced, and booed the decision announced in his favor.

In the top prelim battle of light-heavyweight contenders, Dave Clark decisioned Tiger Jack Fox.

Billy Conn also had a large throng of backers from Pittsburgh and the New York Irish community. But Bettina's fans outnumbered and outshouted them, holding up signs all over the Garden in support of their hero. Just before the bell Conn, noticing the Bettina supporters, told Fierro, "I hate to ruin the night for these people, but Beacon ain't gonna have a champion an hour from now."

In the first round Billy circled to the left and Bettina followed. Both fighters landed a number of lefts, but Bettina landed more. All three judges gave him the round. In the second, they closed and fought, each landing punches inside. Conn landed a right to the jaw that rocked Bettina. Again, both landed good lefts. All three judges gave the round to Conn. Bettina landed a good left early in the third. They fought at close quarters, with Bettina getting the better of it and landing some good body shots. All three judges gave him the round. In the fourth they fought in close again. Conn landed two good rights, one an uppercut; Bettina landed several good lefts and rights. They continued fighting after the bell, as partisan fans rose, cheering and jeering. All three judges again gave the round to Bettina, giving him a three to one lead on all cards. Billy was starting slowly again, and having some difficulty with Bettina's southpaw stance. But the right did seem to be a more powerful weapon. Johnny Ray made several adjustments in Billy's tactics. In the fifth Billy landed two good rights to the jaw, staggering Bettina. Billy followed with two good left hooks late in the round. He walloped the champ with a good one as the ref broke them. Billy had dominated the round, but the ref awarded the round to Bettina because Billy had hit him on the break. After five rounds, Billy trailed badly, but seemed to have solved the champ's awkward style. In the sixth Billy landed a right to the jaw early, and again took the fight to the champion. Bettina landed one good left, but Billy followed up by landing lefts to the jaw repeatedly. Near the end of the round Billy landed another solid right to the jaw.

Bettina was wobbly as he returned to his corner. The jubilant Pittsburgh fans were now outshouting the Beaconites. In the seventh Billy landed a series of lefts that had Bettina's head snapping back, and then landed a right that shook him. Billy continued to score with solid punches throughout the seventh and eighth to the cheers of his fans. Although the judges had it even at this point, Billy Conn was in full control of the fight. In the ninth Billy circled and danced, making Bettina miss punch after punch while landing on the champion repeatedly. At one point Billy landed nine unanswered lefts to the jaw. The tenth, eleventh, and twelfth rounds were much the same. Bettina rushed, Billy danced away and came back with accurate punches. Always moving to his left, Billy jabbed at will, and followed with hooks and straight rights. Bettina could barely land a punch, as Billy skillfully blocked with his elbows and gloves. Bettina at times swung and missed at a dancing Conn that wasn't where he was supposed to be. The champion looked increasingly frustrated as the fight was becoming one-sided. The Beaconites stopped beating their bass drum. In the eleventh Bettina nearly went down after a hard left and right to the jaw by Conn. Billy's piston-like jabs kept popping Melio's head back. Several times the crowd counted the stiff jabs, which Melio was unable to block or counter. In the thirteenth Melio rallied, landing a hard left to the head and following with a flurry of punches to the body. A solid left opened a small cut under Billy's left eye that had never seemed to heal from previous fights. Billy attacked back, battering and hurting the champion for the latter half of the round. In the fourteenth Billy jabbed and danced, following Johnny Ray's instructions to protect his lead and not take any chances.

As they touched gloves for the fifteenth and final round, the bass drum roll sounded again. Bettina's title was slipping away. He needed a knockout to win. The game but outclassed champion made a valiant effort, rushing and wrestling Conn. Johnny Ray had given Billy strict instructions to jab and move, giving Bettina no chance to land a knockout punch. Early on Billy obeyed, blocking Bettina's punches with his gloves and elbows. He landed a couple of left hooks to the jaw to break up Bettina's momentum. Near the end of the round Billy could contain himself no longer. They engaged in a furious exchange, both landing multiple power shots and flailing away to the end. When the bell sounded, ending the fight, Melio Bettina's reign was over. He had won the round, but lost the fight. Billy Conn was the new light-heavyweight champion of the world! From the streets of East Liberty and a dilapidated gym above the Enright Theater, Moonie and Junior had made it to the top.

Wild Bill Conn was the first one into the ring to congratulate his son, with brothers Frank and Jackie following right behind him. The fight grossed over $50,000, giving Billy another big payday of $8644. Bettina received over $15,000, but lost the lucrative title.

After the fight Billy came back to Pittsburgh and checked in with his personal physician, Dr. Harold Kehner at Mercy Hospital. Kehner especially wanted to check the cut beneath Billy's right eye, which had never completely healed since the Corbett fight and had reopened several times in other fights. After the checkup, Billy spent a few days resting at Kehner's summer estate.

In the aftermath of winning the championship, the Conn team received a plethora of enticing offers. Besides Mike Jacobs in New York, Detroit and Cleveland were eager to feature the popular new champ. Philadelphia wanted him for an outdoor bout at Shibe Park, home of the American League Athletics. (And near the current residence of Miss Mary Louise Smith). The new Pittsburgh promotion team of Art Rooney and Barney McGinley wanted him for Forbes Field.

Gus Lesnevich was now the number one light-heavyweight contender, based largely on a spectacular first round knockout of fellow contender Dave Clark. A Conn-Lesnevich bout would be a big draw anywhere. Reports surfaced that they would fight in late July at Forbes Field, promoted by Rooney-McGinley in conjunction with Mike Jacobs, who still had a legal hold on Billy's next few fights. But Bettina still had a guarantee of a return bout within four months.

On Monday, July 17, Billy attended a big Rooney-McGinley card at Forbes Field featuring welterweights Fritzie Zivic and Charley Burley, light-heavyweights Teddy Yarosz and Al Gainer, and lightweights Sammy

Angott and Petey Sarron. (Zivic, Burley, Yarosz, and Angott would all one day earn a spot in boxing's Hall of Fame). Billy had not fought in Pittsburgh in over eight months, and some Pittsburghers grumbled that he had abandoned the city for the fame and fortune of New York. When he was introduced to the crowd as the new light-heavyweight champ, he heard a smattering of boos from resentful local fans. He and Johnny Ray were both hurt by the reaction, and vowed to hold the next fight in Pittsburgh. They signed for the return bout with Bettina for September 25th at Forbes Field.

With his new wealth, Billy bought a solid brick house on Fifth Avenue for the family. It was only about a mile away, but in a much nicer neighborhood. It was much larger than the little East Liberty row houses they had grown up in. His mother feared moving, because she didn't know anybody on Fifth Avenue and would be leaving her friends. Billy told her to just invite them all over.

In the meantime Mike Jacobs worked out a deal for a lucrative bout in Philadelphia at Shibe Park versus Gus Dorazio, a ranked heavyweight. The money was good, the title would not be at stake, and Ray and Conn wanted to test their skills in the heavyweight division. Jacobs and the Conn team expected Billy to turn into a full time heavyweight in 1940 and take on Joe Louis for the really big bucks, after the still growing youngster added a few pounds. The Dorazio date was August 14th, prior to the Bettina title bout.

Jacobs took a liking to his hot new prospect. Fred Fierro wrote, "A father-son relationship developed. Jacobs called Conn 'my boy.' Billy spent his weekends on Mike's rolling showplace at Rumson, New Jersey. He vacationed at Uncle Mike's Miami estate. And used his Central Park West duplex. He was chauffered around in Mike's Cadillac until the promoter gave him a flashy, cream-colored convertible as a stringless gift. Billy wore expensive suits styled by Jacobs' tailors and ten-dollar ties Mike picked out for him."

Despite the resentment and booing at Forbes Field, most Pittsburghers and the Pittsburgh media were proud of their new champion. Feature articles appeared in the local papers. Harry Keck wrote a full page Sunday spread in the *Sun-Telegraph* called "Great American Family: The Billy Conns, A Peak into the Private Life of a Champion." A beautiful picture of the entire family of seven had Frank, 20, Billy, 21, and Jackie, 17, in the back row. Seated in front were Mary Jane, 18, Mom and Pop, and Peggy Ann, 9. The article emphasized mostly the rambunctious and playful fighting nature of the boys, including the father, and the difficulty that Mom had keeping them in line.

Billy bought himself a new black Cadillac and added to his extensive, fashionable wardrobe. Jackie often used the car and the clothes without Billy's consent. Billy was voted best-dressed sportsman of the year, and quipped that Jackie should be runner-up because he wore the same clothes.

Not one to easily forget a slight, Billy had a few scores to settle. He went back to East Liberty to find some of the local toughs who had ridiculed him when he was starting out with Johnny Ray and said he would be a champ some day. As told to Frank Deford in a 1985 *Sports Illustrated* article: "They were loafing in a bar. 'Remember the messenger boy you laughed at?' he asked, and they nodded, cowering. Billy brought his hands up fast, and they ducked away, but all he did was lay a lot of big bills on the hardwood. 'Well, all right,' Billy said, 'stay drunk a long time on the light-heavyweight champeen of the world.'"

In another incident, an older bully who had picked on Billy years ago was walking by the Conn home as Billy was on the porch. Enraged by the sight of him, Billy, now older and stronger and skilled in boxing, administered a prolonged, savage beating to the young man on the street as the Conn family watched. "My father finally had to pull Billy off of him," related Frank Conn.

Billy arrived in Philadelphia a week before the Dorazio fight to a hero's welcome, despite being a Pittsburgher battling a hometown boy. His recent accomplishments were well known to boxing fans and ballyhooed by the local press. The Philadelphia Irish especially turned out to greet their ethnic hero. After arrival by train at the Broad Street station, the Conn team proceeded to City Hall to be greeted by Mayor Wilson and top city officials. A crowd of supporters met him with signs and cheers. Billy looked resplendent in a sport coat and open-necked black shirt. With Johnny Ray, brother Jackie, and heavyweight sparring partner Mickey McAvoy he went on to a welcome luncheon at Tendler's Tavern. Owner Lew Tendler was a former lightweight contender from Philadelphia. After the luncheon they went on to Jimmy Dougherty's training camp in Leiperville, outside the city. Billy got to work immediately, sparring two rounds each with Jackie Conn and heavyweights Mickey McAvoy and Dan Hassett.

Local observers felt that Conn looked frail compared to the bigger Dorazio. Billy responded with the cocky sound bites that reporters love. "There are no 'ifs' or 'buts' about it. I'll be the heavyweight champion of the world in two years."

He dismissed his lack of weight as no drawback: "No doubt some of them will have a lot of weight on me, maybe twenty or thirty pounds. That won't make any difference. Wait and see how I handle Dorazio."

The Pittsburgh papers continued to feature the champ and his family. On the day of the Dorazio fight the *Post-Gazette* ran a big picture of his mother at the stove making her potato salad, Billy's favorite food. The accompanying article included great detail about the recipe, and also listed other favorite foods of the champ, his daily diet, and his training routine.

The fight drew over 12,000 fans to Shibe Park. Billy received the customary champion's share of 37.5 %, even though his title was not on the line. The crowd included heavyweight contenders Lou Nova and Tony Galento, scheduled for September 7th at Municipal Stadium in Philadelphia, Melio Bettina, Fred Apostoli, former light heavyweight champ and Philadelphia native Tommy Loughran, and Mike Jacobs. Dorazio supporters from Southwark, a tough Italian neighborhood near the Italian Market in South Philly, comprised a large part of the crowd.

Billy bought twenty tickets for Mary Louise Smith and guests at nearby Rosemont College. The Mother Superior's watchful eye prevented Mary Louise and her friends from escaping to the fight. Billy was sorely disappointed when no one showed up, not even the Mother Superior. The tickets went unused.

Johnny Ray had told the press that Billy would come in at about 180, but he scaled 173 ½, to 186 ¼ for Dorazio. At the weigh-in Billy told Dorazio, who was arguing about the color of trunks he would wear, "Listen, dago, all you're going to need is a catcher's mitt and a chest protector."

Dorazio's ranking was based largely on his victory over Bob Pastor the previous November, which included two knockdowns. Pastor was scheduled to fight Joe Louis for the heavyweight title September 21. At 5'10 3/4" and 186 ¼ pounds, 23-year-old Dorazio was a solid but small heavyweight. He had good punching power and a durable chin, but lacked the speed and skill of a Billy Conn. Conn would be expected to outmaneuver the bigger man. Oddsmakers made Billy a prohibitive 4 to 1 favorite.

Dorazio told reporters that he would come after Conn and give him a beating like he gave Bob Pastor. Conn told John Webster of the *Philadelphia Enquirer*, "He won't have to look for me either. I'll be punching right with him."

Dorazio came out aggressively, crowding Conn while landing left hooks to the body. He threw big right hands that missed as Billy danced away. Billy tried to figure out a plan of attack for the swarming heavyweight. Near the end of the round Billy landed a left hook to the jaw that rocked Dorazio, and followed with a right that opened a cut over his left eye. In the second Dorazio landed one of his big rights high on Conn's head, stunning Billy. Billy responded by charging and slugging toe to toe with the heavier man as the crowd cheered them on. Conn got the best of it, landing lefts and rights repeatedly on Dorazio's chin, his superior speed the telling factor. In the third and fourth Billy landed frequently on Dorazio's cut left eye. The blood flowed onto his shoulders and splashed onto Conn. Dorazio landed some good left hooks to the body. In the fifth Billy continued his assault, forgetting about the fine points of boxing. Dorazio landed a big left hook to the chin, just the punch that had knocked Pastor to the canvas. Conn shook it off. In the sixth Billy jabbed the cut eye, continuing the blood flow. A left hook to the jaw stunned the Philadelphian. Billy added several powerful rights that hurt him more. The round ended with Dorazio looking dazed and bleeding badly. Courageous Gus came out winging for the seventh, as Conn unleashed a barrage of left hooks and overhand rights that hurt him again. The cut was a bad one. Dorazio's corner could not stop the bleeding, and the whole left side of Dorazio's face was a gory red as the seventh ended. The ringside physician examined Dorazio and recommended that the fight be stopped. Dorazio's corner pleaded with referee Leo Houck to let it continue, which he did. As a desperate Dorazio came out for the eighth, his trainer Joe Martino screamed "One good punch Gus!" Dorazio missed with wild punches. Conn stood flat-footed, jarring Dorazio with hard rights and sharp left hooks that left him helpless. At 1:52 into the round Houck stopped it.

It was an impressive victory against a good heavyweight. Billy had shown that he could outslug the bigger man and take his punches, punches that had knocked good heavyweights off their feet. Billy had not a mark or bruise on him. The Associated Press gave Dorazio only the second round.

Tommy Loughran, a slick boxer much like Conn in his day, praised Billy to Regis Welsh, but sounded a warning: "He's a great, grand boxer – but he fights too much. Conn's unlimited courage is a detriment to him because he's fighting when he should be boxing these big, slow fellows. It gets him into trouble, then, when he is in trouble, or maybe because he's Irish, Billy wants to slug. He looks classy when moving around, flecking that left; he looks great when he is slugging and trying to kayo a fellow – but, he will burn out his seemingly unlimited endurance doing things like that and it will begin to tell on him in those fifteen rounders he sooner or later will have to fight against heavyweights."

Philadelphia sportswriters were lavish in their praise, entranced by Conn's glamour. Davis Walsh of the *Philadelphia Record* said he was

"...handsome as a male ingenue outside the ropes and a deadly, merciless executioner inside." Others called him "Sweet William," and "Bill the Butcher," and referred to his "Robert Taylor profile."

Dorazio protested that he was winning when the fight was stopped, but one local writer quipped that the only thing he was winning was a trip to the Wills Eye Clinic.

Talk of Joe Louis inevitably surfaced, now that Billy had decisively beaten a good heavyweight. Loughran said that Conn could be a heavyweight champ: "I think it will be a boxer like Conn who will beat Joe Louis. A slugger won't do it. Louis hits too hard. But a brilliant prospect like Conn might do it in two years if he improves with weight and time as one believes he will."

Mike Jacobs salivated in anticipation of a future Conn-Louis gold mine. This kid was going to be a legitimate heavyweight contender, one of the most popular and charismatic in years.

After the fight Billy returned to Pittsburgh by car. The next day he flew to New York to be honored at an Irish celebration at the World's Fair. When he returned home again he began training for the return bout with Bettina on September 25th.

On August 19th the Rooney-McGinley team put on another successful show at Forbes Field, featuring middleweight champ Fred Apostoli with Glen Lee in a non-title bout. A strong undercard featured middleweight contender Ken Overlin, local welterweight contender Charley Burley, and local lightweight contender Sammy Angott. Nearly 16,000 attended for a net gate of $24,000. Billy Conn attended with Mike Jacobs, who would promote his upcoming bout with Bettina. Local fans gave Billy a better reception, now that he was scheduled to fight in his hometown. Apostoli, Overlin, Burley, and Angott all won by decision, although the Pittsburgh media criticized Apostoli for a lackluster performance.

Bettina came to town early and began workouts at Ketchell's Gym on Pittsburgh's South Side. He griped that he had received a bad decision in the last bout, and was determined to win back the title. Hype Igoe of the *New York Journal* wrote that Bettina had foolishly tried to match his right jab with Conn's left one in the first bout, and had suffered the consequences of Conn's superior speed. This time he would work on a right to the body, a better strategy for the shorter man. Bettina hired the highly respected Jimmy Bronson as his chief second. Bronson had masterminded Gene Tunney's two brilliant wins over Jack Dempsey in the 1920's. One week before the fight Conn weighed 177, Bettina 176 ½ - right on schedule. Jack Dempsey, in town to referee some Catholic Youth Organization amateur bouts, visited the Conn camp briefly.

Observers reported that Bettina looked impressive in training, battering opponents and scoring a clean knockdown against sparring partner Whitey Schramm. His trainer Jimmy Grippo boasted: "Melio has knocked out twenty-one men in fifty-five bouts. It will be twenty-two after the next bout, you can bet your boots."

Johnny Ray countered, "I am willing to bet Conn will knock out Bettina. To those guys who say Billy can't punch I'll tell them he could have stopped Bettina in New York last July if I hadn't held him back with the title sure in our hands by the decision route."

Igoe penned an interview in which the new champion Conn relished the luxury his newly found wealth had brought.

"You know the Conns were always poor," he told Igoe. "I never had a job. There wasn't much money for so many of us. When I started to make money with my fists it seemed like a dream. It's wonderful to have money and some of the comforts and the pleasures it brings. I'll fight until I die to get more money. I said once that I was aiming for fifty thousand dollars. Now I want one hundred thousand dollars and I suppose when I get that much I'll want a million. That's all right, too. Others made it and I'm only a kid.

"We moved out of the old house where I was raised not long ago. Moved into a new house. I fitted it out with wonderful new furniture. I have a beautiful new room all for myself. You should see my bed. Fit for a king, I tell you. I have an extension phone right at my elbow. The Conns never had that kind of luxury before.

"When it was installed I used to call up all my friends. I'd get them up out of bed the first thing in the morning, just to get the kick out of the extension. A lot of them thought I was daffy, but Santa Claus had come and I was playing with the new toys.

"I have a radio and a swell shower in my room. I take four or five splashes a day. The other afternoon I had six of the old gang of mine up in my room taking showers just so they could get the feel of it. I sat there on an expensive easy chair, watching them and thinking what a sweet thing in life money really is. You don't think I'm going to let Melio Bettina take that away from me. I'll be thinking of that radio, my beautiful bed, the shower, the easy chair, and the rest of the furniture all through the fight.

"If I get tired in the fight, I'll suddenly remember that it isn't all paid for yet, and – boff, boff, boff – Melio will get it again."

Conn, who liked to tease his mother, told Igoe that he called her on the downstairs extension from his upstairs extension. He told his mother, "Good morning, Missus William Margaret Conn, of East Liberty, State of Pennsylvania, U.S.A. The top of the mornin' to you, gracious Madame."

Befuddled, she asked who it was. He told her, "You are speaking to the light heavyweight champion of all this wide, wide, world, your son, William David Conn, of the East Liberty Conns, who will be downstairs in ten minutes for his creamed quail on toast."

His mother quickly set him straight. "Look here, Willie Conn," she told him. "You stop putting on such airs. We're the casual Conns around here, still. You'll come down and get ham and eggs and like them."

Two days before the fight, Jackie "borrowed" Billy's Cadillac and drove a gang of friends around. When Billy found out, he and Jackie slugged it out bare-handed, Billy foolishly risking injury before the bout. Johnny Ray and Mike Jacobs heard the commotion and broke it up. Both were horrified to see splattered blood, fearing that Billy was cut. The blood was all Jackie's, to the relief of all concerned, except maybe Jackie. Billy suffered no injury, but Jackie was beaten and bloodied.

Ticket sales were good for the Monday night, September 25th Forbes Field title tilt. Jacobs alone promoted the bout, and had already scheduled Conn for a November 17th Madison Square Garden date with Gus Lesnevich, providing, of course, that he beat Bettina. A bright silver moon shone on the ring, set up between second base and the pitching mound. The 5,000 infield seats sold out before fight day. Attendance reached 18, 422. It was the largest gate ever for a fight in Pittsburgh, but second in attendance to the 20 thousand plus crowd that saw Teddy Yarosz take the middleweight title from Vince Dundee at Forbes Field in 1934. KDKA radio station broadcast the bout, beginning at 10 p.m. The crowd may have been larger were it not for the local broadcast.

Boxing writers from around the country covered the bout, including large contingents from New York, Philadelphia, and Cleveland. A trainload of boisterous Beacon fans showed up to support Bettina. Manager Pie Traynor led a contingent of Pittsburgh Pirates to the fight, including Billy's favorite players, Jimmy Tobin and Arky Vaughan. Gus Lesnevich attended with Mike Jacobs.

Billy weighed in at 172 ½ to 174 ½ for Bettina. He joked and bantered with reporters, while Bettina appeared irritable and sullen. Johnny Ray almost didn't make it to the fight, due to a reported "sudden illness." But Ray recovered and was in Billy's corner by fight time. Billy was a solid two to one favorite to retain his title.

In the first round Billy danced and jabbed, landing some light lefts. Bettina pressured him, pounding his arms and landing an occasional head or body punch. Both men missed a lot, not yet finding the range. In the second Conn landed a good right to the jaw early. He sidestepped Bettina's rushes and slipped most of his punches, but Bettina forced most of the action. It was another indecisive round. In the third Bettina crowded Conn against the ropes, landing some punches. They shouted at each other, Billy claiming that Bettina butted him. They fought mostly on the inside and against the ropes, with Bettina landing slightly more punches. In the fourth Bettina again crowded Billy into the ropes, landing more punches in close. In the fifth Billy landed some good lefts while Bettina scored with both hands and kept Billy against the ropes much of the time. Billy was off to a slow start again, and had dug himself a hole in the scoring. It was time to get going. In the sixth Billy stood flat-footed, and landed powerful rights to the body and jaw, taking the round. In the seventh Billy attacked, landing solidly with punch after punch as Bettina missed. Bettina appeared to be hurt. The crowd responded, screaming for a knockout as Billy landed at will. By the end of the round Bettina was cut over the left eye. In the eighth Billy backed up Bettina with power rights and lefts, cutting him over the right eye. Bettina stopped the attack momentarily with a good left to the jaw, but Billy responded with a vicious body attack that had Bettina holding by the end of the round. In the ninth Billy rocked Bettina early with a right to the jaw, and continued to score with both hands to the head and body. Bettina offered little in return. Billy was firmly in command – Bettina was tired and hurt, and cut over both eyes. Billy started the tenth dancing and jabbing, easily avoiding Bettina's rushes. He landed hard rights and lefts to Bettina's head, further opening the cut over the left eye. Bettina held for most of the eleventh, but Billy managed to land some good inside shots. The twelfth was much the same, with a groggy Bettina holding on and trying to smother Billy's punches, while attempting few of his own. Bettina kept holding for much of the thirteenth, but made a courageous effort, landing some good punches off of clinches. In the fourteenth Bettina tired again as Billy landed solid punches. Bettina could only hold on or cover up; he offered virtually no attack. As they touched gloves for the fifteenth, Billy was well ahead. The only question was whether or not Bettina could survive the round. He tried holding on, as Billy periodically pushed him off and rocked him with solid punches. The fight ended with Bettina badly beaten, but still on his feet. The fighters embraced after the final bell.

Bettina had to be helped from the ring, and vomited the water he was given as he lay on the rubbing table in the locker room. Bettina's trainer Johnny Romano felt that the fifteen round distance worked in Conn's favor, and conceded that Bettina would never beat Conn at that distance. "In ten rounds, yes," he told Claire Burcky of the *Pittsburgh*

Press. "But he can't go fifteen against a man with as much stamina and boxing skill as Conn."

The fight was strikingly similar to their first bout, with Bettina taking the early rounds and Conn coming on strong midway in the fight to take command until the end. Billy explained his early round difficulty to Jack Mahon of the *New York Daily News*, "I had trouble trying to figure him out. It's not easy to get used to those southpaws."

Bettina had little to say, murmuring tersely to Mahon, "I got tired."

The record gate of over $58,000 landed Billy his biggest purse ever, $21,794. And there was more to come: next stop, Madison Square Garden on November 17th to face the number one contender Gus Lesnevich.

Billy was going back to New York after one title defense in Pittsburgh, but he was still a Pittsburgh kid. He told Regis Welsh, "Some call me Broadway Billy, but you can tell them for me that any alley in East Liberty looks better to me than Broadway. I go to New York because it's the place to get the dough – but you notice how quickly I get away from it to get back home. I like New York for what it brings me – but I'll take Pittsburgh for what it has made me."

As he was about to turn twenty-two years of age, Billy was making his mark on the sport of boxing. The boxing press compared him favorably to the great light heavyweight champs of the past. His speed, skill, stamina, and toughness were of rare proportion. His indomitable will wore down other outstanding fighters. He was exciting to watch. The kid was destined for greatness.

New Jerseyan Gus Lesnevich had earned his number one contender status with a first round knockout of fellow contender Dave Clark, a stable mate of Joe Louis. Lesnevich was ruggedly built, with legs like tree trunks. He could punch with knockout power. Hype Igoe wrote that he had more power than previous Conn victims Yarosz, Apostoli, Krieger, and Bettina, and had a knack for hurting opponents' ribs with vicious body punches. But he felt that Gus could only win by an early KO against a fighter with the skill and stamina of Conn. Conn was an early 8 to 5 favorite, a betting line that showed respect for the challenger. The odds were 2 to 1 by fight day, still respectable against a fighter of Conn's reputation.

The fight drew national attention, as Lesnevich was widely considered the best light heavyweight after Conn. Billy would receive the customary champion's share of 37.5% of what was expected to be a good Madison Square Garden crowd.

Just a few days before the fight, Billy had been missing for more than 24 hours. Johnny Ray suspected, correctly, that he had hopped a quick flight to Pittsburgh to see a woman. (It was not Mary Louise. Billy was unable to get to her for the time being.) Billy called Ray from Pittsburgh and assured him he'd be back in time for the fight.

Lesnevich manager Dan Morgan used Conn's well-publicized disappearance to hype the fight: "I'll tell you why Conn flew to Pittsburgh. He wanted to forget about Lesnevich, if only for twenty-four hours."

Billy showed up for the weigh-in the day of the fight, scaling 171 ¼ to 174 ½ for Lesnevich. Attendance reached 13,704, for a gate of over $45,000, guaranteeing Billy an excellent payday of over $15,000.

Despite Billy's profession of loyalty to Pittsburgh, he had won so many big fights in New York that the Big Apple had taken him to heart like one of its own. He walked down the aisle to the ring to a tremendous ovation, and not just from Pittsburghers who had made the trip by train. The vast majority of New Yorkers cheered the Pittsburgh kid like a hometown boy despite the fact that his opponent was from nearby New Jersey. Billy responded with his characteristic wave and heart-winning, dimpled smile.

Hollywood legends Robert Taylor and Barbara Stanwyck attended, but no star shone brighter than Billy Conn that night. And he might soon join them: the papers were reporting that a Hollywood studio was considering Billy to play the lead role in a movie biography of Gentleman Jim Corbett.

Morgan continued his taunting of Conn: "Billy belongs in Hollywood, not in the ring. He's just too handsome for a fighter. He'll be taking care of those good looks tonight and that's why Lesnevich will beat him."

Despite Morgan's taunt, Billy had never worried about protecting his "good looks." His real fault was fighting too much and giving lesser skilled opponents a chance to land a big punch. As Regis Welsh wrote in the *Pittsburgh Press* on fight day, "But Conn, despite all the glamour draped about him, is inherently Irish. As such, he will fight when he gets hit. He did it with Apostoli and Krieger – and he will do it with Lesnevich."

Joe Louis, now quite aware of the potential challenger from the light heavyweight ranks, attended with his entourage as guests of Mike Jacobs.

The fawning crowd had no idea of the incredible drama that had taken place in the locker room just minutes before Billy made his ring entrance. A few weeks ago Jackie Conn had lost his first fight in a four round decision to University of Virginia boxer Mutt Wormer on a Madison Square Garden undercard bout. Billy told Jackie that he had embarrassed Billy and the Conn family name by losing. Billy, with reverse snobbery, berated his brother for losing to a "college boy." Billy had long wanted Jackie to give up professional boxing, knowing that he didn't have the skill to advance much beyond four-rounder status. Johnny Ray arranged a rematch with Wormer. Billy laid down the law to Jackie: if he lost to Wormer again, he would have to quit boxing. Jackie went into the bout determined to save his short career. The bout ended in a disaster for Jackie. Wormer dominated, flooring him twice in the first round with left hooks. The referee stepped in and rescued Jackie from a terrific beating with just one second remaining in the first round. Jackie had suffered the ultimate humiliation: a first round TKO in front of the large crowd waiting to see his brother.

Jackie, still only 17, came into the locker room heartbroken and sobbing, seeking consolation from his big brother. Billy, all keyed up just moments before a big fight, showed no mercy. He screamed at Jackie that he had disgraced the family, and that his boxing career was over. Jackie got hysterical. He ran to the shower stall, turned on the hot water, and started banging his head against the wall. Several trainers grabbed him and tried to calm him, to no avail. They called in a doctor, who administered a sedative shot and recommended hospitalization. Jackie was taken to Polyclinic Hospital across the street and put to bed, heavily sedated. He would never fight again, at least inside the ring.

In his second title defense, Billy started slowly. Jackie's hospitalization affected him. He appeared to be distracted. Lesnevich took the first three rounds on all cards with excellent body punching. Billy landed a lot of jabs and a few hooks, but Gus went hard to the body with both hands. Gus also landed a few good shots to the jaw. Despite the Lesnevich reputation for power, Conn took the early barrage with little apparent effect. In the fourth Billy picked it up, trading hard punches with Gus in the early part of the round. Billy landed a big right that finally backed Gus up, and followed it with a series of lefts that cut Gus over the right eye. Billy then attacked the body and had Gus holding on by the end of the round, a big one for Conn. In the fifth they fought at close quarters, a strategy which would seem to favor the powerful Lesnevich. But Billy got the best of it, taking the challenger's punches and giving more in return. Billy kept up his close-quartered assault in the sixth, staggering Gus with a big left hook near the end of the round. Conn attacked the body to lead off the seventh, and then started to dance and jab. He landed jab after jab from an outmaneuvered Lesnevich. Seemingly bored, Billy closed and slugged near the end of the round, cutting Gus over the left eye with a big right hand. Billy scored at will during the eighth, landing jabs, hooks, and uppercuts with barely a miss. Lesnevich was bleeding from cuts over both eyes, and totally baffled by Conn's speed. Billy easily avoided Gus's wild rushes in the ninth, landing some well-placed shots and taking another round. Billy now had a big lead and was on his way to a smashing win. In the tenth, true to form, Billy chose to slug it out and received a small cut under the left eye from a big Lesnevich right. Wounded and desperate, Gus was still dangerous. He took the fight to Billy in the eleventh, and got the better of the close exchanges. Billy picked up the already fast pace in the twelfth, calling on his marvelous stamina. He had Gus backing up most of the round, outslugging the slugger. Billy dominated the round, staggering Gus several times. Gus had no answers, and held for most of the round. The fourteenth and fifteenth were Conn's rounds too, as Gus appeared to have little left. Billy was content to win a clear cut decision, and did not seem to go all out for a knockout.

Except for a small cut under the left eye, Billy was unmarked. He looked as fresh as he had all night, never showing the slightest sign of fatigue throughout the bout. Gus Lesnevich was battered, bruised, and cut over both eyes. He had barely survived the ordeal, despite a strong showing in the first three rounds and a rally in the tenth and eleventh. Billy praised Gus for his toughness, but said, "I thought it was one of my worst fights."

He was wrong. He had been utterly dominant against a challenger regarded by most experts as the second best light heavyweight in the world at that time. He had been in full control, beating Lesnevich at his own forte of slugging when he chose to. (Lesnevich was an excellent fighter who would go on to win the light heavyweight title in 1941 and dominate the division for several years.) The lack of a knockout caused pundits to again question Billy's punching power, although he had staggered the durable Lesnevich several times in the bout. Fred Fierro said that Billy had taken a liking to Gus and didn't want to press for a knockout with the decision well in hand. In boxing lingo, he had "carried" Gus.

Syndicated columnist Joe Williams was impressed that Conn had been so dominant. He proclaimed Conn as difficult to hit as legendary Cleveland Indians pitcher Bob Feller. He wrote, "On the attack, Conn would be in and out with a clean score before Lesnevich knew where he was. It was the same on the defense. There would be a clean opening. Lesnevich would strike and up from nowhere would come Conn's gloved fist, his forearm, or his elbow to block the punch."

In less than half a year, Billy had made the light heavyweight division his own. No top challenger appeared. He had beaten the best.

At the end of 1939, Billy Conn, just turned 22, was on the cusp of boxing immortality. He had beaten the best middleweights and light heavyweights, decisively, establishing himself as one of the world's elite boxers. No fighter, not even the great Joe Louis, ever had a better year than Billy Conn did in 1939. He had won all seven fights, six over reigning, former, or future world champions. All were in their prime at the time. The other was a one-sided victory over a good heavyweight. Although barely over 170 pounds, the only challenge left for Billy was in the heavyweight division.

ROUND TEN

1940: Challenging The Heavies

In 1940 the European situation worsened. Germany invaded Denmark, Norway, Holland, Belgium, Luxembourg, and France. The French army collapsed, and Nazi forces entered Paris, marching through the Arche de Triomphe down the Champs Elysses. Winston Churchill became Prime Minister of Great Britain. The German Luftwaffe undertook a bombing campaign that rained terror on the British. FDR won an unprecedented third term by defeating Wendell Willkie. Hit songs that year were "When You Wish Upon A Star" and "You Are My Sunshine." Ernest Hemingway published *For Whom the Bell Tolls*. Pittsburgh and East Liberty native Gene Kelly starred on Broadway in *Pal Joey*. The Pirates finished fourth.

At the dawn of the 1940's Joe Louis stood at the pinnacle of the boxing and sports world. He had held the heavyweight title for over three years, and had already defeated the best challengers available. He had stunned the entire world with a devastating first round knockout of Max Schmeling in the most hyped and politicized sporting event in modern times. Though the phrase is shopworn, he truly was "a legend in his own time." He had nearly reached the heroic level of a Babe Ruth or Jack Dempsey, both now retired.

The new kid in the world of boxing fame was Billy Conn, who had beaten the world's best middleweights as a teenager and now stood head and shoulders above his light-heavyweight rivals. The sporting public awaited Conn's maturity into a heavyweight. No one else on the horizon had the skill to pose a serious threat to Louis. Louis continued to defend the title often. On February 9 the slick-boxing Arturo Godoy of Chile became only the second man to go the distance with Louis in a title fight; Louis won by a fifteen round decision. In April Louis knocked out Jack Roper in the second round. In June he "avenged" Godoy's lasting the distance with an eighth round knockout of the Chilean. It was Joe's eleventh successful defense, nine by knockout. Louis title defenses had become mere formalities – a question of in which round the knockout would occur.

Conn was now 22 years old and had gained very little weight over the past few years. The hope that the tall youngster would grow into a 190-pound heavyweight was fading. Yet so skilled was Conn that even in the low 170's he posed the greatest ultimate threat to Louis. Billy had shown that he could take a heavyweight punch. Although he scored few knockouts, his relentless pace and volume of punches battered and wore down the toughest of men. He was young, cocky, quotable, Irish, and strikingly handsome – traits that enhanced his box office appeal. He reaped lots of honors for his great year in 1939. He won the Edward J. Neil trophy by vote of the New York sportswriters, given to the outstanding boxer of the year. Joe Louis beat him out for *The Ring* magazine's fighter of the year. The Dapper Dan club of Pittsburgh voted him "Man of the Year," as the sports figure who had done the most to publicize the Pittsburgh area.

Among the light-heavyweights, Gus Lesnevich again defeated contender Dave Clark on January 1st. Melio Bettina, in what was billed as a possible elimination bout for a shot at Conn's title, knocked out Fred Apostoli on February 2nd in the 12th round.

With no big money challenger looming, the Conn team decided to try another heavyweight, this time a bigger one than Dorazio. Henry Cooper, of Brooklyn, fought at around 190 pounds. Though not ranked in the top ten, he was an experienced, competent foe. Johnny Ray wanted Billy to get used to the size and strength of a good-sized heavyweight. The bout was booked for January 10th at Madison Square Garden.

Conn had sparred a few rounds with Cooper prior to the Lesnevich fight, as Cooper was training for a bout with contender Gunnar Barland, won by Barland. Cooper had won 10 of 13 bouts in 1939, losing decisions to Barland, Nathan Mann, and Melio Bettina. Conn was established as a 13-5 favorite.

To appeal to his Irish fans, Billy wore green trunks with a white shamrock. Billy weighed in at 173 ½ to an even 190 for Cooper. About 7,000 fans attended at the Garden. Billy was again treated like a local favorite against a local fighter. The atmosphere had nowhere near the electricity of Billy's previous Garden bouts, as the outcome was considered a foregone conclusion. Even starting slowly as he customarily did, Billy won the first three rounds easily, his jab and defense much too quick for Cooper. Cooper captured only the fourth and sixth rounds of the twelve round bout, and those only because Billy seemed content to jab and back off as the bigger man bulled him into the ropes. Cooper landed very few punches in any round, and none solidly. Conn put on a brilliant boxing exhibition, baffling Cooper from the start. Billy landed jabs, hooks, and rights at will, but rarely chose to slug it out. When he did, he even got the better of that due to his superior quickness. Many times Billy landed a long succession of punches while Cooper landed nothing in return. At the end, Conn was fresh and unmarked. Cooper had a cut over the left eye, but was not badly hurt. It was an easy win for Conn.

Pittsburgh fighters were making an impressive mark on the sport. In May, Sammy Angott won a share of the lightweight title. Fritzie Zivic continued to rank as the number one welterweight contender, preparing for a showdown with the great champion Henry Armstrong. Billy Soose, Charley Burley, Jackie Wilson, and Teddy Yarosz were all ranked in the top ten in their respective divisions. And Billy Conn, of course, ruled the light-heavyweights.

Billy had to defend his title again. The Conn team decided to give the shot to Gus Lesnevich again rather than to Bettina. They had already beaten Bettina twice, and Detroit made a good offer for a Conn-Lesnevich bout. No hot new contender was on the horizon at the moment.

Conn-Lesnevich was scheduled for the Detroit Olympia June 5th. Billy was heavily favored at 3 to 1. About a week before the fight he weighed 180 pounds, good for his heavyweight future but above the light-heavyweight limit. He shed 6 ½ pounds quickly to weigh in at 173 ½ on fight day. Lesnevich weighed the same. A somewhat disappointing crowd of 6,075 showed up for a gate of about 17 thousand dollars. Several hundred Pittsburghers came by train. Billy boxed and jabbed to win the first two rounds, but Lesnevich was watching and waiting. In the third he landed a good left to the body, followed by a right to the head. He took the fight to Billy, who hadn't yet accelerated into high gear. In the fourth and fifth Gus continued to rush Billy and land well to the body. He had to make the most of his chance for an upset quickly, but it was not to be. In the sixth Billy was in sync, landing hard jabs and a big right to the side of the head that hurt Gus. Billy stabbed and jabbed at a torrid pace for the next few rounds, landing combinations that had the challenger befuddled. Billy was in his groove, and all worry about an upset was put to rest. Late in the tenth Billy floored Gus with a left to the chin, but lost the round by a referee's penalty for a left that landed low. The eleventh through fourteenth were all Conn, as Billy battered Gus relentlessly. In the fifteenth and final round Gus gave it all he had, trying to land a big punch. Billy mixed willingly, and had Gus in trouble and holding on. Gus stayed on his feet, but Billy retained the title with a unanimous decision by a wide margin. The fight was prototypical Conn: slow start, fast middle and finish, and nearly untouchable once he found his groove. As usual, he slugged it out when he could have won easily by boxing. Yet that strategy no longer seemed so foolhardy – Billy was now able to take big shots from powerful punchers without much ill effect. He had an "iron chin."

According to Fred Fierro, Billy again "carried" Gus because he liked him, and saw no reason to press for a knockout with a win already cinched by decision.

Mike Jacobs, in attendance, praised Conn: "Conn showed tonight that he has everything a great fighter needs. Some people say he can't punch hard enough to mingle with heavyweights. Well, you saw what he did to Lesnevich – had him wobbly, down, out on his feet, cut and bleeding like no one else ever had him."

Jacobs had plans to start Billy on the road to a heavyweight title shot by matching him next with top contender Bob Pastor. Said Jacobs, "I'm going to give Billy a chance to prove what I think he is worth. Pastor is the chance I had in mind."

Conn took on Pastor September 6th at Madison Square Garden. Pastor was an excellent boxer with a good chin, a small heavyweight who had fought his way into contention by ring smarts and boxing skill. He was a product of the New York area, and had played football at New York University. He was nicknamed "Bicycle Bob" because of his preference to dance and jab rather than to slug it out. Pastor was one of few men to go the distance with Joe Louis. In January of 1937 he had lost a ten round decision to then number one contender Louis, avoiding a knockout by using his quick feet. He earned a title shot versus Louis in September of 1939, lasting eleven rounds before the Brown Bomber finally got to him. It was the only knockout Pastor ever suffered. Against Conn he would not have the advantage of foot speed and boxing skill as he did against most heavyweights.

A crowd of 14,448 paid about $49,000 to see Conn and Pastor. Champion Joe Louis was in attendance. Pastor weighed 180 ¾, a few pounds below his normal fighting weight, to 174 for Conn. Pastor knew he would have to be in top shape to match the pace and stamina of Billy Conn. Both men appeared to be in excellent condition. Oddsmakers established Conn as a 3 to 1 favorite.

Billy started in typically slow fashion, dropping most of the early rounds as Pastor outboxed him. Pastor took three of the first four rounds, with the second being even. In the fifth Billy stepped up his attack, landing hard left hooks to the body against a retreating foe. After a lackluster sixth, Billy took it to Pastor's body again in the seventh, although many of his punches were dangerously on the belt line. Pastor winced a number of times as Conn hit the body hard again in the eighth. Pastor appeared to be slowing from the body blows just as Billy was finding his groove. Though Conn dominated the eighth, the ref awarded it to Pastor because of two low blows by Conn. In the ninth Conn landed a big left hook to the chin that sent Pastor to the canvas. He followed it up with a power attack to the head and body. Pastor was in trouble as the round ended, though he still led on the scorecards. In the tenth Billy battered a fleeing Pastor around the ring, driving him into the ropes and bloodying his mouth. Billy jabbed most of the eleventh, looking for an opening. Near the end of the round he attacked and had Pastor wobbly again as the bell rang. In the twelfth Billy landed a huge left hook to the body. Pastor crouched in pain and covered up as Billy unleashed a torrent of punches to the head and body. Near the end of the round Conn landed a right to the chin that sent Pastor to the canvas again. The bell rang as referee Cavanaugh reached the count of nine. Pastor lay flat on his back, but the bell had saved him. Pastor courageously answered the bell for the thirteenth, his mouth gushing blood and his ribs and stomach red from the vicious body attack. Cavanaugh warned Conn again to keep his punches up. Billy attacked with rights to the head and hooks to the body. A right to the head hurt Pastor, followed by a wicked left hook right on the belt line. Pastor doubled up in pain, and fell to the canvas clutching his groin. This time he couldn't beat the count, and the bell didn't save him. He was counted out at 2:54 of the thirteenth round. Conn had his second knockout in three heavyweight bouts.

Conn received much criticism for the many low blows, but his relentless body attack had resulted in only the second knockout in Pastor's long career. Billy had shown a killer instinct against a very good heavyweight. Pastor's manager Jimmy Johnston announced that he intended to file a protest with the New York State Athletic Commission over the repeated low blows. Referee Cavanaugh told the press "The punch that ended the fight was not foul – but pretty close to it. Had Pastor been able to get up, I would have taken the round from Conn for low punching."

Billy responded, "A few of my punches might have been low. But Pastor just can't take it to the body."

Pittsburgh's Fritzie Zivic upset Henry Armstrong to win the welterweight crown on October 4th at Madison Square Garden. After losing most of the early rounds, Zivic dominated the middle and late rounds, cutting Armstrong over both eyes and in the mouth. Zivic floored Armstrong as the fight ended – only the bell saved him from a knockout. Another Conn victim had won a world championship. Billy had now defeated eight world champs: Risko, Dundee, Corbett, Yarosz, Krieger, Apostoli, Bettina, and Zivic. Yarosz, Krieger, Apostoli, and Bettina were double victims, giving Billy 12 wins over world champs at age 23. (Dundee was slightly over the hill when Conn beat him. Zivic, like Conn, was a young prospect. All of the others were outstanding fighters at their peak when Conn bested them.)

Jacobs next matched Billy with Al McCoy in McCoy's hometown of Boston for a ten round bout at Boston Garden on October 18th. McCoy was a decent small heavyweight who had worked his way into contender status by winning the New England heavyweight championship. He was coming off of an impressive decision win over Melio Bettina in June. He had a record of 115 wins, 30 losses, and 20 draws. Despite the name, he was not Irish. He was of French ancestry, born Florien LaBrasseur. A crowd of over 15,000 packed the Boston Garden. Many Boston Irish turned out to see the local hero take on this Mick from Pittsburgh who had shaken up the boxing world. Conn weighed 172 ¾ to 181 ½ for McCoy.

Billy started slowly as usual, losing two of the first three rounds. The third was McCoy's best round. The stocky, powerfully built Bostonian shoved Conn about the ring and landed a series of short left hooks. Near the end of the round, Billy countered and drove McCoy back with combinations. After an even fourth round, it was all Conn. Billy shifted gears and outboxed McCoy easily. In the seventh Billy slipped on a water spot in the middle of the ring. McCoy tried to take advantage and nail him when he was down. Billy slipped the punches on his knees, but was so angered that he got up and spat in McCoy's face. Billy attacked and battered McCoy about the ring for the remainder of the round. McCoy had drawn Billy into a slugging match for the last three rounds, to his own misfortune. Conn's power combinations staggered McCoy and completely closed his left eye. In the ninth and tenth McCoy struggled to survive: staggering and covering up, he threw few punches. Billy had another decisive win over a heavyweight.

After the fight the Conn team drove to New York to meet Mike Jacobs and plan the next steppingstone to Joe Louis. Ex-champ Max Baer and Arturo Godoy were possibilities, but they decided on Lee Savold of Iowa. Savold was ranked in the top ten, and had racked up an impressive string of knockouts. He was bigger than McCoy or Pastor. He could punch and take a punch, but like all of the heavyweights, he had nowhere near the skill of Conn.

Conn-Savold was scheduled for twelve rounds at Madison Square Garden on November 29th, 1940. Savold had done most of his fighting in Des Moines and St. Paul, and had built a record of early knockouts. He was a ruggedly built blonde with a powerful right hand that had earned him the nickname "Lethal Lee." He had fought once in Madison Square Garden, in January of 1940, and KO'd Big Jim Robinson in three. Ring had him rated the number eight contender. Conn was expected to win, but Savold would be a difficult man to knock out. The New York crowd of 12,750 knew that Conn liked to fight and would try to KO Savold. Billy was never content to box his way to an easy victory, and the fans loved him for it. Conn weighed 174 ½ to 186 ¾ for Savold.

Johnny Ray had Billy shadow box hard for several rounds in the dressing room to get him off to a quick start. This time it worked. Billy set a fast pace that had Savold confused and missing. Billy's lightning jabs kept him off balance for big left hooks to the body. By the end of the first round, Savold was bleeding from the nose and had angry red welts on his body. Billy landed jabs, hooks, and rights almost at will for eight rounds. He staggered Savold several times. Billy easily avoided the slower man's rushes. In the ninth Savold landed his first good punch, a big left hook that bloodied Conn's nose. Lee came to life in the tenth as Billy slugged with him, landing three good rights to Conn's chin. Conn barely flinched, and fought back with renewed fury. Lee's "lethal" right proved unable to hurt the iron-chinned light-heavyweight champion in front of him. Conn put on a boxing exhibition in the eleventh, dancing, jabbing and hooking. In the twelfth Billy attacked in a last ditch attempt at a knockout. He threw a barrage of punches, many to the body, some of them low. Referee Art Donovan took the round away from Conn for hitting low. Battered and bloody, Savold survived. He had won only the tenth and twelfth rounds, the latter on a penalty.

Conn was again criticized for a lack of punching power because he failed to stop Savold. But his critics were missing the point. So superior was Billy to even the top-rated heavyweights that he could dominate a bout even without a big heavyweight punch. Critics accustomed to recent heavyweight champs like Dempsey, Baer, and Louis declared that punching power was a must. Their short memories forgot slick boxers like Jim Corbett and Gene Tunney, who defeated power-punching opponents. Conn's skills rivaled or exceeded those of Corbett and Tunney. And he could sure take a heavyweight punch: powerful hitters like Savold, Bettina, and Lesnevich could not hurt Conn even when landing their best punch. Despite his small size, Conn was too good for any heavyweight in the game – except Joe Louis.

Joe Louis had run out of quality opponents, and had not fought since June. The only possible big draw was Billy Conn. The Conn and Louis people met with Jacobs and agreed on a June match. Jacobs wanted to wait for the summer of 1941 to have the Louis-Conn match outdoors. In the meantime, Louis initiated a series of monthly title defenses against mediocre opponents, to keep active and keep the money rolling in. The bouts became known as the "Bum of the Month Club." He began with a December match in the Boston Garden against Al McCoy, recently defeated by Billy Conn. Louis KO'd McCoy in the sixth.

At the end of 1940, Billy Conn was the hottest thing in boxing. He had beaten the best of the light-heavyweights and some worthy heavyweight contenders. *The Ring* magazine would name him the "Fighter of the Year" for 1940. He was wealthy beyond his wildest dreams, with an elegant Fifth Avenue address, a long way from the streets of East Liberty. Much more wealth was in store. He looked forward to a shot at the heavyweight title, the "greatest prize in sports."

ROUND 11

1941: Preparing For Joe Louis And Greenfield Jimmy

War raged in Europe and Asia throughout 1941, as Nazi Germany and Imperial Japan continued their offensive thrusts. Most Americans did not want war, but it seemed inevitable. Sports provided a great diversion: Joe DiMaggio of the New York Yankees hit in 56 consecutive games, a record that still stands. Ted Williams of the Boston Red Sox batted .406, the last major leaguer of the twentieth century to hit over .400. Whirlaway won the Triple Crown. The boxing world awaited the Joe Louis-Billy Conn battle in June. Also in June, Yankee legend Lou Gehrig died of a neurological disease that would become known as "Lou Gehrig's Disease."

Hollywood produced *Citizen Kane*, *Meet John Doe*, and *Sergeant York*. Hit songs included "You Made Me Love You" and "Chattanooga Choo Choo."

After beating Savold, Billy officially relinquished his light-heavyweight crown. He would campaign as a heavyweight only, and expected a shot at Joe Louis in the summer of 1941. The Conn and Louis people had a written agreement with Mike Jacobs for a June fight at the Polo Grounds in New York. Home of the New York Giants, the baseball stadium in Harlem could hold over 50,000 people. Conn would receive 20% of the gate to 40% for Louis. Jacobs hoped for a gate of half a million dollars, the biggest in boxing since Louis-Schmeling in 1938.

Anton Christoforidis of Greece and Melio Bettina fought for the vacant light-heavyweight crown in January, with Christoforidis winning a 15-round decision. Gus Lesnevich took the crown by decision from Christoforidis in May, becoming the seventh world champion who had lost to Billy Conn. Lesnevich defended the crown successfully five times until losing in 1948.

Louis continued his monthly title defense series with a fifth round KO of Red Burman at Madison Square Garden January 13th. In February Louis knocked out Gus Dorazio in the second round in Philadelphia. (Conn had stopped Dorazio in eight in 1939.) In March Louis battered big Abe Simon (6'5" 254 lbs.) into submission with a 13th round TKO in Detroit. In April he KO'd Tony Musto in the ninth round in St. Louis. Louis was giving himself a lot of national exposure. Jack Miley dubbed the tour the "Bum of the Month" club, which really was unfair to the opponents. They were competent, courageous professionals who fought hard against Louis and took serious punishment. The weren't "bums." Simon and Burman were ranked in the top ten. They were just outclassed by the marvelous skill and power of Louis, perhaps the greatest heavyweight champ of all time.

Conn, in the meantime, began his own "Bum of the Month" tour to keep sharp while awaiting the summer showdown. For the first time in his career, Billy had an easy "tune-up" fight. He took on Ira Hughes, a journeyman Pittsburgh light-heavyweight, in Clarksburg, W.Va. Conn won easily by a fourth round knockout. Billy took on 204- pound Philadelphia heavyweight Danny Hassett in March in Washington, D.C. Conn weighed 181, his heaviest ever. After boxing the first four rounds, Billy opened the fifth round with a vicious body attack, followed with a left hook to the jaw that felled Hassett. Hassett was counted out a mere 35 seconds into the round.

Billy took on another big heavyweight, Gunnar Barland of Finland, in Chicago on April 4th. The fight violated the terms of the agreement with Jacobs for the Joe Louis fight in June. In December the Conn team had agreed to no new fights after Hassett, which had already been scheduled. Jacobs wanted to avoid any risk that Conn could lose or suffer an injury and jeopardize the big gate. Ray and Conn figured they could fight Barland and still get the Louis fight, since Conn was the hottest thing in boxing and would make a big gate for Jacobs. Conn easily outboxed Barland and put him away in the eighth round.

Each fighter took an outdoor stadium bout in May to keep sharp and, of course, earn more money. Louis put his title on the line against the number seven contender, 6'6 ½" 237-pound Buddy Baer, the brother of former champ and Louis victim Max Baer. The bout was on May 23rd at Griffith Stadium in Washington, D.C. before over 20,000 fans, many of them blacks from the South and the D.C. area. Baer surprised Louis in the first round with a combination that sent Louis through the ropes. More embarrassed than hurt, Louis proceeded to punish Baer for the next several rounds. Baer showed a great chin and heart, absorbing the Brown Bomber's punches and inflicting a cut over Joe's left eye that would require three stitches. But the Louis punches were taking a toll. In the seventh he knocked Baer down for a count of seven. Toward the end of the round he decked Baer again. This time Baer struggled to make it up at the count of nine. The bell rang, but Louis did not hear it. Louis knocked Baer down after the bell, and this time Baer didn't get up. He had to be dragged to his corner. Referee Arthur Donovan had three choices: disqualify Louis for hitting after the bell, disqualify Baer for failing to answer the bell for the seventh round, or give Baer time to recover. He ruled it an unintentional foul and a TKO for Louis. The controversy gave the press something to write about in an otherwise routine title defense. There is no question that Louis was winning and had Baer ready to go, but in hindsight it appears that Baer should have been given time to recover from the illegal blow.

Conn headlined a Forbes Field card on May 26th against Buddy Knox, considered a tough trial horse with a good chin. Knox, an Irish-American from Dayton, Ohio, weighed 190 to 180 ¼ for Conn. He had an impressive of 85 wins, 13 losses and 4 draws. The 27,000 plus crowd was the largest ever to witness a fight in Pittsburgh, and a huge success for the local promotion team of Art Rooney and Barney McGinley. Again, the Conn team violated the agreement with Jacobs. The money was just too much to pass up. It was a risk, as a poor showing by Conn or a cut sustained in the bout could imperil the June date in New York.

The Pittsburgh papers wrote that Joe Louis would be in attendance to "scout" Conn. Louis did not attend, although several of his handlers did. A large contingent of New York sportswriters came to view Conn.

The top prelims were both heavyweight bouts. Hot prospect Pat Comiskey knocked out James Johnson in the first one. The ethnic-conscious press of the time described Comiskey as a "giant Jersey Hibernian" and Johnson as a "towering North Carolina Negro." Johnson, who trained with Conn for the bout, was often referred to as a "colored boy." In the top prelim Pittsburgh heavyweight Harry Bobo won an upset split decision over Lee Savold.

Billy started slowly as usual, feeling Knox out for the first four rounds and taking no chances. In the fifth he shifted gears, setting a fast pace of jabs, hooks, and rights that baffled Knox. In the seventh Billy landed some big shots to the body, and followed with a right to the jaw that decked Knox for a count of eight. Billy quickly decked him again with a left hook for another eight count. Near the end of the round Billy hit Knox with a right to the temple that knocked him down for the third time in the round. He didn't beat the count this time, but the bell saved him. Knox was unable to come out for the eighth round, so Conn was awarded an eighth round TKO. Although Knox was not a top heavyweight, Billy showed impressive power against a man with a reputation for a good chin.

The huge crowd paid over $68,000, of which Billy got $19,000, his second biggest purse ever. The paid gate was the largest ever in Pittsburgh, breaking the record of the Conn-Bettina fight in 1939.

The next stop for Billy would be June 18th at the Polo Grounds for the heavyweight title in the biggest fight since Louis-Schmeling in 1938. Meanwhile, Billy's personal life was in turmoil.

Over the past year or so, Margaret McFarland Conn had become fatigued and quite ill. When her symptoms persisted, she sought medical help. The diagnosis was terminal ovarian cancer. Her eldest son was heartsick as he watched the disease destroy his mother's body. She became bedridden. Billy spent enormous sums of money for her medical bills and to provide round-the-clock nursing care for her. He brought her champagne, which she loved and could never afford when they were poor. Her health continued to decline; only a miracle could save the 41-year-old mother of five.

Billy fell ever more madly in love with the beautiful young Mary Louise Smith. He wanted to marry her and spend the rest of his life with her. They informed her parents of their intentions. But her father forbade it due to her young age and Billy's profession. "It wasn't anything personal against Billy," Mary Louise says, "…it was because he knew what that world was like and didn't want that for me."

Family lore holds that Greenfield Jimmy promised the Bishop of Pittsburgh that he would kill him if any priest in the diocese married his daughter and Billy Conn. None did, in spite of the earnest attempts of the lovebirds to arrange a Catholic wedding. As both came from devout Irish Catholic families, a civil ceremony was out of the question. Mary Louise, the love of her father's life, had to sneak around with the man she loved to avoid her father's wrath.

Two days after the Knox fight, May 28, Billy and Mary Louise drove to Brookville in Jefferson County, in northwestern Pennsylvania, to take out a marriage license. The license listed her age as 21. Billy listed his age as 23 and his profession as "pugilist." Pennsylvania law at that time required parental permission for anyone under 21 years of age. Despite what the application said, Mary Louise had just turned 18. But the law required that a disapproving parent file a legal objection within three days after a marriage license was filed. Rumors surfaced in the papers that the two had already been married. Greenfield Jimmy threatened them in the print media: "Champion or no champion, I'll punch hell out of that fellow. I know where those people end up. I'm not going to have him for a son-in-law and I want him to stay away from my family."

Wild Bill Conn took offense and countered with a statement to the *Daily Mirror*: "Who does this guy think he is? There is one thing certain, he ain't never punched a Conn. And it'll be a sorry day for him when he tries. My Billy is the greatest guy in the world. Yes sir, and this Joe Louis will know he's in the ring with a man. So he'll punch my boy Billy, will he? Listen, that guy never punched anybody without having a couple of guys hold the other fellow's arm. He was even a light hitter with a baseball bat."

The family feud raged through the newspapers. Despite the rumors, no wedding had taken place. The young lovers planned to marry at her home parish, St. Philomena's in Squirrel Hill, the Friday after the fight. Billy seemed amused by the whole thing, telling reporters, "I wish it were true about Mary and me being married already. I'd be the first to tell everybody about it. Now I see I got to lick two guys, Louis and Smitty. I know I can lick Louis, but that Smitty is pretty tough. I think I'll steer clear of him."

Before leaving for New Jersey, Billy visited his mother and presented her with a huge diamond bracelet. She insisted that he give it to Mary Louise, and marry the girl despite Greenfield Jimmy's rantings. Like a true Irish mother, she told Billy that he was good enough for anybody, including Mary Louise Smith. He took her advice. He told her proudly, "Mom, the next time you see me, I'll be the heavyweight champion of the world." Maggie, sensing her downhill course, responded, "Son, the next time you see me will be in Paradise."

While Billy was driving to Brookville, Johnny Ray flew to New York to sign the final contract with Mike Jacobs. The percentage remained 40% for Louis and 20% for Conn. Louis was guaranteed a return bout within 60 days if he lost. Jacobs demanded exclusive rights to promote Conn for five years if he won. Ray objected, and the confrontation nearly came to blows. Jacobs was used to getting his way with managers of contenders, and was startled by Ray's reaction. Jacobs threatened to call off the bout and have Louis fight contender Lou Nova. Only when Jacobs made the offer to Nova's manager, who was present, did Ray relent.

Ray requested of the commission that Conn stay in the locker room while the dignitaries were introduced. He was concerned about Billy's tendency to start slow, and he wanted him warmed up when the fight began. The commission granted none of his requests.

The Conn team drove to New York on Sunday, June 1st. Billy sparred briefly on Monday with welterweight Johnny Creegan at the Pioneer Club. Afterward he and Joe Louis appeared together at Mike Jacobs' office for the official signing and newspaper pictures. Conn and Ray had to sign a one-year contract to conform to New York rules. All previous business between them had been by mutual understanding. After the signing, they headed for training camp at Pompton Lakes, New Jersey, a mere hour's drive from the city. Louis and company headed for Greenwood Lake, New York. They announced that Joe's cut was healed and that he would begin sparring Friday.

The Pompton Lakes camp included a large entourage of trainers, sparring partners, and hangers-on. Pittsburgh city detective Joe Becker accompanied Billy everywhere, even on morning runs. "Gabby" Ryan, an old East Liberty friend, chauffeured Billy's Cadillac. "Gabby" earned his nickname by rarely speaking. Business manager Milton Jaffe watched over his financial interests. Omnipresent Jackie Conn kept up a lively verbal and physical banter with his brother, to the eternal dismay of Johnny Ray, who supervised Billy like a mother. They borrowed a cook from Lindy's, German immigrant Willie Handeler. Jack Miley wrote that he feared Billy would contract "fresh air poisoning" in the country air after growing up in smoky Pittsburgh.

Johnny Ray gave up drinking for the first time since Billy had known him. The years of heavy drinking had taken a toll on his body, resulting in several recent hospitalizations. He was often drunk in the corner during Billy's bouts. Billy flippantly mused, "Everybody knows Jews don't drink. I gotta get the one that does. But Johnny Ray drunk knows more about boxing than anybody else sober."

Billy trained hard, concerned more with speed than weight. He expected to scale at considerably less than his recent bout weights of about 180. Louis, quite concerned with Conn's speed, insisted at coming in at around 200, a few pounds less than his normal fighting weight. His handlers disagreed with him, feeling that the weight loss might drain him after six fights in six months. Joe got his way, and got down to an even 200 by fight day.

Reports from Conn's camp portrayed a relaxed, almost nonchalant challenger. Most Louis opponents were tense and fearful in the days leading up to the bout; Conn was quite the opposite. Yet Conn trained very hard and would ultimately come in at his lowest weight in years. He looked sharp and fit in sparring sessions. He called his ailing mother daily. He also called Mary Louise and spoke of their secret plans to marry. The twin crises worked on his mind, yet the youngster was able to focus on his work as well as ever.

The papers carried quotes to hype the fight. Louis co-manager John Roxborough told United Press that Louis considered Conn "…the most dangerous man he ever met," and hinted that Louis might try for a quick knockout to keep Conn from getting in a groove. Undoubtedly Conn, with his unusual speed and skill, would be a different opponent than the ones Louis usually faced. The typical heavyweight was made to order for Louis' fast, accurate, and devastating punches. Conn's speed of foot was the biggest worry, and Louis trained with a lot of fast-stepping sparring partners.

United Press reported a Louis response to a rumor that Conn had called him "dumb." The wire service wrote that Joe was angry, and told them, "Maybe I ain't the smartest feller in the world, but who is Conn to go callin' me dumb? I never heard of him getting' no college degrees. He talks too much, and I'm gonna push some of his gab right down his throat."

Conn had said no such thing, but it helped to hype the fight. The *Post-Gazette* carried letters written by Conn from training camp. The first one, dated June 9th, responded to Louis' saying that he talks too much.

Billy wrote, "What am I supposed to do – ask the great Joe Louis for permission to talk? My answer to Joe is 'Nuts.' Say, you don't suppose the Brown Bomber could be getting cold feet and starting to crack up already, do you?"

On June 10th Billy received a plaque from *The Ring* magazine for being voted the fighter of the year for 1940. Pittsburgh Pirate star Arky Vaughan also visited that day. The next day Billy went through a long, tough sparring session with several different heavyweight partners and received a small cut on his left cheek. He refrained from sparring the next day on Ray's orders. In a letter dated June 13th Billy lauded Jim Corbett, Gene Tunney, and Jim Braddock as Irish fighters who had won the heavyweight title in a major upset. He wrote, "They weren't lace curtain Irish either. They were shanty Irish, like me. And if they could do it, I guess I can. I'm going to give it a good two-fisted Irish try for I'm proud to bat in that league and I'd be an awful hound if I let those other great Irish underdogs down."

The general consensus was that Conn had better sparring partners and was mixing it up more than Louis was. Billy worked hard with his two "Negro heavyweight spar mates" George Higgs and Battling Monroe. Higgs, a native of Harlem, had worked previously with Louis. He told the press, "That Louis, he hits hard, but after he hits you he lays off or hits you some other place. This Conn, he hits you in the same place so often and so fast you don't get a chance to recover."

Higgs also touted Conn's defense: "You just can't hit him, even with a jab. I've been out there a week and I haven't caught him with a solid punch yet."

On Sunday, June 15th, Billy ended his roadwork and attended Mass at St. Mary's Church in Pompton Lakes. That afternoon he boxed two rounds each with Higgs, Monroe, and fleet-footed Teddy Wint, another "Negro spar mate."

Billy worked out Monday and broke camp that night, checking in at his headquarters in the Edison Hotel. He worked out at the Pioneer Gym on Tuesday. Weigh-in and fight night were the next day. He was in great shape and full of confidence.

Billy's last letter ran the morning of June 18, 1941, dated June 17, New York. Billy wrote, "Well, folks, I guess it is all over but the shouting. The only thing we can do now is wait for the returns from the outlying districts, particularly those around the Polo Grounds, some time between 10 and 11 o'clock tomorrow night.

"I feel great. I'm in the best shape of my career. And if I don't beat Joe Louis, I'll have nobody to blame but myself.

"For my manager, Johnny Ray, has gotten me into perfect condition. I'm not too heavy but I feel as strong as a bull. I'm boxing sharply and I never felt keener in my life with the gloves than I did those last few days over at my camp at Pompton Lakes.

"Strangely enough, I can't seem to get too excited about what the near future holds for me. I know I'm just a kid and that I'm pretty lucky to get this shot at the champ. But I'm not nervous or fidgety or fretting about matters.

"The newspapers ask me if I'm not excited and they don't know what to make of me when I tell them I'm not. They seem to think I should feel like a June groom or something. But I don't feel any different about fighting for the title than I used to feel on the eve of some scrap in Duquesne Garden.

"My friend, Jimmy Braddock, thinks this is a good sign. He says it is just the way he felt when he fought Max Baer. Of course, Jim was a lot older than I am now and he'd had more experience. But I can't see where a fellow should get more excited fighting a champ than a chump. Either one of them may or may not tag you, so why worry about it until the time comes?

"I honestly think that I'm coming home to Pittsburgh with that title. When I left camp I told the people there to reserve the place for me late in August. Because in the event I do win the championship, I have already agreed to give Joe Louis a rematch within 60 days, so that means I'll be back working at Pompton before the summer is over.

"They tell me Louis is rarin' to go. I understand I've got Joe's goat a little bit by popping off. I hope so, for that is okay with me. All the curbstone quarterbacks seem to think that the champ is going to come tearing out of his corner and punch me right back to Pittsburgh. That's okay, too. If he tries those tactics, Johnny Ray and I have worked out a little scheme, which I'm not going to talk about before the fight, that might make Joe regret it.

"I think the fight'll go 15 rounds and that I'll win on a decision. Ray is sure I'll stop Joe. He's going in there with a newly healed cut over his eye that Buddy Baer gave him. If that opens up, I may win on a TKO. But I'll settle for a decision right now. I'm signing off now and going to a movie. So until after the fight, goodbye and wish me luck!"

Five to six thousand Pittsburghers invaded New York by train and car. The special chartered trains had names like "Shamrock," "Ham and Cabbage," "Dapper Dan," and, ironically, "Brown Bomber." Some Pittsburghers arrived a few days to a week early and congregated in the "Forties" streets, especially at the Edison Hotel. They were a rowdy bunch, and woe to the New Yorker who told them their Billy didn't have a chance. They crowded the saloons, restaurants, sidewalks, and street corners of the Big Apple.

The weigh-in was scheduled for noon at the New York State Athletic Commission office. Over 100 writers and 100 photographers awaited the arrival of the fighters. The Louis team decided to come late to rattle Conn. They phoned the office that they would be ten minutes late due to traffic. The Conn team arrived early. At noon Billy stepped on the scale, which showed a shockingly low 169. "One seventy-four!" yelled Mike Jacobs to the press, and that became the official weight. Only Jacobs, Conn, and Ray knew the truth. After a few minutes, Conn barked at John Phelan, Chairman of the New York Boxing Commission, "Where is that Louis? I was told to be here at noon. I was fifteen minutes early. I'm not going to wait for him."

Phelan requested that they wait for Louis, who was expected soon. The photographers wanted the traditional pictures of the two together. Conn underwent exam by Dr. William Walker, who found a pulse of 64 and blood pressure of 128/70. If Louis and company had hoped to rattle Conn, the physical exam showed no signs of it. Many previous

Louis opponents had shown visible signs of fear when fight day arrived, and often manifested elevated blood pressure and pulse rate. Conn appeared to be fearless. (On the day of his first Liston fight, Cassius Clay/Muhammad Ali was hysterical, and his blood pressure was dangerously elevated, nearly causing postponement of the fight.)

Conn posed for pictures and told the press, "I'm in great shape. I think I got a good chance. I'll give him more fight than he ever got before – and I'll beat him."

Conn dressed and prepared to leave. Johnny Ray told Phelan, "Louis ain't gonna make no chump out of us. We were here at twelve o'clock. We weighed – and we are leaving."

As they departed, a buzz rose among the press crowd. The Louis team was walking in. The Conn team passed them on the way out, not even exchanging glances. Louis stepped on the scale, which read an even 200. "One ninety-nine and a half!" yelled Jacobs. He wanted to soften the actual 31- pound difference so that it didn't look like such a mismatch. The official fight record showed 199 ½ for Louis to 174 for Conn, a spread of 24 ½ pounds. The official measurements showed Louis bigger in nearly all areas, but Conn had a 17 ½" neck to 17" for Louis. His thick Irish neck was one factor in Billy's extraordinary ability to take a punch. He would need it against Joe Louis.

The sports headlines screamed that Conn had walked out on Joe Louis at the weigh-in, hyping his image as the cocky young kid. Conn went to Dinty Moore's for his pre-fight meal of eggs and fruit salad. Pittsburgh Post-Gazette reporter Havey Boyle wrote that Conn looked very thin, with his face drawn and his chin sharply outlined. Boyle was right on the money – Conn was eleven pounds lighter than in his previous fight. Conn retired to his room at the Edison Hotel after the meal.

In the hotel, Billy and Jackie got into a spirited wrestling match. As Fred Fierro describes it, "I flung open the door and sure enough, there they were rolling around on the floor trying to belt the be'Jesus out of each other. Johnny and I both blew up. 'What the hell are you doing, Billy, you're fighting for the biggest thing in the world tonight, it's the greatest night of our life and here you are taking a chance getting your head busted open on a bed post or a cut eye or something that will call the fight off.'

'We were only playing,' Billy smiled."

Moments later Billy and Jackie got into it again. Billy squirted a seltzer bottle into a sleeping Jackie's mouth, causing him to choke. He chased a laughing Billy through the halls and knocked over a food cart, splattering the food all over the walls.

According to Fierro, "Just think of it, here Billy was going to fight Joe Louis for the heavyweight championship of the world in less than nine hours and what was he doing? Resting like he should have been? Not him."

The Conn men – Wild Bill, Frank, and Jackie, were in New York to attend the fight. Frank was in Army training at Indiantown Gap in central Pennsylvania, but received a furlough to attend his brother's fight. The women gathered at the Conn home on Fifth Avenue to listen to the radio broadcast at 10 p.m. Billy's sisters and aunts surrounded the radio on the porch while his mother lay in bed alone upstairs. Her doctor ordered her not to listen to the fight because he felt the stress would be too much for her. Maggie prayed hard for her son, and ordered the others to do the same.

At Forbes Field the Pirates had scheduled a rare night game for June 18th against the New York Giants, whose own home field, the Polo Grounds, was staging the fight. To avoid a conflict, the team announced that the game would be stopped to broadcast the fight over the Public Address system. The fans responded – nearly 25,000 attended, about four times the season average that year. Starting time was 9:15 p.m., much later than night games today. In the fourth inning, with the Bucs ahead 2-1, play was stopped, and the broadcast on WCAE was fed into the PA system. Pittsburgh fans heard the voice of Don Dunphy in his first broadcast of a big fight. (Dunphy would eventually become known as the "Voice of Boxing" and be inducted into the Hall of Fame. He kept broadcasting fights until 1981.)

In the South China Sea, the commander of the U.S.S. Ticonderoga stopped the ship and ordered all hands on deck to listen to the broadcast of the fight.

Over 500 sportswriters from around the nation and world attended the bout. On a warm night, the crowd of nearly 55,000 filled the Polo Grounds early. With tickets ranging from $2.50 to $25, the gate would be the largest since Louis-Schmeling in 1938.

The Pittsburgh contingent included Mayor Cornelius Scully and future mayors David Lawrence and Joseph Barr, promoters Art Rooney, Barney McGinley, Jake Mintz, and Jules Beck, welterweight champ Fritzie Zivic , and many prominent businessmen. Leo Wise, *Pittsburgh Post-Gazette* business manager and great uncle of this writer, attended. Former champs Jack Dempsey, Jim Braddock, and Tony Canzoneri attended. Bob Hope, Olivia DeHavilland, Robert Taylor, Barbara Stanwyck, and Burgess Meredith represented the entertainment world.

Mary Louise Smith was not allowed to attend the fight, but got a room at the Waldorf-Astoria in Manhattan, with her Aunt Catherine as chaperone. Billy planned to see her after the fight.

Just hours before the fight, Johnny Ray fired up the Pittsburgh crowd with a pep rally speech outside the Edison Hotel. Afterward, thousands of boisterous Pittsburghers made their way to Harlem and the Polo Grounds to cheer on their hometown boy.

Betting odds began at 5 or 6 to 1 in favor of Louis several weeks before fight night. By June 18th Louis was about a 3 to 1 favorite, with some fluctuation. Louis was 8 to 5 to win by knockout. Both Billy and Johnny Ray bet thousands of dollars on themselves.

The vast majority of experts and boxing scribes picked Louis to win. Most who picked Conn had a Pittsburgh or Irish connection, with a few notable exceptions. Syndicated sports columnist Jack Cuddy called Conn "the greatest natural fighter I have ever seen," and predicted the upset. Damon Runyan, famous for the quote "The race is not always to the swift or strong – but that's the way to bet," chose the swift Conn in this one. Hype Igoe felt that Conn would be too fast and smart for Louis.

Former foe and reigning world welterweight champion Fritzie Zivic liked Conn: "I think Billy, my pal, will be the next heavyweight champion if he gets past the third round. Billy, a slow starter, will befuddle Joe with his speed and stinging left."

Venerable sportswriter legend Grantland Rice observed that Louis had never faced anyone with the speed of Conn, and Conn had never faced anyone with the power of Louis. Perhaps no fighter ever faced anyone as powerful as Louis, and no heavyweight ever faced anyone as fast as Conn.

ROUND 12

The Fight Of The Century

Joe Louis had defended the heavyweight title successfully 17 times - winning 15 by knockout - since wresting it from Braddock in 1937. At 27, he was a mature, seasoned, complete fighter. He had a marvelous jab, good boxing skills, and knockout power in either hand. Conn, though only 23, had more fights than Louis, 67 to 53. Conn had beaten nine world champs, five of them twice. He had not lost a fight in three years.

Billy was just a kid when he outboxed those champs. He had matured physically, developing punching power and an even stronger chin as he aged, with no loss of speed. He had knocked out five of his eight heavyweight opponents. He had the reputation of a light puncher based on his middleweight and light-heavyweight careers, but he had shown over the past year that he could hurt heavyweights. Dorazio, Pastor, Barland, and Knox could testify to that. Big punchers like Krieger, Bettina, Lesnevich, and Seelig had landed their best shots with little effect on Billy. Gus Lesnevich told the Pittsburgh Post-Gazette, "They say Billy will fall apart when Louis tags him, but I doubt it. I'm no cream puff puncher myself, but when I connected with Conn, he never even blinked an eye. The Louis crowd thinks he can't hurt you, but Billy had me out on our feet in our Detroit fight."

Louis had a jab that could break your nose. Opponents who tasted it wondered what a hook or right would be like, and shortly they found out. Billy's chin and toughness would surely be tested.

Billy had shredded the middleweight, light-heavyweight, and heavyweight divisions. Pound-for-pound he was already one of the all-time greats. In many ways he had more ring experience than Joe Louis. Louis had no memory of the seventeen-year-old, 140-pound kid who held the spit bucket for him in Pittsburgh in January of 1935, but that boy had grown into a formidable physical specimen who had survived a meat grinder schedule of the toughest fighters in the world. He would be no "Bum of the Month."

No Pittsburgher had ever won the heavyweight title. Native Dominic McCaffrey lost a decision to John L. Sullivan in 1885. Frank Moran, a former Pitt football player and a top contender for several years, lost by decision to Jack Johnson in 1914 and to Jess Willard in 1916. John Henry Lewis, Pittsburgher by adoption, lost to Louis by first round knockout in 1939.

Ethnic and racial considerations, so prevalent in boxing, played a part in this fight too. Louis was a god-like hero to black Americans, and one who was accepted as a hero by white Americans as well. No African-American had ever been so widely admired and emulated. Many Irish-Americans identified with Conn's quest as an attempt to recapture the crown that was rightfully theirs. At this point in the history of boxing the Irish had produced more champs than anyone else. Conn could restore the legacy of Sullivan, Corbett, Dempsey, Tunney, and Braddock. The bout took place in Harlem, the "capital" of "Black America," surrounded by a city with a large Irish population.

At the Conn home on Fifth Avenue in Pittsburgh, seventeen relatives – sisters, aunts, cousins - gathered around the radio on the porch. A slew of reporters and photographers surrounded the porch, waiting to record the family's emotions during the fight.

The Polo Grounds, home of the New York Giants, opened on June 28, 1911, bordered by Eighth Avenue, 159th Street, 157th Street, and the Harlem River. Seating capacity was about 55,000. The famous

Dempsey- Luis Firpo fight took place there in 1923, in which the Argentine knocked Dempsey through the ropes and out of the ring in the first round. Dempsey proceeded to knock Firpo down seven times in the first round and three times in the second before the referee counted Firpo out. The stadium would be demolished in 1964.

Johnny Ray put Billy through an eight round warm-up in the locker room, hoping to avoid his typical slow start. Billy normally used the early rounds to watch and learn, taking punches and getting a feel for his opponents' moves and power. Against Louis that could be fatal. He kept his robe on in the ring until the last minute, to stay warm. Joe wore black trunks, his body streamlined and muscular in its light brown, even yellowish skin. When Billy took off his white robe with green "Billy Conn" lettering, he revealed royal purple trunks as a statement that he, too, was a champion – the "king" of the light-heavyweights. He had relinquished his 175-pound crown, but had never been defeated as a light-heavyweight. His white skin glowed in the lights, his body lean and lithe.

The ring announcer intoned, "Presenting the present world heavyweight king, from Detroit, Michigan, weighing one-ninety-nine and a half – he's wearing black trunks – Joe Louis! From Pittsburgh, Pennsylvania, weighing one seventy-four, wearing purple trunks, the very capable challenger – Billy Conn!" The crowd roared at the sound of "Billy Conn."

The bell rang and the seconds left the ring. Only Joe, Billy, and referee Eddie Josephs remained. As the fighters came toward each other, one could see that Louis was of heavier build, but there was not much difference in height. Billy danced around the ring, keeping his distance. Louis threw a jab that missed. Billy landed a few light jabs, never getting very close. Early in the round Billy slipped and fell as he threw a jab. Billy moved in and exchanged with Joe briefly a few times, always dancing away cautiously. Louis continued to stalk. Joe landed a few punches inside during the close exchanges, but nothing heavy. It was Joe's round, as Billy fought defensively for most of it.

In the second Billy started off dancing as Joe pursued. Billy stopped and fought several times. Joe landed a good left hook to the head and several punches to the body. Conn fought back, landing some good lefts himself. Louis was landing well to the body. He got in some good head shots that rocked Billy. Joe was dominating the round. Near the end of the round Billy landed a good right to the jaw, but it was Joe's round all the way.

In the corner between rounds Billy must have felt warmed up and ready to go. He had seen Joe's moves and tasted his power. Just before the bell rang he told Johnny Ray, "All right, Moon, here we go." Billy came out for the third round a different fighter. He started dancing, and then landed a hard lead left hook. He threw it again, landing effectively. He closed and fired beautiful combinations inside, snapping Joe's head back. He landed jabs and hooks from a distance. Joe had difficulty with the left, unable to react quickly enough. Billy repeatedly closed and slugged with Joe, getting much the better of it inside – he was too quick for Joe. The crowd roared as Billy took full control of the round. Just before the bell he landed a leaping left hook.

Billy started the fourth dancing again, but soon landed lead lefts and a big left-right combination. Billy kept landing effective combinations as Joe looked bad, missing again and again. Near the end of the round they clinched. Billy held his own as Joe tried to wrestle and muscle him. It was another big round for Conn. In the corner Billy told Johnny Ray, "This is a cinch."

"Don't talk like that!" Ray screamed back at him.

In Pittsburgh the Conn clan cheered on the porch as the radio blared. Billy's Aunt Rose reported to Maggie in her upstairs bed that her son was doing well. Maggie sent her orders down to the women below: "Keep prayin'." At the Waldorf-Astoria, Mary Louise could no longer stand to listen. She went into the bathroom and turned on the shower so that she couldn't hear the broadcast. Aunt Catherine kept her ear to the radio.

In Louis' corner his worried handlers told him to pick up the pace – he was letting the smaller man dominate the fight. Joe came out determined. Billy started the fifth with another lead left followed by a right to the jaw. Louis attacked the body. Conn fought back, but Joe pounded the body with hard, accurate punches. He landed some big shots to the head that rocked Billy. Joe had gotten himself back into the fight with a big round.

In the sixth Louis again worked the body, and used his weight in the clinches to smother Billy's punches. He followed with some good head shots, rocking Billy again and opening a small cut over the right eye. Joe had, for the time being, stopped Billy's vicious inside attacks, and taken back control. The Forbes Field crowd shuddered as it sounded like Joe was landing effectively and setting Billy up for the knockout. New York Giant pitcher Cliff Melton started warming up, anticipating an imminent end to the bout.

Joe had landed some big shots in the past two rounds, but Billy had shown that he could take them. There would be no early knockout, although Billy trailed in the scoring after six rounds.

In the seventh Billy started out dancing and landing a few jabs. He landed some good left hooks. Joe landed some body shots and a left hook to the head. Billy landed a solid right to the jaw late in the round. Neither man dominated in what was essentially an even round.

In the eighth Billy landed some good combinations early, and continued to assault Joe with quick inside shots. Joe seemed baffled. Billy landed some solid rights to the jaw. He worked the body and head with brilliant combinations, and landed a big left hook at the end of the round. It was a big round for Conn. The seesaw battle had swung back to Billy. At some point during the middle rounds Billy told Joe, "You're in a fight, Joe." Joe responded, "I know it." At Forbes Field, Melton stopped warming up and returned to the dugout.

Billy followed his strong eighth with an even better ninth. He continued to fire beautiful combinations in succession. Joe was unable to figure him out, and now appeared to be in real danger of losing. Joe landed few punches as Billy put on a boxing clinic of smooth, fast, three and four punch combinations. "Joe, I got you," Billy told him. For the time being, Billy was right. Joe had no answer.

In the tenth Billy showed more confidence, closing with Joe several times and getting the better of it. Joe landed a hard right to Billy's jaw, a punch that had felled many a large heavyweight, but Billy took it well, fighting back and beating Joe to the punch again. Joe continued to stalk. At one point Billy slipped and grabbed onto the ropes, leaving himself open. Joe could have punched him in that vulnerable position. Instead, in a great display of sportsmanship, Joe allowed him to regroup. Though he was losing, Joe refused to take a cheap shot at Conn. The incident became part of the Louis legend, that of a supreme sportsman who always played fair. It also displayed Joe's confidence. He was indeed losing, but he never counted himself out. He knew he had the punch to come back and win. The tenth was another good round for Conn.

Maggie Conn received periodic reports from her relatives below, and gave the same response: "Keep prayin'." Billy's 20-year-old sister Mary Jane told reporters after the tenth round, "Yeah, and the smart guys said he wouldn't even last that long."

Conn came out aggressively for the eleventh, landing multiple shots to the head and body as Joe landed only an occasional body shot. The crowd roared as Conn attacked, landing series after series of quick, accurate combinations. Louis landed a big right on Conn coming in, but Billy shook it off and kept pounding Joe. It was an astonishingly brilliant round for Conn. No one had ever beaten Louis like that. It drove the crowd into a frenzy that echoed throughout Harlem. Panic swept the community as they heard the radio accounts and the roaring crowd that confirmed the unthinkable: *Joe Louis was losing!* As Billy walked back to his corner, he shot his fist into the air in response to the screaming crowd. Joe didn't have much time left to turn it around.

Conn rooters were starting to believe it could really happen. At Forbes Field, in Irish enclaves in New York and around the nation, in the bars and humble homes of smoky Pittsburgh, they clutched beer mugs, rosary beads, and each other. On 44th Street in Pittsburgh, Mary Louise Bulger, this writer's mother, gathered around the radio with her family. She heard her father, like Billy Conn the son of an Irish immigrant mother, muse aloud in disbelief, "He's gonna do it. He's gonna beat Joe Louis."

It got worse for Joe in the twelfth. He started out landing some jabs and a right to the jaw, but Billy responded, pounding him to the body and following with power shots to the head. Billy landed a lightning-fast four-punch combination that stunned Joe, and followed it with a big left hook to the jaw. Joe was hurt and in real trouble. He held on to Billy to keep from falling. "Louis is hurt!" screamed Dunphy's voice through the radio. Billy pushed Joe around the ring as Joe grabbed Billy's arms and tried to smother the attack. Joe had difficulty getting his legs under him. Billy landed a good left to the stomach. The round ended – a big one for Conn – one that gave him the confidence that he, the boxer, could knock out Louis, the slugger.

Louis' handlers told him he needed a knockout to win. They told him to throw rights, as Billy was winding up with his left hook to try for the big KO punch. Joe was indeed hurt in the twelfth round, but throughout his career he had shown an ability to recover quickly. Most of the crowd was on its feet screaming, watching an upset in the making as two of the greatest fighters of all time, both in their prime, battled to a climax. Hopes and fears reached a fever pitch for the millions of listeners around the nation. At the Conn home on Fifth Avenue, Maggie continued to pray. She had willed herself to stay alive for this moment. Mary Louise Smith kept the shower running, but she could hear her Aunt Catherine cheering. In the black ghettoes of America millions of worried rooters hoped that somehow their Joe could pull it out.

No one has described the scene better than Frank Deford in his 1985 article for *Sports Illustrated*, "The Boxer and the Blonde."

"...There was bedlam. It was wonderful. Men had been slugging it out for eons, and there had been 220 years of prizefighting, and there would yet be Marciano and the two Sugar Rays and Ali, but this was it. This was the best it had ever been and ever would be, the twelfth and thirteenth rounds of Louis and Conn on a warm night in New York just before the world went to hell. The people were standing and cheering for Conn, but it was really for the sport and for the moment and for themselves that they cheered. They could be a part of it, and every now and then, for an instant, *that* is it, and it can't ever get any better. This was such a time in the history of games."

In Conn's corner the handlers were optimistic but cautious. Louis still had the biggest punch in boxing. Billy was bursting with confidence, aching to get back in there and finish Joe off. Fred Fierro told him to play it safe. Billy scoffed. "Did you see that, Fat? I staggered him. I'll knock him out next round."

Johnny Ray told him to box, keep away, win by decision. Billy replied, "I'm gonna knock him out." Ray threw up his hands and muttered, "You're on your own."

Contrary to popular lore, Billy did not rush out for the thirteenth like a wild man and start slugging. For nearly a full minute, he danced and jabbed, waiting for the right opening. Billy started his attack by landing a lead left hook, the same punch he had used so effectively all night. He danced briefly, and attacked again. Joe landed a hard right to the jaw, followed by a left hook and a right uppercut. Conn was stunned, but shook it off. He rushed at Joe and they engaged in a furious slugfest in which they stood toe to toe and each man threw 20 to 30 punches in barely ten seconds. Billy was faster and landed more. At one point Billy landed seventeen straight punches. It was Joe who finally clinched. The referee broke them, but Billy went right after him again. At this point it became obvious that Billy meant to end it all here and now, one way or the other. Joe landed a good right, Billy a good left, Joe a good uppercut, Billy another good left. Both men were landing heavy punches and not retreating. Billy Conn was slugging it out with the hardest hitter the game had ever seen, a man who outweighed him by 30 pounds. Joe's big shots stunned Billy. Joe came to life – this was the shot he had been waiting and praying for! He fired a series of devastating shots with his trademark speed and accuracy, yet the smaller man refused to fall. "Conn is staggering but he won't go down," said Dunphy at ringside. Billy was out on his feet. His incredible will kept him up through the final seven punch combination, after which he finally fell. The ref counted "One.. two..three…" At about "eight" Billy sat up, not fully lucid. He rose just after the ref yelled "Ten!" Two seconds remained in the round. "The referee says it's all over," said Dunphy to millions of listeners around the nation.

At the Conn home, Mary Jane collapsed into a chair and sobbed. All of the Conn women were crying except the feisty eleven-year-old youngest, Peggy Ann, who held court with reporters. "If only he could have gotten up," she told the *Associated Press*. "But he'll get another match and he'll beat Joe Louis then. I'll bet you!"

To the *Post-Gazette* she said, "Billy was wonderful – if only he had a few more seconds. He'll get another chance – and then you watch!"

She ran off into the night, and Mary Jane called after her, "Don't you go fighting with anybody, no matter what they say!"

Aunt Rose went upstairs to tell Maggie, who already knew. She could tell from the crying she heard downstairs. Rose relayed Maggie's last message to the reporters: "I am very proud of him."

At that moment Billy's voice came through the radio: "Hello, Mother. I hope you're all right. I'm okay."

When the fight ended, Johnny Ray rushed into the ring and wiped Billy off with a towel. Joe and Billy shook hands. Their respect for each other would only grow over the years. The Polo Grounds throng was stunned, but cheered for the valiant effort of both warriors.

Hundreds of reporters crowded both the Conn and Louis locker rooms. Joe told them, "Billy Conn is a great fighter with a lot of heart. He was much faster than I was and I had a hard time catching him. I would like to meet him again, and maybe the game won't go thirteen innings like it did tonight."

Asked if Billy had hurt him, he responded with refreshing honesty: "Yes he did. Anyone who says Conn can't hit hard enough to hurt you doesn't know what he is talking about. I was dazed in the twelfth but I shook it off right away and was all right when I walked back to my corner. I knew I was behind when I went out in the thirteenth and had to go after him or lose my title. I was just hopin' he would mix it with me because if I stung him, I knew he would fight back. He did, and I finally caught up with him."

In the Conn locker room Johnny Ray held off reporters while Billy sat with his back to them, chin on chest, sobbing audibly. "Wasn't he swell?" said Ray. "You bet he was – he was swell in defeat – but we'd rather have won."

Billy got it out of his system. He was ready to face the press again as smiling, irrepressible Billy Conn. He told them, "I fought a good man and he beat me. But if Uncle Mike will give me another chance, I think I can beat him – yes, I'll knock him out."

Asked why he went for the knockout instead of playing it safe, he said, "I guess it's the Irish in me. I knew I hurt him and had him going in the twelfth round and was going for a knockout, but he got to me first."

He added, "Maybe I had too much guts – and not enough common sense."

After talking with reporters, Billy showered, dressed, and mysteriously disappeared. He slipped out of the Polo Grounds onto Eighth Avenue. He walked alone through Harlem, heading for the Waldorf-Astoria and the woman he loved. Many of the African-Americans on the street recognized him, and applauded him for the brave effort that had nearly toppled their hero Joe Louis. For almost five miles Billy walked, alone with his thoughts. He was not one to brood over the missed chance in the fight – he was young and expected more opportunities. His concern now was for two women: Mary Louise Smith and his dying mother. Tired but determined, he made it to the famous hotel and into the arms of his sweetheart. She saw a Billy who was slightly bruised and cut, but who by now had put the loss behind him. "I tried my best, Matt," he told her. He stayed there that night, with Aunt Catherine remaining as chaperone.

Joe Louis won the fight, but Billy Conn was the story. His valiant effort as the "little guy who went for it all" won the hearts of America. For over half a century his strategy has been second-guessed and analyzed. It began in the aftermath of the fight. Most analysts felt he had won and lost the title in the same night. Syndicated columnist Red Smith dissented, writing that Billy was living on the edge all night and finally got caught. Hype Igoe suspected that Billy went after Joe because he and Ray bet a bundle on a Conn KO. Regis Welsh captured the thoughts of the majority in the *Post-Gazette* the next day: "Conn hit a home run but was thrown out trying to stretch it into a five-bagger."

Frank Deford wrote 44 years later in *Sports Illustrated* that Billy went for the knockout to impress Mary Louise and her father. Billy himself never wavered from his original assertion that he tried to knock Louis out because he thought he could. He felt that the big left hook that hurt Louis in the twelfth caused the change in strategy. "If I don't land that punch, I win the fight," he said.

Other quotes famously attributed to Conn were "What's the sense of being Irish if you can't be dumb?" and "I had too much Pittsburgh in me."

Louis put a humorous spin on it when Conn asked him years later "Joe, why didn't you just lend me the title for six months?"

"You had it for twelve rounds and didn't know what to do with it," Joe deadpanned.

Billy and Mary Louise planned a wedding for Friday, June 20, at her parish, St. Philomena's in Squirrel Hill. They invited friends and relatives and hoped to pull it off despite the objection of her parents. The wedding was scheduled for 9:30 a.m. About 150 fans gathered outside the church to catch a glimpse of the couple. Greenfield Jimmy found out about it and came to the church. Billy pleaded with him to bless the marriage. They argued alone together, amicably, for nearly two hours as the guests and fans waited. Finally, Billy gave up – for now. There would be no wedding that day. Father Augustine Smith (no relation), pastor of St. Philomena's, informed the crowd that the wedding was called off.

Greenfield Jimmy drove Billy home to Fifth Avenue. Newspaper reporters caught Billy leaving the car and surrounded him. The *Sun-Telegraph* wrote that Billy had his hands in his pockets and looked despondent. "No wedding today," he told them. "I'd love to be married now, but I can't."

Mary Louise was in tears when Billy left her at the church. He had his brother Jackie drive him to the Smith home later that day so he could comfort her.

A few days later, Mary Louise's parents whisked her off to Ocean City. Billy followed. Shortly after arriving there, he received a call that his mother was dying. He flew back to Pittsburgh to be by her side. Maggie was gravely ill, but she rallied and was not in immediate danger. Billy returned to New Jersey. On June 28th he received a call from his sister Mary Jane. Mary Louise watched him as he listened and the tears flowed down his cheeks. She knew before he told her that his mother had finally lost her long battle with cancer.

Billy flew home again, leaving Mary Louise in New Jersey. The funeral took place in the Fifth Avenue home on June 30th. Maggie was buried in Calvary Cemetery.

Billy and Mary Louise made plans to elope, and acted quickly. Billy picked up Father George Schwindlein, a priest friend from Erie, and the two drove to Philadelphia with Billy's chauffeur Gabby Ryan. Father James Vallelly, pastor of St. Patrick's Church in Philadelphia, agreed to let Schwindlein marry the young couple. Billy met Mary Louise in Atlantic City on Tuesday, July 1st, and drove her to St. Patrick's. The wedding took place with no guests other than Ryan, who served as best man. Mary Byrne, a Rectory housemaid, acted as maid of honor. Mary Louise wore a blue dress and Billy's mother's wedding ring. After the wedding Billy told reporters, "In the Catholic Church, when a priest marries you, you're married forever. It goes for keeps – and I'm mighty happy about it."

From the church Ryan drove the new Mr. And Mrs. Billy Conn to Mike Jacobs' luxurious estate in Rumson, New Jersey. They informed her parents by phone from Rumson. Billy spoke with her father, who threatened him physically and unleashed a tirade of profanity. He told reporters that the only thing Smith said that he could repeat was "I'm still against it and I always will be."

Billy pleaded his own case to the press: "Just because a fellow's a boxer, you shouldn't hold it against him. I think I'm a fine gentleman.

Everybody in the world says I'm all right. My wife loves me because she believes I'm an all right guy – with no fancy airs like a lot of people might want me to have. Just a plain, everyday guy with nothing phony about me. A real sincere fellow."

Smith was in a rage, but the wedding was a done deal. He called Jacobs and vented with vicious invective. Mary Louise's brother Jimmy told her that he had never heard anyone swear like that.

Billy and Mary Louise took off by train for a Hollywood honeymoon. Pictures of the happy couple graced newspapers around the country. Upon arrival, they stayed with movie stars Robert Taylor and Barbara Stanwyck, fans of Billy's who had become friends. Taylor and Stanwyck were veterans of many popular movies. They married each other in 1939. Stanwyck received an Oscar nomination for *Stella Dallas* in 1937 and would receive three more in her career, although she never won one.

Bob Hope and his lovely wife Dolores held a big party for the Conns shortly after their arrival. They had a big cake with a boxing ring on top, featuring Billy in one corner, Greenfield Jimmy Smith in the other, and Mary Louise in the center of the ring as referee. The Conns got a big kick out of the cake.

The Hopes had an 18-room English Tudor mansion in the Toluca Lake section of Hollywood with a swimming pool, tennis courts, golf course, office building, and expansive guest quarters. Bing Crosby was a neighbor. Hope was a former amateur boxer himself, and was especially fond of Billy Conn. Hope had starred in many films with Bing and others, and had a popular weekly radio show. Mary Louise remembers the Hopes as generous and kind, especially Dolores.

Billy had signed with Republic Pictures for $25,000 to star in an adaptation of the boxing novel *Kid Tinsel*. It was to start shooting in ten days. Republic changed the title of the film to *The Pittsburgh Kid* with Billy using his real name in a fictional tale of a handsome young boxer.

Shooting of *The Pittsburgh Kid* was expected to take about five weeks. Jack Townley directed. He was better known as a screenwriter, with 48 credits to his name. He would be directing his sixth movie. Jean

Parker co-starred, playing Billy's love interest. Only 25 years old, she had already appeared in 39 movies. She began her movie career at age 17. The cast also included veteran actors Dick Purcell, Veda Ann Borg, and John Kelly. Professional boxers Henry Armstrong and Freddie Steele played themselves, as did referee Art Donovan. Former heavyweight contender Jack Roper played "The Champ," Billy's rival in the film.

Billy and Mary Louise had a few days of honeymoon, after which Billy had to work long hours on filming. He was with Jean Parker for much of the time, and posed for countless pictures with young starlets on his arms to hype the movie. Eighteen-year-old Mary Louise was overwhelmed by all the glitter and celebrity. She didn't know anyone but Billy, and he was gone most of the time. She became quite lonely and jealous. She sat and cried for much of the day. She was so pretty, even crying, that they asked her to do a screen test. They wanted her to be in the movie as a girl selling cigarettes. She refused. Billy agreed with her. After a week or so of tantrums and tears, Billy and Mary Louise decided that she should go and stay with a girlfriend in San Diego. She did, and her mood improved. When the shooting finished, she and Billy returned home to Pittsburgh. "We were young and in love," Mary Louise says, "…but not smart. We could've stayed and been movie stars."

She says that Billy was offered the part of heavyweight champ Jim Corbett for the movie *Gentleman Jim*. He turned it down, and Errol Flynn got it. Billy's famous footwork appears in the film, showing him from the waist down as the fleet-footed Corbett.

The real "Pittsburgh Kid" and his sweetheart had had enough of Hollywood. He was not "Kid Tinsel." They were much happier on their home turf.

The film came out quickly, showing in Pittsburgh and around the country before the end of 1941. It never pretended to be anything but light-hearted B-movie entertainment, but Billy called it "a real stinker." He wanted nothing to do with Hollywood ever again.

Back home, the newlyweds bought a beautiful red brick home on Denniston Street in Squirrel Hill, not far from the Smith home on

Beechwood Boulevard. While it underwent remodeling, they lived in the elegant William Penn Hotel downtown. Mary Louise hoped to patch things up with her parents, but her father refused to speak with her or Billy. She saw him on the street in town one day and he passed by without acknowledging her. That broke her heart. When he found out a month later that she was pregnant, he made up with her, but still refused to speak with Billy.

Billy had done no serious training since the Louis bout in June. Louis signed for a September bout with top contender Lou Nova, a big, strong heavyweight from California. Mike Jacobs felt he could get a good crowd for Louis-Nova and tantalize the public by prolonging the buildup for the Louis-Conn rematch until the summer of 1942. He was right. The Louis-Nova bout drew 56,000 to the Polo Grounds.

Billy felt that Nova was made to order for Louis and wouldn't last long with the Bomber. He was right, too. After boxing cautiously with Nova for five rounds, Joe floored him in the sixth with a right. Nova beat the count, still reeling. Joe finished him off with a wicked combination to register a sixth round TKO.

War continued to rage in Europe, with Germany in control of much of the continent. The British held out desperately, hoping for American help. In the Far East the Empire of Japan, ally of Axis powers Germany and Italy, rampaged through China and other Asian nations. On December 7, 1941, as a Japanese delegation engaged in peace talks with the Americans in Washington, Japanese bombers hit Pearl Harbor in Hawaii, killing over 2,000 Americans and crippling our Naval fleet. The United States declared war on Japan. Germany and the U.S. declared war on each other, and America found itself facing a full-blown war on two fronts.

The Selective Service Act of 1940 required all males 21-36 to register for a military draft. After Pearl harbor, the drafting accelerated. Joe Louis got his draft notice in late December, despite an upcoming title bout with Buddy Baer in January. As a married man, Billy Conn would be deferred for now.

The year 1941 ended darkly, with war looming on the immediate horizon. But it had been a great year for sports, with the baseball exploits of Ted Williams and Joe DiMaggio, and the Louis-Conn fight. Joe Louis won *The Ring* magazine and Edward J. Neil awards as the outstanding boxer of 1941. Billy Conn won the hearts of America with his brilliant effort.

It was a turbulent year for Billy, with the Louis fight, his mother's death, and all of the controversy surrounding his marriage. He became famous for all time as a boxer, and starred in a Hollywood movie. He "won and lost" the heavyweight title in the same night and lost his mother, but won the hand of Mary Louise Smith. They were expecting their first child in April. Greenfield Jimmy Smith still refused to speak with his son-in-law, but Billy had Mary Louise. They would remain together "until death do us part."

ROUND THIRTEEN

Private Billy Conn

In 1942 America mobilized for all-out war with the Axis powers. Millions of patriotic young men enlisted or were drafted into the armed forces. Civilians did their part on the "home front" growing "victory gardens," buying war bonds to finance the effort, and sending goods overseas. The government imposed rationing of gasoline, rubber, shoes, sugar, butter,, and meat, among other materials. Factories converted their facilities to war production of jeeps, tanks, and weaponry.

Professional sports struggled, as many of its finest athletes were in the military. Due to a manpower shortage, the NFL's Pittsburgh Steelers and Philadelphia Eagles combined to form the "Steagles." President Roosevelt urged owners to continue the games, as he felt it was good for the national morale.

Melancholy songs about absent lovers dominated, such as "Don't Sit Under the Apple Tree," "I'll Never Smile Again," and "As Time Goes By." Dark, war-themed movies like *Casablanca* and *For Whom the Bell Tolls* were popular, as was the patriotic *Yankee Doodle Dandy*.

As the war dragged on, hundreds of thousands of American mothers received a "Gold Star" for the death of a son. Many more young men suffered serious injuries. FDR won re-election to a fourth term in 1944, and died in office on April 12, 1945. Vice-President Harry Truman became President. American industrial and military might made the difference on both the European and Pacific fronts, forcing the surrender of Germany on May 7, 1945, ("VE" Day) and of Japan on September 2, 1945 ("VJ" Day).

The U.S. government permitted the Joe Louis-Buddy Baer heavyweight title fight to go on at Madison Square Garden on January 9, 1942. Louis donated his entire 40% purse to the Navy Relief Fund. Louis decked the 6'6" 250 lb. Baer three times in the first round. Baer couldn't beat the count after the third knockdown, and Joe had another first round knockout, his fourth as heavyweight champion. The next day Louis entered the Army. He received his physical at Governor's Island, New York, on January 11th with heavy press coverage.

Private Joseph Louis Barrow received permission to defend his title on March 27 at Madison Square Garden against Abe Simon. This time he donated his entire purse to the Army Relief Fund. Joe KO'd the 255 pound Simon in the sixth.

Billy Conn took on heavyweight Henry Cooper, whom he had decisioned in 1940, at the Toledo University Field House on January 12 in a twelve round bout before 8,000 fans. Scaling 182 to 197 for Cooper, Billy jabbed his way to an easy decision win, closing Cooper's left eye early in the bout. Billy donated his purse to a local relief fund for police and firemen.

Billy took on J.D. Turner, a 227 ½ pound heavyweight, on January 28 in St. Louis. Conn weighed 181 for this one. He won an easy ten round decision before 7,000.

Billy kept busy, as he, Louis, and Mike Jacobs looked forward to a lucrative summer rematch. He signed for a 12 round bout with middleweight champ Tony Zale for February 13 at Madison Square Garden. While in training, he visited Private Joe Louis at Camp Upton, New York. It was the first time they'd seen each other since their fight the previous June. The press covered the visit, and wrote that Billy would soon be in the Navy. Billy told reporters that he expected to enter military service within six weeks, but wasn't sure which branch. At that time he could have received a deferment because he was married, but he was patriotic and wanted to join the armed forces.

Conn scaled 175 ¾ to 161 for Zale. The bout drew over 15,000. Tony had won the middleweight title in November by decisioning Georgie Abrams. Known as the "Man of Steel," the Gary, Indiana, native could punch and take a punch. He was tough, but would be giving up considerable height and weight to Conn. He would also give up speed. Billy's long jabs and quick combinations were much too fast for Zale. He staggered Zale in the seventh and ninth rounds, but for the most part was content to box his way to an easy win. Some in the crowd booed Billy for not knocking out a middleweight. The Associated Press had Conn winning 10 of 12 rounds. Some observers felt that he had won every round.

Lieutenant Commander Gene Tunney, former Marine, former heavyweight champion, was director of physical training for several Navy bases in the Northeast. Conn and Tunney had never hit it off too well. Tunney fancied himself an intellectual. He liked to read books and quote Shakespeare. Billy felt that he put on airs - the ultimate sin to a Pittsburgh guy of that era. Tunney wasn't too fond of Billy's brash style either. Nevertheless, Tunney wanted the popular Conn in the Navy to help train sailors in physical culture. Billy didn't like the bell bottom Navy pants, and wasn't too thrilled about working with Tunney. He visited the Navy recruiting office in New York and spoke to an official there. After identifying himself, he told the official to ask Tunney if he could somehow get out of wearing those "funny pants." After a phone call, the official told Billy, "Mr. Tunney says you will wear the same uniform as all the other Navy men."

Billy responded, "You tell Mr. Tunney that he can shove the Navy up his ass."

Billy went right to the Army recruiting office in New York and enlisted in the Army the same day, March 7, 1942.

The Tunney-Conn feud would flare up again shortly. A hot new prospect, Sugar Ray Robinson, was undefeated, and had just KO'd tough

Fritzie Zivic in the tenth round. Tunney told some people that Robinson was so good he could even beat Conn. Conn heard about Tunney's remarks and was insulted. One day he walked into Mike Jacobs' office and Robinson was there. Conn insisted that they step outside and test Tunney's hypothesis in the parking lot. Robinson pleaded that he had nothing to do with Tunney's statement and refused to fight Conn.

Billy was inducted into the Army at Fort Wadsworth in New York on March 16 and sent to Fort Campbell, Kentucky, for basic training.

Although Conn and Joe Louis were both in the Army now, Mike Jacobs planned a rematch for June at Yankee Stadium. Proceeds would benefit the Army Relief Fund. But Billy had important family business to take care of first. On April 12, Mary Louise gave birth to a son, whom they named David Phillip, after two of his McFarland great uncles. Billy received a furlough to attend his son's christening, which would be May 10 at St. Philomena's. David Phillip's grandfather, Greenfield Jimmy Smith, still refused to speak with Billy. Art Rooney, who was the baby's godfather, decided that it was time to patch things up. He arranged a post-christening party at Smith's home on Beechwood Boulevard. Smith agreed to acknowledge Billy and forget the past conflicts.

The lavish party included the Al Turner Orchestra, fancy hors d'oeuvres, and rented Oriental rugs. The large guest list included many priests. When Billy, Mary Louise, and the baby arrived, Smith and his son-in-law shook hands and made up under the supervision of Art Rooney. As the party progressed, Smith continued drinking, and his disposition turned sour. "He still had it in for Billy," says Mary Louise. In the kitchen Smith cornered Billy and launched a tirade, berating him for not attending church regularly and not being a worthy member of the family. Mary Louise says Billy did not want to argue or fight - her father provoked him to the breaking point. Smith continued his verbal assault, telling Billy that he could beat him up, and approaching him in a threatening manner. Billy had had enough. As Smith came at him, he threw a left. Smith ducked, and the punch landed on top of his skull. Billy knew immediately that he had injured, perhaps broken, his left hand. They grappled as several onlookers grabbed them. In the confusion Smith viciously raked Billy's face with his fingernails, drawing blood. Milton Jaffe toppled down the steps into the basement and broke his ankle.

"Why is it that when you get into a fight, your friends hold you instead of the other guy?" Billy asked.

Frustrated by the hand injury that he knew would jeopardize the upcoming Joe Louis fight, Billy punched his right hand through a glass door, cutting it badly. The party ended abruptly. Billy went to the hospital, where X-rays showed a fracture in the left hand. They casted his left hand and bandaged his right hand. The Louis fight was off for now.

Incredibly, Smith showed up the next morning at the Conns' Denniston Street home, still raging and demanding to continue the battle. With both hands injured and immobilized, Billy was not eager to renew hostilities. Smith refused to leave. Billy had to call the Pittsburgh Police to have his father-in-law removed from the porch.

The next day Billy flew to New York and returned to Fort Wadsworth with his broken left hand. The Louis fight was postponed indefinitely.

Mary Louise was left at home alone with her baby. Her mother and sisters helped her with the care. Her father called the baby "Timmy" because he thought "David Conn" sounded "too Jewish." The name stuck. Billy and Mary Louise's eldest son is still known as "Tim."

A month or so later Billy tested his left hand on the heavy bag and pronounced it healed. Jacobs went to work on putting the bout together, and in September announced the Louis-Conn rematch for October 12, with proceeds again to benefit the Army Relief Fund. The bout would be held during daylight hours at Yankee Stadium, due to wartime restrictions on night lighting. Under the contract Louis and Conn would earn just enough to pay off their debts. Louis owed Jacobs $59,805 and owed his manager John Roxborough $41, 145. Conn was in debt to Jacobs for $34,500.

Conn started training September 14 at Jacobs' estate in Rumson, New Jersey. Louis opened camp at Greenwood Lakes, New York. NBC offered a record $71,200 for the radio rights.

On September 25 Secretary of War Henry Stimson announced that he was cancelling the bout. He felt that it was not fair that the fighters had an opportunity to work off their debts when other servicemen did not have the same opportunity. Jacobs pleaded with Stimson, offering that both fighters would work for nothing. Stimson refused to reconsider. The bout was off. The Army immediately transported Conn back to Fort Wadsworth and Louis back to Fort Riley, Kansas.

The heavyweight title was "frozen" because the champion was in military service. Other titles were also frozen. Light-heavyweight champ Gus Lesnevich was in the Coast Guard; middleweight and welterweight champs Tony Zale and Fred Cochrane were in the Navy. There would be no title fights in those divisions for the duration of the war.

In December Conn, now a corporal, was moved to Camp Lee, Virginia, to serve as boxing instructor. In April of 1943 he joined the 12th Armored Division in Kentucky as coach of the boxing team. He spent the rest of 1943 and early 1944 in Kentucky.

On June 6, 1944, the Allies invaded the northern coast of France and began the liberation of Nazi-controlled Europe. Billy arrived in England on June 29 to begin a boxing exhibition tour. As the Allies liberated much of western Europe, he toured England, France, Italy, Corsica, and Sicily. He boxed exhibitions four nights a week and visited wounded American soldiers in hospitals at every opportunity, logging over 50,000 miles in six months.

An amusing incident occurred on the boat going over to England. A big, intimidating Southern drill sergeant threw out a challenge to the men lined up for exercise: "Anybody here who thinks he can kick my ass - step forward!"

Billy did so. Infuriated, the sergeant rushed over to him. "And who the hell do you think you are?" he barked. "Billy Conn," Conn replied.

Recognizing the famous prizefighter, the sergeant announced, "That goes for anybody but you."

On December 18, 1944, the *Associated Press* reported, "Corp. Billy Conn and his troupe of boxers touring Army bases in Britain, France, and Italy rescued an American fighter pilot from his burning plane in Italy, it was disclosed today. The plane crashed in a swamp. Conn and other boxers riding near by in a jeep fought through the flames and dragged out the unconscious pilot."

December 28, 1944, was a day Billy would never forget. He and his boxers took off from Paris, only to discover that the controls were locked. The pilot had to make an emergency landing. He asked Billy and several others to run to the back of the plane to bring the tail down. The odds did not look good. Billy prayed for his life, promising $5,000 donations to missionary priest Dan Rooney (Art's brother) and Sacred Heart Church if he survived. The plane hit the runway at 150 miles per hour, but the pilot managed to stop it without crashing. Miraculously, all on board escaped serious injury. Sacred Heart Church used the donation for a statue of the Blessed Mother that still stands on the parish grounds.

That same night the Germans bombed Paris for the first time in four months. One blast blew out the windows in Billy's hotel, but he was not injured. The *New York Times* reported the next day: "Corp. Conn Has Two Close Calls In a Day on French Boxing Tour."

During the war Billy was unable to call home much, but he sent frequent letters and gifts. "He sent me perfume from Paris and leather from Italy," says Mary Louise. In January of 1945 he received word that Mary Louise had give birth to another son, Billy Junior.

Conn was not fond of Army life. He called K-rations "the worst food in the world" and lamented having "nine million bosses" as a corporal. But he enjoyed boosting soldier morale with his boxing exhibitions and hospital visits.

The boxing shows were three rounds, fought in a relaxed manner to show off the ability of a top-notch boxer like Billy Conn. No one took them too seriously. Billy had a bout with professional middleweight Costello Cruz of California in Reims, France, on April 20, 1945. Cruz boasted loudly to his fellow servicemen that he would show up Conn and "fix his handsome face." Billy heard about it, but figured it was just talk. In the first round Cruz attacked aggressively, stunning the surprised Conn with a big right. Billy's temper flared. He proceeded to punish and batter Cruz, knocking him down twice in the second round and hurting him badly. The referee attempted to stop the contest to protect the nearly helpless Cruz. Billy told him, "If you stop this the same thing will happen to you." He continued to inflict just enough punishment on Cruz to hurt him, but keep him on his feet. Finally, in the third round, Billy knocked him cold with a right. The soldiers got a better show than they expected that day.

In May of 1945 Nazi Germany surrendered to the Allies. The war in Europe was over, but many American servicemen remained. Bob Hope added Billy to his USO tour. Billy met the Hope troupe at Mannheim, Germany, and toured through Germany, Austria, and Czechoslovakia. Billy was with Hope at Nuremberg on "V-J Day" in September of 1945, when Japan surrendered to the Allies.

Billy returned to the U.S. on September 12. Mike Jacobs greeted him at LaGuardia Airport. The *New York Times* published a large photograph of Jacobs kissing half of his big meal ticket. Billy was discharged within a few weeks, as was Joe Louis. Jacobs eagerly anticipated a lucrative rematch.

Although he arrived in New York at 1:50 a.m., Billy called Mary Louise and the boys and spoke with them by phone. He had yet to meet his second son Billy. He hopped a flight to Pittsburgh and visited them for only a day - he had to report the next day to Camp Lee, Virginia. From there he received his discharge.

With Louis and Conn out of the Army, Jacobs announced his plans. The fight would be held in June of 1946 in Yankee Stadium. He hoped to build a record-setting three million dollar gate, with ringside seats at an unprecedented $100. Louis signed a preliminary contract on October 14. Conn and Johnny Ray met with Jacobs to review terms. Jacobs insisted that there be no tune-up fights. Ray vehemently objected. He knew that Billy was not sharp after nearly four years of inactivity. Although Billy fought over 300 exhibitions in the service, those bouts were not real fights, and were mostly against amateurish opponents. Billy needed a couple of tough fights to get him ready for Louis. Ray knew that Conn depended on finesse and speed much more than Louis, and would need more work. Jacobs refused to budge: no fights for either Conn or Louis. He knew that both had suffered a decline in skill with their long layoff. He feared that a loss or injury for either would jeopardize his pending gold mine.

After a heated session, Ray walked out of the negotiations. The next day Jacobs agreed to allow two exhibitions for Conn, but no real bouts. Ray was not happy, but money talked - he and Conn stood to earn up to half a million dollars. They agreed to the terms and signed the contract. Billy started training a few days later at the Pittsburgh Lyceum.

Billy's old nemesis Gene Tunney spoke out against the fight. He felt that it was a travesty because neither man had fought in four years. Said Tunney: "The public will not stand for this phoney-baloney when the heavyweight championship is at stake.

Billy felt that Tunney was jealous because the gate might surpass his own record-setting gates from the Dempsey fights of the 1920's.

Billy's first three round exhibition took place on October 29 against sparring partner Bearcat Jones. The New York Times reported that Billy looked fat, but moved well. Jones weighed 198. Billy's weight was not announced, but was reportedly 192. Both fighters pulled their punches in typical exhibition fashion. Jones threw punches only at Conn's body and arms.

Conn and Jones put on another exhibition in Kansas City on November 7 before 4,000 fans. Billy weighed 194 and was obviously not in top shape. Afterward Billy said he was finished with exhibitions and would go to Hot Springs, Arkansas, to rest before starting serious training for Louis.

At the end of 1945 the country was in a jubilant mood. The war was over; things were getting back to normal. Billy stood to make an enormous sum of money, much more than he had ever made before. And he would get another chance to defeat Louis and win the heavyweight title.

ROUND FOURTEEN

1946: Another Shot At Louis

With the war over, millions of veterans returned home. The birth rate soared, creating a "Baby Boom" that persisted into the 1960's. Many veterans took advantage of government-funded tuition through the "GI Bill" to attend college. The American economy boomed, led by housing, automobiles, and appliances, and would take the country to unprecedented prosperity. A devastated Europe struggled to rebuild.

Hollywood produced happier movies like *It's A Wonderful Life*, *The Best Years of Our Lives*, and *Song of the South*. Sports enjoyed a surge in popularity, as many top athletes returned to action. The St. Louis Cardinals beat the Boston Red Sox four games to three in the World Series. The Chicago Bears won the NFL, and Notre Dame won the mythical college football championship. Joe Louis and Billy Conn prepared for their long-awaited rematch.

During the war years, Greenfield Jimmy Smith grew attached to his grandchildren, Tim and Billy Junior. He was ready to drop the feud with his famous son-in-law. When Billy returned home, they set up a meeting through a mutual priest friend, Father Getty, at the Bachelors Club, owned by Smith. They shook hands and agreed to "let bygones be bygones." Smith proposed a drink in honor of the reconciliation. Father

178

Getty, remembering that Smith's drinking had led to the infamous fight at the christening, nixed the idea. Billy and Smith remained friends for the rest of their lives. The two headstrong Irishmen discovered that they actually liked each other.

Wild Bill Conn remarried during the war, to a woman named Henrietta. They had two young sons, half-brothers to Billy. They lived on East End Avenue, in the Frick Park section of Pittsburgh. Billy's youngest sister Peggy Ann, now sixteen, lived with her father and stepmother. Mary Jane had married Vincent Cunningham. Frank Conn, who had served with the U.S. Army in Europe, was now married and beginning a family. He would eventually have five children. Jackie served in the Army, too. When he exaggerated his exploits, telling people that he was a paratrooper, Billy corrected him by saying, "You never even jumped off the front porch."

Billy traveled to Hot Springs, Arkansas, a gambling haven run by mobster Owney Madden, in early 1946 for some rest and relaxation. He did some running to begin getting himself back into condition. Afterward, he returned to Pittsburgh and worked out at the Pittsburgh Lyceum. The Conn team set up camp in Greenwood Lake, New York, in early June to begin serious training for the June 19 Louis fight. Louis chose Pompton Lakes, New Jersey; the two had switched training sites from their first fight.

Billy did not have the top quality sparring partners he had before the first fight, but he did look good in training and worked himself into excellent condition. About one week before the fight a physician tested him before and after a hard sparring session. His pulse returned to normal quickly, and his blood pressure was actually lower after the workout, astonishing the physician.

Billy rocked his sparring partners with jarring shots to the head and body, impressing observers from the media and boxing worlds. At times he looked brilliant. But a few saw some troubling signs. He was getting hit with right hands too often. That could be fatal against Louis. His feet looked blistered and raw, unaccustomed to the phenomenal footwork that had carried him to so many victories in the past. He was in great shape, but did he still have the reflexes and skill to defeat Louis after so long a layoff? According to Fred Fierro, Billy himself had doubts. Fierro said Billy told him, "They're getting to me, Fat. I can't get out of my own way."

By some accounts, Johnny Ray was barely involved in the training. He had "fallen off the wagon," and was drunk and bedridden for much of the time. But Ray did tell reporters that Billy was more focused this time because he did not have a wedding to worry about.

Louis did not look sharp in training. He explained that he was training to win the fight, not to look good in sparring. Neither man could possibly expect to be in 1941 form after not fighting for over four years. But Louis still had the big punch. Some had the more cynical view that Jacobs manipulated reports to say Conn looked good in training and Louis looked bad, thus building the gate by making the public believe that it would be a good fight and that Conn had a real chance.

Billy was spirited in camp, graciously receiving celebrity visitors from Pittsburgh and elsewhere. When Gene Tunney predicted that Conn wouldn't last two rounds, Billy invited him to visit training camp so that he could punch him out.

On Sunday, June 16, three days before the fight, Billy boxed six rounds before a crowd of 800. He battered three sparring partners, cutting one of them on the nose, and looked great. He had put in 279 rounds of sparring. It seemed that the Pittsburgh Kid was ready.

Jacobs worked tirelessly to promote the fight, hoping to break all previous monetary records. He charged robust ticket prices, including $100 for ringside seats, the highest ticket price in boxing history. Although the threat of rain held the crowd down somewhat, over 45,000 fans poured into Yankee Stadium and paid top dollar. They had been waiting five years for this rematch. The gate fell just short of two million dollars, second only to the second Tunney-Dempsey bout of 1927.

Louis-Conn II remained the second highest grossing boxing match for thirty years. Even the Ali-Frazier battles (1971, 1974, 1975) grossed less despite decades of inflation. In 1976 the Ali-Ken Norton bout at Yankee Stadium grossed 2.4 million, taking second place on the all time list.

Louis-Conn II was the first fight ever televised, drawing a closed circuit audience of 146,000.

Pittsburgh fans followed their hero to the Big Apple by train, car, and even plane. Seven TWA planes packed with 147 fight fans took off from Allegheny County Airport the day before the fight and landed in New York. The "Ham and Cabbage Special" chartered trains brought many more. A total of over 5,000 Pittsburghers journeyed to New York City for the fight.

The *Post-Gazette* had a front page article stating that "Mrs. Billy Conn" would stay home with her two sons and listen to the fight on the radio. She told the paper that Billy would win, and that she was not too excited about it.

A crowd of 24 Conn relatives assembled in the living room of Wild Bill's East End Avenue home. Another group of relatives listened at the home of Billy's sister Mary Jane, now Mrs. Vincent Cunningham.

The Conn team broke camp early. Billy's last workout was to take place at 2 p.m. on June 18, the day before the fight, at the Metropolitan Life Insurance Company gymnasium. When word got out that the handsome Conn was coming, 250 female workers in the building swarmed into the gym and refused to leave. Company officials persuaded the Conn team to move to the New York Athletic Club, and ordered the disappointed women to return to work.

Joe and Billy weighed in on the morning of the fight with much fanfare, and with hundreds of reporters from around the world in attendance. Joe weighed 207, about seven pounds above his weight for the first fight. Billy weighed 182, 13 pounds more than in 1941. Billy looked thicker in the face and torso; the "kid" had matured into a 28-year-old man. His neck now measured an incredible 18 inches. He was upbeat at the weigh-in. He and Joe exchanged friendly words several times. Oddly, Billy had dark circles under his eyes.

Never before had a title fight taken place between two men who had been idle for over four years. Although Joe was 32 and Billy 28, they were not in top fighting shape. Both had worked themselves into good condition, but understandably lacked the reflexes and finely honed skills they had before the war. After such a long layoff, it could not be otherwise. It figured to affect Conn more; his speed would require more fine-tuning than Joe's power.

A slew of celebrities from different walks of life paid the high ticket price to witness the first big fight following the war. From the boxing world retired champs Jack Dempsey, Gene Tunney, Jim Braddock, Barney Ross, Tony Canzoneri, Mickey Walker, and Max Baer attended. From the active ranks were Gus Lesnevich, Fritzie Zivic, and Teddy Yarosz, all previous Conn victims. Promoters Art Rooney, Barney McGinley, and Jake Mintz led a Pittsburgh contingent that included Mayor David Lawrence. New York Governor Thomas Dewey and New York City Mayor William O'Dwyer attended, as did Mayor Kelly of Chicago and Mayor Frank "I Am the Law" Hague of Jersey City. Clark Gable, Frank Sinatra, Irving Berlin, Ann Sheridan, George Burns, and Gracie Allen were just a few of the entertainment personalities present. Andrei Gromyko, Soviet ambassador to the U.N., and Bernard Baruch, United States representative at the U.N., lent international gravitas, as did nuclear scientist J. Robert Oppenheimer.

By fight time the skies had mostly cleared. Millions gathered around their radios to hear the Gillette-sponsored broadcast with Don Dunphy and Bill Corum, hoping for another thrilling battle like 1941. Pittsburgh's streets were deserted, much as they would be today for a Super Bowl involving the Steelers.

A national poll of boxing writers found 57 picking Louis to win, while 17 picked Conn. Pittsburghers Harry Keck, Havey Boyle, and Chet Smith, who had all followed Conn from the birth of his career, picked the local boy by a decision. The betting odds generally favored Louis by about three to one, very close to the odds on the first fight.

Louis uttered his now-famous quote about Conn to Arthur Daley of the New York Times: "He can run but he can't hide."

In the locker room at Yankee Stadium Billy told his father-in-law Jimmy Smith, "This is going to be the worst fight you ever saw." Billy knew he was nowhere near his 1941 form. Hopefully, Joe wasn't either. Smith felt that something was wrong with Billy - more than just ring rust. He suggested postponing the fight. Referee Eddie Joseph also expressed concern at the way Billy looked. At this point, with nearly two million dollars paid, postponement was out of the question.

Billy made his entrance first, to a huge ovation. Joe followed shortly, to an equally impressive ovation. Both men had been linked in the public mind for four years as the top two heavyweights in boxing. Billy had in effect been the number one contender for all that time in a nation and world deprived of entertainment by the sacrifices of war.

Billy wore a white robe with "Billy Conn" in green on the back, and black trunks with red trim. Joe wore his usual blue robe with a red "Joe Louis" on the back, and his royal purple trunks with "JL" on the left front side.

Broadcaster Bill Corum said of Conn's near-victory in the first bout: "The cup of victory trembled and sloshed over as he lifted it to his lips."

With the fighters in their respective corners, ring announcer Harry Balogh took the microphone and intoned, "From Pittsburgh, Pennsylvania, weighing one hundred eighty-two pounds, wearing black trunks, undefeated light heavyweight champion and the very capable challenger for the heavyweight crown - Billy Conn! And his opponent, weighing two-o-seven, he's wearing purple trunks, the internationally famous Detroit Brown Bomber, always a credit to his chosen profession and the race he represents, the heavyweight champion of the world - Joe Louis! And may the best man emerge victoriously. [sic]"

Referee Joseph brought the fighters and their seconds to the center of the ring and gave the pre-fight instructions. Billy made the sign of the cross as he returned to his corner.

The bell rang and Billy moved cautiously about the ring, staying on his toes. Joe stalked him, but not too aggressively. Both men threw a lot of jabs, but few of them landed. Billy retreated for most of the round. When Joe started throwing more punches near the middle of the round, Billy told him, "Take it easy, Joe. We have fifteen rounds to go.," drawing a laugh from Joe. When Joe landed one, Billy laughed and said, "That's no way to treat an old pal."

Billy started the second with a good right to the head, and followed with a good right to the body. After that, he kept moving away. Joe landed some good jabs, but missed repeatedly with rights and hooks. All three judges gave the first two rounds to Louis, since Billy retreated most of the time. The fight had displayed little action so far. Billy was known as a slow starter, so the fans expected the pace to pick up. But it was already obvious that neither man was as quick or as polished as in their first fight.

In the third round Billy landed two good hooks in a row, to the head and body. Joe landed a few long left jabs, but Billy blocked several others. Joe rarely threw a right. Late in the round Billy landed another double hook combination. Conn had stood and fought more this round, and all three judges awarded it to him. In the first fight Billy had come alive in the third round, boxing brilliantly. This time he showed flashes of his old self and did enough to win the round.

In the fourth Billy jabbed lightly and danced on his toes. Joe stalked him harder, looking more determined. Joe cornered him and landed a hard right to the head, followed by a good combination to the body. Joe continued his effective assault with several jabs and a hook to the head, opening a cut on the bridge of Billy's nose. It was Joe's best round so far.

In the fifth Billy began circling, as Joe stalked. Billy kept one step ahead of Joe, who kept missing as Billy retreated. Finally, Joe landed a long right to the jaw that snapped Billy's head back. Billy took it well. Joe followed with another short crisp right to the jaw. Joe was finding the range. He landed two more jabs, and then trapped Billy on the ropes and scored with a good body combination. Billy landed three quick hooks from the ropes just before the bell, but it was Joe's round all the way.

In the sixth Joe kept stalking and landing jabs. Billy moved in and out, landing several jabs and hooks. Joe cornered him on the ropes and landed a good left to the head and several rights to the body. Billy responded with a good hook, and kept moving. They traded hard jabs several times. It was Joe's round again. He was in control and well ahead now. Billy needed to start winning some rounds. To do so, he would have to take some chances punching and stop retreating so much.

In the seventh Billy circled, landing light jabs. He moved his fists in a rapid motion, trying to confuse Joe. Billy landed a hard left hook to the head. Joe responded with a hook to Billy's head. Joe trapped Billy on the ropes and got in a good right to the ribs. Billy had traded more this round, and the pace was much faster than in any previous round. Joe landed several good rights to the body near the end of the round.

After seven rounds, Billy had shown little of the brilliance of the first fight. In 1941 he had taken control by getting inside and baffling Joe with quick combinations. He showed neither the speed nor the confidence to do that now. He had taken a lot of hard shots, especially to the body, yet was still able to move about well on his feet. He still had his chin.

Curiously, they touched gloves at the start of the eighth round. Don Dunphy commented, "They touch gloves… usually they touch gloves at the start of the last round. Could that mean something?" Billy was moving fast, and Joe was stalking fast. Joe kept jabbing, hitting some and missing some. Midway through the round, Billy stopped dancing. He jabbed and hooked Joe to the head. Joe landed a good left and a right to the jaw. Billy stood and fought, more willing to slug with Joe than at any other time in the fight. Billy landed a hook, and Joe came back with a right. Billy was smiling as Joe kept coming. Joe landed a "one-two," a stiff jab followed by a powerful right hand that buckled Billy's knees. Billy staggered forward, still stunned as Joe landed a right uppercut that nearly took Billy's head off, and follwed it with a left hook that snapped Billy's head again and floored him. Billy didn't beat the count, struggling to rise as the referee counted "ten."

"And it's all over... Conn is knocked out!" screamed Dunphy. "Joe Louis knocks out Billy Conn!" Louis retained his title by knockout at 2:19 of the eighth round.

The fight was far inferior to the 1941 classic. Billy was nowhere near top form. Joe still had the marvelous punching power that had earned him 22 successful title defenses, 19 by knockout.

Afterward, Louis was gracious but blunt. "Billy wasn't the fighter he was the last time. He was much slower and didn't bother me at all."

Billy, with small cuts on the bridge of his nose and under the left eye, told the throng of reporters in the locker room, "He's a terrific puncher. I didn't have to go in there to find that out, but I figured I cound tire him out. You know - play safety first with him for a while. The next thing I know, he's knocked me down. I heard the count, but I just couldn't get up."

Johnny Ray wept quietly in a corner, saddened that the brilliant career of his "Junior" was apparently over. Billy told the press that he intended to retire: "It's the kid's last fight. I'm putting the cue stick back on the rack."

Ray concurred : "There's no use kidding ourselves. He hasn't got it any more."

The Conn women in Pittsburgh were quiet throughout the bout. Edith Rosenblatt, *Post-Gazette* reporter on the scene at East End Avenue wrote: "Every blow that struck the Pittsburgh Kid last night shook the women of his family who sat tense by their radios."

Sixteen-year-old Peggy, so tough and defiant after the first bout, took it hardest. Rosenblatt wrote: "When Conn took the staggering blow that sent him down, Peggy cried out, and as he took the count of ten, she wept bitterly."

The fight grossed $1,924,564, of which Billy received $312,958, a huge sum in those days. He was able to pay what he owed Uncle Sam, "Uncle Mike" Jacobs, and Johnny Ray. At age 28, he was independently wealthy from a successful career. He didn't have to fight again. Louis received over $600,000, most of which went to pay off debts to the IRS and Jacobs.

The question remains as to why Billy Conn, only 28, performed so poorly in the second Louis bout after a brilliant career in which he was nearly invincible from 1939 to 1942. Referee Eddie Joseph, who had the best view of the fight, told Pat Robinson of the *International News Service*, "I don't care what the doctors or anyone else may say; I say Billy Conn was not in condition. Now don't give me a song and dance about his heart and his pulse and his blood pressure. I say he wasn't in proper condition for a tough fight and I knew it as soon as I saw him step into the ring. I knew there was something wrong when I saw those circles under Conn's eyes. I don't know whether he was overtrained or not, but I do know he wasn't in shape for a battle against one of the hardest punchers the ring ever saw."

Harry Keck of the *Sun-Telegraph* had visited the camp and said that Conn was brilliant in training. "What happened?" he asked suspiciously.

Some circumstantial evidence suggests that it was more than ring rust. Members of the Conn family believe that Billy was drugged before the fight by a mob conspiracy that was hoping to get an edge in the betting, which was massive. According to the Conn family, Billy and manager Milton Jaffe were missing for nearly 24 hours prior to the fight. When Billy returned for the morning weigh-in, he wasn't himself. He had dark circles under his eyes and acted "goofy." Greenfield Jimmy Smith was with him in the locker room prior to the fight, and felt that he was in no condition to fight. He demanded that Billy call the fight off. Billy refused, telling Smith that he had caused the first rematch to be called off by breaking his hand in the fight with Smith, and didn't want to be blamed for a second postponement. Johnny Ray was reportedly drunk and sick for most of training camp, including the day of the fight. He was in no condition to watch over and protect his protégé. Conn may have been drugged the day before the fight to ensure a poor performance and a Louis win.

The notorious Abe Attell, former featherweight champ who allegedly helped mobster Arnold Rothstein fix the 1919 World Series, was seen hanging around the Conn camp several times. Jaffe reportedly gave Conn huge wads of cash over the years for no apparent reason. Greenfield Jimmy Smith believed that Jaffe betrayed Conn, and was trying to assuage his guilt. Smith spoke often through the years about what he believed to be Jaffe's betrayal. Billy himself refused to talk about it.

Is this theory plausible? The evidence is all circumstantial, and all possible participants in such a plot are dead. We'll never know for sure.

Louis defended his title again in September, knocking out Tami Mauriello at Madison Square Garden in the first round. He laid off for a year after that, and then took on Jersey Joe Walcoot in December of 1947 at the Garden. Although a 20-1 favorite, Louis looked terrible. His skills had declined from the second Conn bout, and were a far cry from his pre-World War II form. Walcott knocked Louis down in the first and fourth rounds, and appeared to have won a decision. To the surprise of all those present , the judges awarded Joe the bout by split decision. The crowd booed the verdict.

Joe had to redeem himself. Six months later, at Yankee Stadium, he knocked out Walcott in the eleventh round. It would be Joe's last fight before announcing his retirement in March of 1949. The Walcott KO capped a notable statistic in the career of Joe Louis. Against every opponent he fought twice, Louis did better the second time. Natie Brown, Bob Pastor, Arturo Godoy, Buddy Baer, Abe Simon, Billy Conn, and Walcott all fell victim to Joe in more decisive fashion the second time around. Only Schmeling had beaten Louis, and Joe KO'd him in the first round in their second bout.

With Louis ready to retire Billy contemplated a comeback. At age 31, he had fought only once in the last six years. Yet he hoped he could work his way into top shape, at least enough to win the title after Louis left. He believed that the rest of the heavyweight field was weak. He signed for two bouts for November of 1948.

On November 15 he knocked out journeyman Mike O'Dowd in the ninth round in Macon, Georgia. He KO'd Jackie Lyons ten days later in Dallas, Texas, also in the ninth round.

After two bouts against mediocre competition, Billy knew that his heart wasn't in it. He and Joe Louis staged a six round exhibition in Chicago on December 10, 1948. The friendly joust was in essence a farewell for both great warriors. Billy never fought again. Joe announced his retirement a few months later.

Walcott and Ezzard Charles met for the vacant heavyweight title on June 22, 1949, at Comiskey Park in Chicago. Charles won by decision.

Due to financial problems and a huge debt to the IRS, Louis came out of retirement for a title bout with Charles at Yankee Stadium on September 27, 1950. Although he had not fought in over two years, his name still had drawing power. Now 36, he weighed in at a bloated 218 pounds. Nevertheless, a faded Louis summoned enough grit to last the distance with Charles, a solid champion who had defended his title successfully three times. Charles won a unanimous decision.

Still desperate for money, Louis won bouts in Chicago, Detroit, Miami, and San Francisco against less than stellar opposition. He KO'd an aging Lee Savold in June of 1951. He won a decision over the respectable Jimmy Bivins in Baltimore in August. He still drew good crowds. In October he met the hard-hitting young contender Rocky Marciano in New York. Joe outboxed Marciano early, winning three of the first five rounds, but couldn't sustain it. Marciano put him away in the eighth round with a devastating combination that knocked Joe through the ropes. The "Hard Rock from Brockton" wept after destroying his boyhood hero. Louis retired for good this time.

ROUND FIFTEEN

Retirement Years: Pittsburgh Icon

After hanging up the gloves for good, Billy gave up physical exercise altogether. He began smoking cigarettes, which he had never done in his life. He had rarely partaken of alcohol as a fighter, but now acquired a taste for Scotch whiskey. He and Mary Louise had two more children - Suzanne in 1947 and Michael in 1952 - thus joining the "Baby Boom."

In the 1950's Billy invested some of his money in oil wells in Texas and Oklahoma, lent his name to a car dealership, and bought some race horses. With his money from boxing and business deals, his financial situation was comfortable.

The kids all attended St. Philomena's Catholic Grade School in Squirrel Hill, where their mother had gone. Billy shunned public appearances, and rarely participated in the children's activities. Despite his bravado in the ring and with the media during his fighting days, Billy was no longer comfortable dealing with the public and became somewhat reclusive in his post-career days. He did not like strangers patting him on the back and calling him "Champ." He had a small group of close friends and a few bars and clubs that he frequented. He and Mary Louise attended the earliest Mass on Sundays, when few people were there. Billy Junior says that he rarely talked of his boxing career, even to his family.

Billy taught his boys how to box on a heavy bag in the basement, but lectured them on the dangers of the sport. He said it was not like baseball or football, in which an average player could get by and enjoy the game. A boxer could get seriously hurt, even if he was very good. When his eldest son Tim took up boxing for a while, sparring with ex-pro Al Quaill at the YMHA, Billy forbade it when he found out about it. He told Tim that he became a boxer because he had to, and that there was no other reason for doing so.

Greenfield Jimmy Smith was much involved in all of his grandchildren's activities, and taught the boys baseball. Tim played baseball for Allderdice High School in Pittsburgh. Billy Junior played football at Allderdice.

Billy occasionally refereed a boxing match, and dabbled in teaching amateurs how to box. The late veteran trainer Frank "Spacky" Delio described Conn as a "genius" in the ring, but an impatient teacher. "He expected everybody to be perfect - like him," said Delio.

The Pittsburgh area, a hotbed of boxing talent since the turn of the century, rarely produced quality fighters after the war. Instead of Greb, Yarosz, Zivic, Burley, and Conn the region spawned football players like Johnny Unitas, Joe Namath, Mike Ditka, Dan Marino, Joe Montana, Tony Dorsett, and Jim Kelly, among many others.

Johnny Ray, retired also, continued to drink heavily. He often visited Billy at home, teasing him to "Get out of bed, you bum!"

As Mary Louise remembers, "He was always drunk."

He developed liver disease, and his health declined. Tim Conn remembers he and his dad visiting Ray in the hospital in his dying days: "He was all yellow, and very sick. He told my dad, 'Get me outta here, Junior. Get me a drink.' Dad told him, 'The only way you're getting out of here, Moonie, is with a tag on your toe.'"

Ray died in 1961 at age 66.

In 1963 Billy received a lucrative offer to manage the casino at the famed Stardust Hotel in Las Vegas, and uprooted the family from its

Pittsburgh home. Mary Louise and the kids objected, but the offer was too good to pass up. The mob-owned hotel had opened in 1958. With 1,470 rooms, it was the largest in Las Vegas at that time. The casino alone was 16,500 square feet. Big time mobsters, gamblers, and entertainers frequented the Stardust. "It was just like the movie *Casino*," says Mary Louise. Tim and Billy Junior worked as busboys in the hotel, and met stars like Frank Sinatra, Don Rickles, and Jackie Gleason. Wealthy oil tycoons sometimes tipped Billy thousands of dollars just to hang out with them while they gambled.

It was a glamorous life, but the Conns missed Pittsburgh. Tim stayed only about eight months before returning east to attend college at Youngstown State University in Ohio. Billy and Mary Louise were increasingly uncomfortable with the Las Vegas lifestyle, particularly for the effect it might have on their kids. Their old friend Bob Hope agreed with them and told Mary Louise, "You get your nice family out of here." After nearly three years in Vegas, they returned to Pittsburgh. They had rented but not sold their home on Denniston Street, so they made arrangements to move back in. This time the Pittsburgh Kid was home for good.

In Pittsburgh Billy "loafed" with Joey Diven, a legendary street fighter from the Oakland section of Pittsburgh. Diven had been written up in books and magazines for his exploits. At 6'5" and a solid 290 pounds, Diven, also of Irish extraction, was reportedly undefeated after decades of barroom and alley brawls against the area's "best." He was most famous for a 1954 incident in which he single-handedly took on most of the University of Pittsburgh football team the night before a game - and won! Many of the Pitt players were unable to play the next day. Diven and Conn became close. An occasional brawl broke out in Billy's presence, making headlines because of his celebrity. According to the Conn family, Diven and his pals did most of the fighting; Billy was for the most part an innocent bystander. Others report a few instances in which Billy lost his temper and scored some unofficial knockouts.

In 1965 Billy was voted into *The Ring* magazine Hall of Fame. He was honored at a fight in Pittsburgh's Civic Arena between Rubin "Hurricane" Carter and Pittsburgher Johnny Morris. The underrated but talented Morris won by decision.

In 1966 Billy received an offer to referee a title bout in Mexico City between lightweight champion Carlos Ortiz, a Puerto Rican living in New York City, and Ultiminio "Sugar" Ramos, a Cuban living in Mexico. The Mexicans had adopted Ramos as one of their own. Ortiz manager Bill Daly wanted an American referee with the guts to be fair to his fighter in a hostile venue, and suggested Conn. Conn accepted the offer. The bout would take place October 22 at El Toreo Bullring in Mexico City. Both the World Boxing Association (WBA) and the Mexican-dominated World Boxing Council(WBC) sanctioned it as a title bout.

Billy arrived in Mexico City a few days early and visited the shrine of Our Lady of Guadeloupe at the cathedral. On fight night over 18,000 Mexican fans poured into El Toreo. Ramos was a top contender who was expected to put up a tough fight. In the second round Ramos floored Ortiz for a count of two. After that, Ortiz dominated, landing frequent rights that opened a nasty cut on Ramos' eyelid. By the fourth round, Conn felt that the fight should be stopped due to the cut. He halted the action to have the ring doctor inspect the cut. According to Conn, Dr. Gilberto Bolanas Cacho told him to make his own decision. In the fifth Ortiz kept landing rights on the cut, making it a gruesome mess. Conn again halted the action and asked the Mexican doctor to support his decision to stop it. Conn said the doctor refused to do so, apparently fearful of the crowd that was growing ever more menacing as they sensed that Ortiz could soon be declared the winner by TKO. As referee, Conn had the authority to stop the bout, but preferred to have the doctor's support. Conn said of Dr. Bolanas Cacho, "He said I was doing the right thing, then he lit out of there like a greased banana."

Conn stopped the bout on his own and declared Ortiz the winner by TKO. He said, "I had to save Ramos' eye. That's what the referee is for."

The fans began throwing things - first peso coins, and then rocks and bottles. Some even invaded the ring and attacked Ortiz and his handlers. The police were nowhere to be found. Trainer Teddy Bentham put the water bucket over Ortiz' head to protect him. Bill Daly was hit in the head with a rock, and blood streamed down his face. He was beaten and kicked, suffering two fractured ribs. Conn suffered multiple bruises to the head and back fending off attackers. He battled his way back to the dressing room without escort. Eventually, all of the foreign parties made it to the safety of the dressing room. Conn said: "There weren't any cops around. The cops were all scared, too, they all hid. I didn't even have Joey Diven with me. Joey enjoys that kind of action. He'd have gone right through like a tank."

In the ring WBC official Ramon Velazquez declared that the bout was not over, and gave Ortiz ten minutes to return and continue the fight. The Ortiz team and Conn refused to return. After 25 minutes, Velazquez declared Ramos the winner. Hundreds of bloodthirsty fans surrounded the dressing room area, dispersing only when military troops arrived and escorted the Americans to their hotel. Conn defended his action to the media: "I knew I was asking for trouble, but at least Ramos will have two eyes tomorrow. I didn't want to see his career ended because I didn't have the guts to stop the fight." It took 28 stitches to close the cut.

The WBA supported Conn's decision, and declared Ortiz the winner by TKO. Nearly all news media and boxing authorities agreed. Tapes show that Conn repeatedly asked the doctor to support him in stopping the fight. Eventually even the WBC relented, overturning its hasty ringside decision and declaring the title vacant. They mandated a January rematch. It had to be postponed for several months due to the severity of Ramos' cut. They fought in San Juan, Puerto Rico, on July 1, and Ortiz won by a fourth round TKO.

The sports world credited Conn with making the right decision in a dangerous situation. He was lauded for displaying the same kind of courage he had displayed in the ring as a boxer. An unimpressed Conn said, "One of the few times in my life that anybody thought I was right and I almost got killed. After this I'm gonna stay home. It doesn't pay to be right."

Billy appeared on NBC's *Tonight Show* the following Tuesday. He handled himself well, joking with Johnny Carson about the incident. What had been a truly dangerous situation at the time was by then funny.

Ortiz told this writer in a 2006 interview that in his opinion Conn was right to stop the bout. He also said the ringside doctor didn't support Conn because he was afraid of the crowd. "It was a scary night," said Ortiz. "I wouldn't have gone back out there for a million dollars."

In 1967 Billy visited his old rival and buddy Joe Louis in England. Joe and Billy had taken a liking to each other since their first fight and remained close through the years. Both were involved in the Las Vegas casino business scene, and accepted an invitation to England to help promote legal gambling interests there. They struck up a friendship with notorious London mobsters Ronnie and Reggie Kray. Both former boxers, the "Kray Twins" adored Conn and Louis. Conn related to his family that when someone asked one of the Krays if they knew the queen, he said, "We don't know her, but she bloody well knows us."

Pittsburgh no longer produced champion boxers, but it revered its glorious past. Billy Conn and Fritzie Zivic became twin icons, frequently attending youth sports banquets. Zivic was more comfortable and entertaining in this milieu, and did it more often. With his quick-witted humor and disfigured nose, he looked and acted the part of an old pug. This writer recalls seeing him speak at a banquet in Garfield. Of his reputation as a dirty fighter, he said, "I was a perfect gentleman in the ring. I said 'Pardon me' every time I fouled a guy. One time I said 'Pardon me' thirty-nine times in one round!"

This writer also witnessed Billy Conn speaking at a 1971 banquet in Point Breeze, near his home. He showed the film of his first fight with Joe Louis, and took questions afterward. Joe Frazier had just beaten Muhammad Ali in their first fight. Billy told a questioner that Ali (he called him Clay) was the better fighter and would beat him the next time. When asked if he could have beaten Ali in his prime, Billy answered, "I would have had a chance." He said that Harry Greb was definitely the greatest fighter of all time. After the Q and A session Conn hung around and talked with some of the kids in the audience, including yours truly. He had a quiet, self-assured dignity about him.

In July of 1972 Muhammad Ali defended his title against Alvin "Blue" Lewis in Dublin, Ireland. The Irish government invited Irish-American ex-champ Billy Conn to Ireland to help promote the bout. Billy accepted, and visited the land of his ancestors for the first time. He was not too thrilled with what he felt were its backward ways. After the fight he was boarding the plane for home when a reporter asked him what he thought of Ireland. Ever blunt, he quipped, "I'm glad my mother didn't miss the boat."

Jackie Conn died of a cerebral hemorrhage in 1975 at age 54. Billy's father died two years later at 79. By the 1970's, most of Billy's famous rivals were gone, including Fred Apostoli, Gus Lesnevich, Babe Risko, Melio Bettina, and Teddy Yarosz. The great Joe Louis died broke and debilitated in 1981. Billy attended the funeral at Arlington National Cemetery, reportedly paid for by Max Schmeling and Frank Sinatra.

Billy's health remained good into his sixties. Despite an affinity for cigarettes and Scotch, he experienced no major health problems, physically or mentally. In his fifties his weight had inched upward. When an old friend mistook him for Jackie, who had ballooned to well over 250 pounds, Billy was insulted. He took the weight off and kept it off. He did not formally exercise, but took long walks through his Squirrel Hill neighborhood.

Fritzie Zivic remained alert until his sixties, when his 230-bout career started catching up with him. He experienced symptoms of "pugilistic dementia" and died in 1984 at a Veterans Hospital in Pittsburgh. Billy visited his old buddy, near death, and for a brief moment Zivic recognized him.

In the 1980's the Billy Conn saga enjoyed a media rebirth. The January, 1981, issue of *The Ring* magazine reported that a poll of boxing historians voted the first Louis-Conn fight as the greatest of all time, beating out the Frazier-Ali and Tunney-Dempsey battles. In 1985 Frank Deford wrote "The Boxer and the Blonde" for *Sports Illustrated*, which recounted the romance of Billy and Mary Louise amidst Billy's quest for the heavyweight title. The beautifully written article became one of the most popular in the magazine's history, and for a time revived interest in one of boxing's greatest stories.

The International Boxing Hall of Fame opened in Canastota, New York, in 1989. The first induction group of 46 boxers was a "who's who" of boxing history, and included Billy Conn. All-time greats Joe Louis, Jack Dempsey, Gene Tunney, Harry Greb, John L. Sullivan, Rocky Marciano, and Sugar Ray Robinson, among others, were inducted posthumously. Present for the initial induction ceremony in June of 1990, in addition to Conn, were Muhammad Ali, Carmen Basilio, Willie Pep, Jake LaMotta, Archie Moore, Sandy Saddler, Ike Williams, Kid Gavilan, Jose Napoles, Jersey Joe Walcott, Emile Griffith, and Bob Foster. Billy attended with sons Tim and Mike. Archie Moore, one of the greatest light-heavyweights in boxing history, asked of Conn, "How come you and I never fought?" "You weren't good enough," Conn told him.

In 1990 Billy's daughter Suzanne was diagnosed with breast cancer, and was undergoing treatment. Billy and Mary Louise began attending a Wednesday morning novena (a series of prayers for a special intention) to Our Lady of Perpetual Help at St. Philomena's. One morning after the novena service they stopped at a convenience store on the way home. Mary Louise went to the back of the store to get coffee. Billy bought a newspaper and waited for her near the counter. A young man burst into the store and pulled a gun on the owner, demanding money. He paid little attention to the elderly man nearby holding a newspaper. Mary Louise saw it all from the coffee area. Knowing Billy, she thought "Someone is going to get killed, either Billy or that kid."

"You leave him alone," Billy said to the robber. As he turned toward Billy, the famous Conn left hook crashed into his face, driving him through the cookie display. His gun fell to the floor. He threw the newspaper rack at Billy, and fled the store. In the confusion his wallet fell out, and he was later apprehended.

"You have to hit him with your best punch," Conn told reporters. "I interrupted him. I mean I fixed him. He won't be robbin' any stores for a couple days."

The story was all over the newspapers the next day, even making the *London Times*. "Do you know who that was?" the cops asked the suspect. He didn't. The eighteen-year-old had never heard of seventy-two-year-old Billy Conn,

June 18, 1991, was the 50th anniversary of the first Louis-Conn fight. Scores of newspapers and magazines carried articles about it. Billy was interviewed at home for ESPN by boxing commentator and former lightweight champion Sean O'Grady. After showing film clips and old interviews, O'Grady posed a final question to Billy Conn: "If you had it to do over again, would you have fought him the same way?" Billy paused for a moment, and then answered: "I woulda done it the same way. What the hell's the difference?"

Shortly afterward Billy began to experience some mental lapses and delusions. At times he would wake up in the middle of the night and get dressed, thinking he had to be somewhere. The problems were sporadic at first, but grew more frequent. The "pugilistic dementia" that had affected so many prizefighters had finally caught up to him. Now 73, he had enjoyed good health longer than the typical fighter who had been a lot of tough fights. Billy had not suffered a lot of damage in his career due to his superb defensive skills, but he had 75 fights, mostly against top competition. He had done thousands of rounds of hard sparring. He probably kept his faculties for so long because he retired at the relatively young age of 31.

In early January of 1993 he was hospitalized at a psychiatric hospital in Pittsburgh, and then transferred to a Veterans Hospital very near to the East Liberty neighborhood where he had grown up. His daughter Suzanne died of cancer in February at age 45. With Billy deteriorating and near death, it was a rough time for Mary Louise and the family.

William David "Billy" Conn died of pneumonia at the hospital on May 29, 1993, at age 75.

"BILLY CONN DIES, CITY BOXING LEGEND," proclaimed the *Post-Gazette* front page headlines the following day. The funeral took place at St. Philomena's with Fathers Getty, Kelly, and McAnulty concelebrating the Mass. Billy was buried in Calvary Cemetery, not far from the grave of Harry Greb. Newspapers around the nation carried obituaries.

He certainly was a "city boxing legend." Jack McGinley, matchmaker for Rooney-McGinley boxing promoters, and Vice-President and part owner of the Pittsburgh Steelers, has been deeply involved in the Pittsburgh sports scene since the 1930's. McGinley says Conn was not only the biggest sports figure in Pittsburgh in his prime, but one of the biggest in the country. Despite Pittsburgh's long history of major sports figures from the Pirates and Steelers, McGinley says, There wasn't anybody bigger than Billy. He could fight, he was fearless, and he looked like a movie actor."

Billy received many honors in death. In 1998, a section of Craig Street in Pittsburgh's Oakland district, near where Duquesne Gardens had stood, was renamed "Billy Conn Boulevard." Billy won 11 of 12 fights there, defeating six world champs. In 2001, he was voted one of the top ten boxers of the twentieth century by an *Associated Press* poll of boxing writers. In 2004, the Western Pennsylvania Sports Hall of Fame opened in downtown Pittsburgh. An entire room is devoted to the area's boxing legacy, with Conn the most prominently featured star. A life-sized cardboard cutout of him greets patrons at the entrance to the room. The light-heavyweight championship belt is on display, courtesy of the Conn family. A videotape of excerpts from the first Louis-Conn fight runs non-stop.

Today Billy and Mary Louise have eight grandchildren and two great-grandchildren. Eldest son Tim lives with wife Ronnie in Pittsburgh. Their son Ryan, who bears a striking resemblance to his famous grandfather, maintains a web site, billyconn.net, devoted to him. Billy Junior lives with his mother in Pittsburgh. The youngest son, Mike, lives with his wife and three children in San Francisco. Mike attended Georgetown University with Joseph Louis Barrow, Jr., the son of Joe Louis.

Mary Louise is still beautiful and vivacious, as alert as ever. Her age is "don't ask," but she was sixteen when she met Billy in 1939. She sold the Denniston Street home a few years ago and moved into an apartment, which has become a Billy Conn shrine. An entire room is wall-to-wall pictures of Billy, Mary Louise, and various celebrities posing with Billy. There are letters and autographed pictures from Presidents Kennedy, Ford, Reagan, and Bush I, and from Attorney General Robert Kennedy. Celebrity posers include such big names as Bob Hope, Frank Sinatra, Muhammad Ali, and Jack Dempsey, among others. Conn nemesis Gene Tunney is not included, but the only man ever to beat him, Pittsburgher Harry Greb, holds a prominent position.

The largest picture in the room is the most striking. Billy and Mary Louise are running from the ocean at the Jersey shore in bathing suits, holding hands, the waves splashing their feet. It's 1941. Both are as beautiful as anyone could possibly be. They are young, happy, and in love. It is how they should be remembered.

EPILOGUE

Billy Conn's Legacy

How great a fighter was Billy Conn? He is certainly deserving of the honors he has received, such as inclusion in the first group of Hall of Famers, ranking by some as the greatest light-heavyweight of all time, and as one of the top ten boxers of the twentieth century. Yet he is still underrated; most all-time rankings by various historians place him far below where he ought to be, often ranking 30 or 40 others ahead of him.

One must consider the methods used to determine such rankings. Pundits often divide fighters by weight class, which can be misleading. One who fought at the same weight for most of his career would then have an advantage. Someone like Conn, or Henry Armstrong, who had success in three weight classes, would be at a disadvantage. For example, Archie Moore was light-heavyweight champ for nine years with nine successful title defenses, while Billy Conn held the crown for less than two years and defended it four times before moving on to pursue the heavyweight title. Is it fair to rank Conn and his short reign as a better light-heavyweight than Moore and his long reign? Conn at his best would almost certainly have beaten Moore at his best. Conn could have stayed a light-heavyweight and held the title for many years, but did not.

He was too good not to go for the heavyweight crown. Does that count for more than longevity?

The Associated Press twentieth century rankings (see Appendix B) consider a fighter's total career in all of his weight levels, and show Conn as the ninth best pound-for-pound fighter of the twentieth century. These rankings were the first to give Conn his due, and even they underrate him a little.

Factors one must consider in any rankings are: ability, record, and longevity.

Ability: Conn was as skilled a boxer as anyone who ever laced on gloves. He had great speed of hand and foot, and ring smarts. He had phenomenal stamina, and an almost inhuman ability to take a punch (after reaching physical maturity at age 20). He was not a knockout puncher for most of his career, yet did increase his power by age 23 as shown by his ability to hurt and knock out some good heavyweights in 1940 and 1941. He had the toughness to take on much bigger quality opponents and defeat them, a trait rare even among great fighters. Sugar Ray Robinson, for example, never did it. Only a few, like Conn, Armstrong, Harry Greb, and Sam Langford, could do it.

Record: His record from November of 1938 to April of 1942, about 3 ½ years, may be unequalled. He defeated both reigning middleweight champs - twice each - as a 21-year-old, and won the light-heavyweight crown a few months later. He was utterly dominant in that class, so much so that only the heavyweight division presented a challenge. Despite his low weight, he dominated the best heavyweights around. He lost to Joe Louis, perhaps the greatest heavyweight of all, but proved in their 1941 fight that he *could* beat Louis. Even Louis conceded that Conn was capable of beating him, and that was when Louis was in his prime. With today's twelve - round title bouts, Conn would have won. Boxing historian Max Kellerman says of Conn's 1941 performance against Louis, " At 169 pounds, he was lighter than I am and he's beating Joe Louis! I consider that the single greatest athletic achievement in the history of this country - even though he lost the fight! He was a total phenom."

Conn fought tougher opposition than anyone. He defeated ten world champions - five of them twice - all in their prime. That's more than Louis, Ali, Armstrong, or anyone else on the top ten list except Robinson, who defeated eleven champs in over 200 bouts. From the Zivic fight of December, 1936, when 19-year-old Billy Conn became a "name" fighter, until the second Louis fight of 1946, 20 of his 37 bouts were against world champs.

Longevity: World War II interrupted Conn's prime, and the four-year layoff permanently ended his period of greatness. We'll never know what might have been. He lacks the longevity of other greats like Louis, Ali, Armstrong, Greb, and Robinson. Therefore, those fighters must be ranked ahead of Conn in the pantheon of boxing legends. Yet Conn's lack of longevity and fading memory cannot obscure this conclusion: Billy Conn at his best might well have beaten any middleweight, light-heavyweight, or heavyweight who ever entered a ring. Pound for pound, *no one was better.*

"What the hell's the difference?" answered Conn when Sean O'Grady asked if he would fight Louis the same way if he had it to do over. It does make a difference. He could have been the handsomest and most charismatic heavyweight champion, an underweight dynamo who baffled the big guys with speed and skill, a hero many times more famous than he became. It was not to be. The hubris of youth and the intrusion of geopolitics dictated otherwise. He will forever be remembered as the guy who almost made it, his matchless record obscured by one heartbreaking loss.

One of life's saddest refrains is what might have been. But Billy Conn's story is not a sad one. He rose from poverty to find fame, fortune, true love, and a blessed family. He had a long and healthy life for a prizefighter. He was the "Pittsburgh Kid," the symbol of a city, and an era. The memory of him is fading, but his phenomenal record stands. In the long and storied history of the sport of boxing, he was one of the greatest.

APPENDIX A

The Fight Record Of Billy Conn

DATE	OPPONENT	Wt	Conn Wt	SITE	RESULT
6/28/34	Dick Woodward	unk	unk	Fairmont WV	Lost 4 rd dec
7/20/34	Johnny Lewis	136	135	Charleston WV	Won KO 3
8/30/34	Bob Dronan	130	135	Parkersburg WV	Won 6 rd dec
9/27/34	Paddy Gray	139 ½	137 ½	Pittsburgh (North Side Arena)	Won 4 rd dec
11/12/34	Pete Leone	140	139	Wheeling WV	Lost TKO 3
1/29/35	Johnny Birek	144	143 ½	Pittsburgh (Motor Square Garden)	Won 6 rd dec
2/25/35	Ray Eberle	142	143	Pittsburgh (Moose Lodge)	Lost 6 rd dec
3/13/35	Stanley Nagy	U	U	Wheeling WV	Won 4 rd dec
4/8/35	George Schlee	142	144 ½	Pittsburgh (Moose Lodge)	Won KO 1
4/25/35	Ralph Gizzy	139 ½	142 ½	Pittsburgh (Motor Square Garden)	Lost 4 rd dec
6/3/35	Ray Eberle	145 ½	146 ½	Millvale PA	Won 6 rd dec
6/10/35	Ralph Gizzy	142	142 ½	Millvale PA	Lost 6 rd dec
7/9/35	Teddy Movan	147 ¾	144 ¾	Millvale PA	Lost 4 rd dec
7/29/35	Ray Eberle	147 ½	145 ½	Millvale PA	Won 5 rd dec
8/19/35	Teddy Movan	147 ½	147 ¼	Millvale PA	Lost 4 rd dec
9/9/35	George Liggins	145	147	Pittsburgh (Duquesne Gardens)	Won 4 rd dec
9/10/35	Johnny Yurcini	U	147	Washington PA	Won 6 rd dec
10/7/35	Johnny Yurcini	143	149	Johnstown PA	Won 6 rd dec
10/14/35	Teddy Movan	150	147 ½	Pittsburgh (Motor Square Garden)	Draw 6 rds
11/18/35	Steve Walters	U	150	Pittsburgh (North Side Arena)	Won 6 rd dec

205

DATE	OPPONENT	Wt	Conn Wt	SITE	RESULT
1/27/36	Johnny Yurcini	U	U	Pittsburgh (North Side Arena)	Won TKO 4
2/3/36	Louis Kid Cook	152 ½	152	Pittsburgh (North Side Arena)	Won 6 rd dec
2/17/36	Louis Kid Cook	150	151 ¾	Pittsburgh (North Side Arena)	Won 8 rd dec
3/16/36	Steve Nickleash	155	152	Pittsburgh (North Side Arena)	Won 6 rd dec
4/13/36	Steve Nickleash	155	155	Pittsburgh (Moose Lodge)	Won 6 rd dec
4/27/36	General Burrows	155	157	Pittsburgh (Moose Lodge)	Won 6 rd dec
5/19/36	Dick Ambrose	U	161	Millvale PA	Won 6 rd dec
5/27/36	Honeyboy Jones	160	156	Pittsburgh (Greenlee Park)	Won 8 rd dec
6/3/36	Honeyboy Jones	157	155	Pittsburgh (Greenlee Park)	Won 10 rd dec
6/15/36	General Burrows	149 ½	154	Millvale PA	Won 8 rd dec
7/30/36	Teddy Movan	155	157	Pittsburgh (Forbes Field)	Won 8 rd dec
8/10/36	Teddy Movan	155	155 ½	Millvale PA	Won 8 rd dec
9/8/36	Honeyboy Jones	154 ½	151	Millvale PA	Won 10 rd dec
9/21/36	Roscoe Manning	166	156 ½	Pittsburgh (Forbes Field)	Won TKO 5
10/19/36	Charley Weise	163	156 ½	Pittsburgh (Islam Grotto)	Won 10 rd dec
10/22/36	Ralph Chong	160	154	Pittsburgh (Duquesne Gardens)	Won 10 rd dec
12/2/36	Jimmy Brown	160 ¾	158	Pittsburgh (Motor Square Garden)	Won TKO 9
12/28/36	Fritzie Zivic	149 ½	156	Pittsburgh (Duquesne Gardens)	Won 10 rd dec **
3/11/37	Babe Risko	160 ¾	160	Pittsburgh (Duquesne Gardens)	Won 10 rd dec *
5/3/37	Vince Dundee	157 ¼	161	Pittsburgh (Duquesne Gardens)	Won 10 rd dec *
5/27/37	Oscar Rankins	161 ½	162 ¼	Pittsburgh (Duquesne Gardens)	Won 10 rd dec

DATE	OPPONENT	Wt	Conn Wt	SITE	RESULT
6/30/37	Teddy Yarosz	161	161	Pittsburgh (Forbes Field)	Won 12 rd dec **
8/3/37	Ralph Chong	U	U	Youngstown OH	Won TKO 6
8/13/37	Young Corbett III	158 ½	163 ½	San Francisco (Dreamland Auditorium)	Lost 10 rd dec
9/30/37	Teddy Yarosz	161	162	Pittsburgh (Duquesne Gardens)	Won 15 rd dec **
11/8/37	Young Corbett III	158 ¼	163 ½	Pittsburgh (Duquesne Gardens)	Won 10 rd dec **
12/16/37	Solly Krieger	162 ½	163	Pittsburgh (Duquesne Gardens)	Lost 12 rd dec
1/24/38	Honeyboy Jones	158	165	Pittsburgh (Motor Square Garden)	Won 12 rd dec
4/4/38	Domenic Ceccarelli	170 ½	167 ½	Pittsburgh (Motor Square Garden)	Won 10 rd dec
5/10/38	Erich Seelig	165 ½	169 ½	Pittsburgh (Motor Square Garden)	Won 10 rd dec
7/25/38	Teddy Yarosz	161	160	Pittsburgh (Forbes Field)	Lost 12 rd dec
9/14/38	Ray Actis	166	169	San Francisco (Civic Auditorium)	Won TKO 8
10/27/38	Honeyboy Jones	161	167	Pittsburgh (Duquesne Gardens)	Won 10 rd dec
11/28/38	Solly Krieger	163	165 ½	Pittsburgh (Duquesne Gardens)	Won 12 rd dec *
1/6/39	Fred Apostoli	160 ½	167 ¾	New York (Madison Square Garden)	Won 10 rd dec **
2/10/39	Fred Apostoli	161	167	New York (Madison Square Garden)	Won 15 rd dec **
5/12/39	Solly Krieger	166	170 ¼	New York (Madison Square Garden)	Won 12 rd dec *
7/13/39	Melio Bettina (Won light-heavyweight title)	173 ¼	170 ½	New York (Madison Square Garden)	Won 15 rd dec *
8/14/39	Gus Dorazio	186	173	Philadelphia (Shibe Park)	Won TKO 8
9/25/39	Melio Bettina (Retained light-heavyweight title)	174 ¼	171 ½	Pittsburgh (Forbes Field)	Won 15 rd dec *
11/17/39	Gus Lesnevich	174 ½	171 ¼	New York	Won 15 rd dec *

DATE	OPPONENT	Wt	Conn Wt	SITE	RESULT
(Retained light-heavyweight title)				(Madison Square Garden)	
1/10/40	Henry Cooper	190	173 ½	New York	Won 12 rd dec
				(Madison Square Garden)	
6/5/40	Gus Lesnevich	173 ½	173 ½	Detroit	Won 15 rd dec *
(Retained light-heavyweight title)				(Olympia Stadium)	
9/6/40	Bob Pastor	180 ¾	174	New York	Won KO 13
				(Madison Square Garden)	
10/18/40	Al McCoy	181 ½	172 ¾	Boston	Won 10 rd dec
				(Boston Garden)	
11/29/40	Lee Savold	186 ¾	174 ¼	New York	Won 12 rd dec
				(Madison Square Garden)	
2/27/41	Ira Hughes	179	182	Clarksburg WV	Won TKO 4
3/6/41	Danny Hassett	204	181	Washington DC	Won KO 5
				(Uline Arena)	
4/4/41	Gunnar Barland	194 ½	178	Chicago	Won TKO 8
				(Chicago Stadium)	
5/26/41	Buddy Knox	190	180	Pittsburgh	Won TKO 8
				(Forbes Field)	
6/18/41	Joe Louis	199 ½	174	New York	Lost KO 13
(For heavyweight title)				(Polo Grounds)	
1/12/42	Henry Cooper	197	182	Toledo OH	Won 12 rd dec
1/28/42	J D Turner	227 ½	183	St. Louis	Won 10 rd dec
				(Municipal Auditorium)	
2/13/42	Tony Zale	164 ¼	175 ¾	New York	Won 12 rd dec **
				(Madison Square Garden)	
6/19/46	Joe Louis	207	182	New York	Lost KO 8
(For heavyweight title)				(Yankee Stadium)	
11/15/48	Mike O'Dowd	201 ½	190	Macon GA	Won TKO 9
11/25/48	Jackie Lyons	184	188	Dallas TX	Won KO 9

U= Unknown

64 wins (15 KO's) 12 losses, 1 draw

* defeated world champion

** defeated world champion and Hall of Famer

Conn defeated 10 world champions, including 5 Hall of Famers

APPENDIX B

Billy Conn's Awards And Honors

July 13, 1939: Light-heavyweight champion of the world

1939: Edward J. Neil Memorial award for fighter of the year

1939: Dapper Dan Award - for the sports figure who has done the most to publicize Pittsburgh that year. Conn was the first to receive it.

1940: Ring Magazine Fighter of the Year.

1940: Best Dressed Athlete of the Year

1945: Dapper Dan Award

1965: Induction into Ring Magazine Hall of Fame

1978: The Boxing Writers Association nationwide poll named Conn the best light-heavyweight of all time

1981: Ring Magazine January issue names the first Louis-Conn bout as the greatest fight of all time

1988: Grand Marshal, Chicago St. Patrick's Day parade

1989: Induction into the initial class of the International Boxing Hall of Fame in Canastota, New York

1998: City of Pittsburgh named the corner of Fifth Avenue and Craig Street "Billy Conn Boulevard"

The site is near where the Duquesne Gardens stood. Conn won 11 of 12 fights there, defeating six world champions

2000: Conn named one of the Top Ten fighters of the Twentieth Century by the Associated Press

Associated Press Fighter of the Century:
1. Sugar Ray Robinson
2. Muhammad Ali
3. Henry Armstrong
4. Joe Louis
5. Willie Pep
6. Jack Dempsey
7. Roberto Duran
8. Benny Leonard
9. Billy Conn
10. Harry Greb

Much of the information on this page is from the billyconn.net web site

BIBLIOGRAPHY

BOOKS:

Bak, Richard. *Joe Louis: The Great Black Hope*. Dallas: Taylor Publishing Company. 1996

DeLisa, Michael C. *Cinderella Man*. United Kingdom: Milo Books Ltd. 2005

Fried, Ronald K. *Corner Men*. New York: Four Walls Eight Windows. 1991

Lorant, Stefan. *Pittsburgh: The Story of an American City*. Pittsburgh: Esselmont Books, LLC. Fifth Edition, 1999

Mead, Chris. *Champion Joe Louis: Black Hero in White America*. London: Robson Books. 1985

Mullan, Harry. *The Great Book of Boxing*. New York: Crescent Books. 1990

O'Brien, Jim. *Hometown Heroes*. Pittsburgh: James P. O'Brien Publishing. 1999

O'Brien, Jim. *The Chief*. Pittsburgh: James P. O'Brien Publishing. 2001

Remnick, David. *King of the World*. New York: Random House. 1998

Roberts, James B., and Skutt, Alexander G., *The Boxing Register: International Boxing Hall of Fame Official Record Book.* Ithaca, New York: 2002

Rosenfeld, Allen S. *Charley Burley: The Life and hard Times of an Uncrowned Champion.* Bloomington, Indiana: Author House 2003

Sugar, Bert Randolph. *The 100 Greatest Boxers of All Time.* New York: Bonanza Books. 1984

Sugar, Bert Randolph, Editor. *The Ring Record Book and Boxing Encyclopaedia.* New York: The Ring Publishing Corporation. 1981

Toker, Franklin. *Pittsburgh: An Urban Portrait.* University of Pittsburgh Press. 1994

Weston, Stanley, and Farhood, Steve. *The Ring: Boxing the 20th Century.* New York: BDD Illustrated Books. 1990

MAGAZINES:

Beeler, Paul. "Pittsburgh Fistic Star." *The Ring* October, 1937

Deford, Frank. "The Boxer and the Blonde." *Sports Illustrated* June 17, 1985

Parker, Dan. "Impulsive Mr. Conn's $1,000,000 Punch." *The American Weekly* June 21, 1942

WEB SITES:

Boxing.about.com
Billyconn.net
Boxrec.com
eastside boxing.com

NEWSPAPERS:

Baltimore Sun. October 24, 1966
New York Daily Mirror. July 14, 1939 to June 20, 1941
New York Daily News. July 14, 1939 to September 26, 1939
New York Sun. September 22, 1939
New York Times. February 11, 1939 to June 20, 1946
New York Word-Telegram. July 13, 1939
Philadelphia Inquirer. August 14, 1939 to August 15, 1939
Philadelphia Record. August 27, 1939
Pittsburgh Post-Gazette. 1934 to November 14, 2004
Pittsburgh Press. 1936 to October 25, 1966
Pittsburgh Sun-Telegraph. 1938 to 1946
Pittsburgh Tribune-Review. March 17, 1996
San Francisco Call-Bulletin. September 15, 1938
San Francisco Chronicle. November 1, 1966
San Francisco Examiner. August 7, 1937
Sports Journal. June 25, 1937

Billy and Mary Louise at Ocean City, New Jersey, 1941

June, 1990, Canastota, New York. Front row: Sandy Saddler, Ike Williams, Kid Gavilan, Willie Pep, Jake LaMotta, Carmen Basilio.
Back row: Billy Conn, Jose Napoles, Jersey Joe Walcott, Muhammad Ali, Emile Griffith, Bob Foster, Archie Moore.

Conn and Louis after their first fight

Conn lands a left hook on Lee Savold

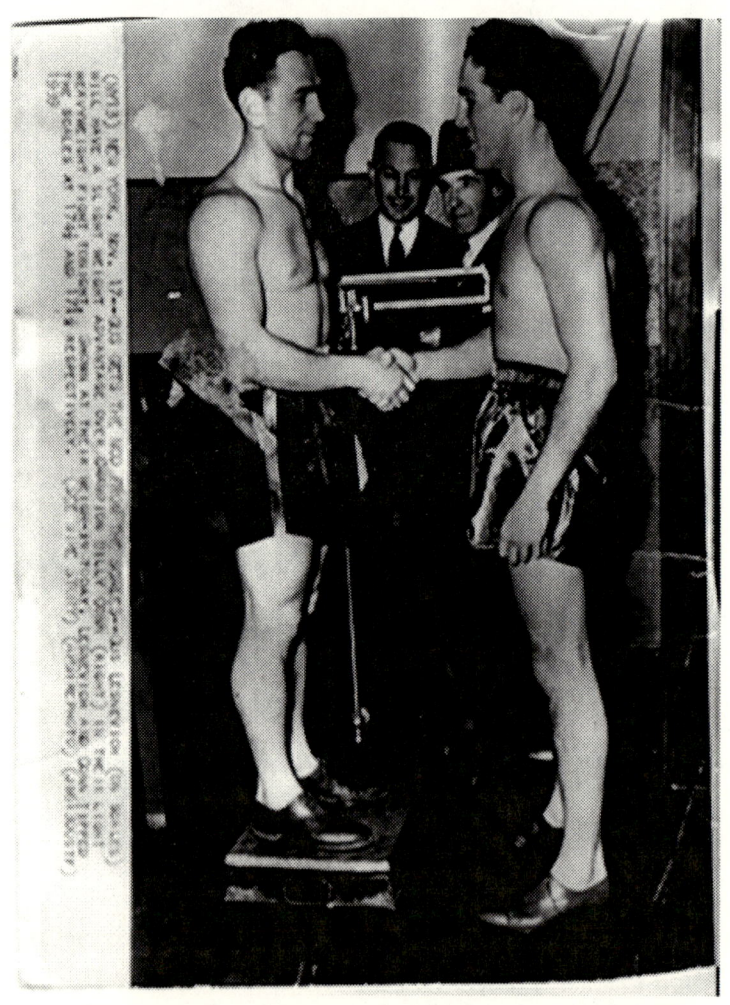

Gus Lesnevich and Conn weigh in for their first title fight

Conn battles Bettina

Conn lands a right on Joe Louis in their first fight

Conn in Shamrock trunks with Bettina

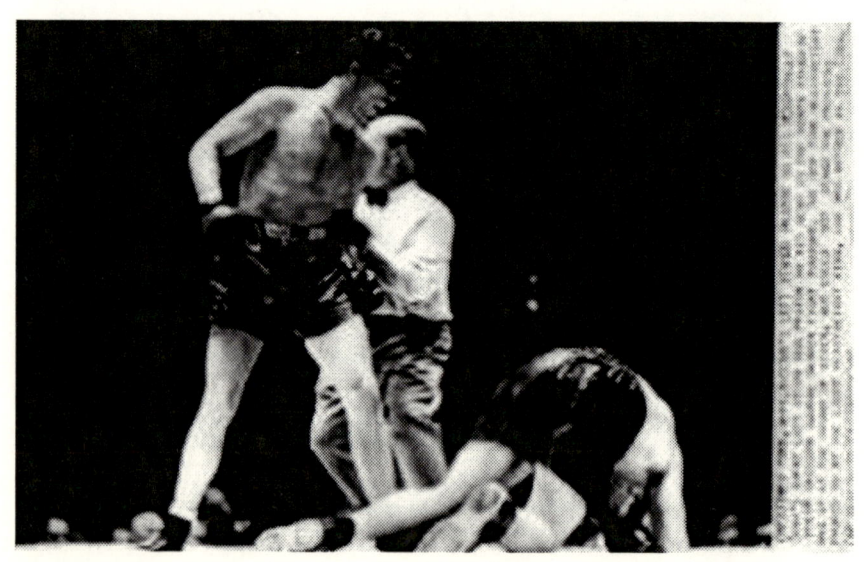

Conn floors Bob Pastor

Billy after breaking his hand in the brawl with his father-in-law

Conn family at dinner

Billy Conn ages 16 to 23

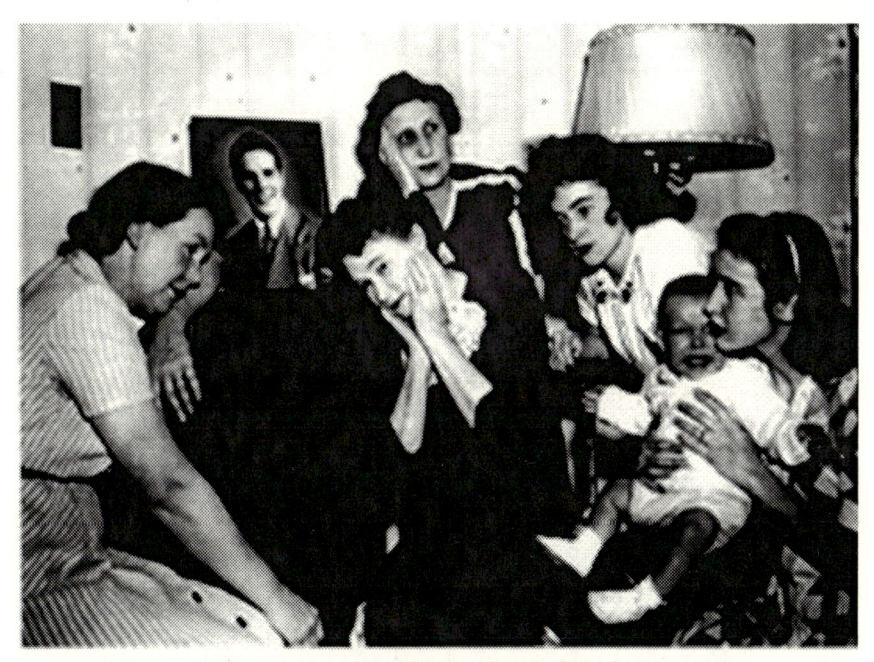

Conn relatives react to the radio broadcast of the first Louis fight

Publicity shot for the movie.

Billy chows down

Conn and Melio Bettina weigh in

Conn and Louis in the Army

Conn with sons Tim and Billy Junior

ABOUT THE AUTHOR

Pittsburgh native Paul F. Kennedy has written over 60 articles for the *Pittsburgh Tribune-Review*, mostly about local history, including Pittsburgh's impressive boxing history. He has published articles, poetry, and short fiction in such diverse publications as *Boxing Digest, Loyalhanna Review, Laurel Highlands Scene, Miraculous Medal,* and *Pittsburgh Quarterly*. In 2001 he published *A Pittsburgh Gamble*, a novel that takes place in Pittsburgh during the 1960 Pirate-Yankee World Series.

Paul is a graduate of Central Catholic High School in Pittsburgh and Indiana University of Pennsylvania. He has a master's degree from Carnegie Mellon University. He currently lives with wife Patricia in Greensburg, Pennsylvania.

As a child, Paul heard tales of the days of the great Pittsburgh boxers, of the time when the Pittsburgh area owned five of the eight world titles between 1939 and 1941. He heard of how Fritzie Zivic won the title from Henry Armstrong, and of how Charley Burley was the best fighter never to hold a title. But the most heralded legend was of how an undersized Billy Conn, young, handsome, and talented, had the great Joe Louis beat, only to lose by getting too cocky and trying to knock him out. As a teenager in Pittsburgh's Point Breeze section, Paul witnessed Conn, who lived in nearby Squirrel Hill, taking long solo walks through the neighborhood. Though elderly at the time, Conn still had a rugged look and formidable physical presence.

Paul has had the good fortune to gain access to the Conn family's vast treasure of information about Billy's life and career. *Billy Conn - the Pittsburgh Kid*, his first biography, is the result.

Printed in the United Kingdom
by Lightning Source UK Ltd.
125100UK00001B/240/A